A Map of
Making Dances

A Map of Making Dances

Stuart Hodes

Forward by Paul Taylor

Ardsley House, Publishers, Inc.
New York

Address orders and editorial
correspondence to:
Ardsley House, Publishers, Inc.
320 Central Park West
New York, NY 10025

ISBN: 1-880157-61-6

Printed in the United States of America

10 9 8 7 6 5 4 3 2 1

For all who make dances

...dreams of a perfect finite
action, free and heedless as the
impulse of a directed will...

Lawrence Durell

Contents

$\mathcal{L}$IST OF PROJECTS

ℱORWARD

𝒜s an experienced guide leading us across the scenic if somewhat bumpy terrain of making dances, my admirable friend Stuart Hodes cannot be beat. This book that he calls a map, however, is much more than a how-to book. It is a whole atlas, one that his old boss and mentor Martha Graham might have called a "landscape of the heart." The creative projects included (count 'em, 247!) are described in a voice that reveals the author's deep commitment and devotion to dance, the joys of serving his chosen profession, his generosity, and his upbeat view of life. Indeed, the voice of our friendly guide is strongly autobiographical.

Along the way a little dance history is offered and notable dancemakers pointed out (see index under Taylor), all in a voice that is clear, enthusiastic, down to earth, sensible, and blessedly free of theoretical clap trap. We are entertained with personal experiences and tickled by appropriate anecdotes. His extensive research has verified a practically photographic memory, one that might otherwise be mistaken for pure fantasy. But, as an indication of our guide's not being above error, he occasionally admits to being a little unsure of his facts. This is a most satisfying trait to reveal, insofar as there is nothing more human than to err, and, in doing so, our momentarily confused leader gives us opportunities to feel connected to him, if not superior.

Over the years the only matter on which my old friend and I have tended to disagree concerns the knotty matter of who deserves the title of the World's Greatest Dancemaker of All Time: him or me? Anyway, whichever of us he believes it to be, an endearing humility has prevented him from tooting his own horn throughout these pages.

Seriously, though, this is a great book by a great guide, and that's the honest truth. Enjoy your trip!

— PAUL TAYLOR

$\mathcal{P}$REFACE

$\mathcal{A}$ MAP OF MAKING DANCES began as classroom handouts for students at the American Dance Festival in 1989. A first draft was completed in China in 1992, where I taught technique and composition to members of the Guangdong Modern Dance Company. Additions and revisions followed.

Like a true map, A MAP OF MAKING DANCES can suggest paths; but since its form is that of a book, it is forced to be sequential, and thus cannot lay out the landscape before your eyes. This presents the problem of finding a rational order for so many concepts, approaches, and processes. Quite simply, I could not find one. I do suggest a way to begin—but after that, dancemakers and their guides must decide what paths to take. That noted: here is the order of topics:

Chapter 1. SETTING OUT — introduces ideas, plus a project for a group on its first day together.

Chapter 2. AVAILABLE MOVEMENT — draws on moves inherent in body action, dance techniques, and the imagination.

Chapter 3. INVENTING MOVEMENT — enlists ideas and concepts that can be transformed into movement, from images of nature to human relationships to tasks and games.

Chapter 4. IMPROVISATION — is presented as a dancemaker's tool. As an experiential, educational, or performance form, it is a field of study in itself.

Chapter 5. DANCE ENVIRONMENTS — includes all that surrounds dances: space, accompaniment, ideas, media, and more.

Chapter 6. DANCE AT WORK: "Applied Dance" — explores forms for general audiences.

Chapter 7. COLLABORATIONS — involves projects that two or more people can work on together.

Chapter 8. DANCING OFF THE *MAP* — is experimenter's turf.

Chapter 9. FORM — considers the basic idea of form and then specific forms generated by dance, music, and language, how these intermix and transform, and possibilities for further transformations.

Chapter 10. VALUE JUDGEMENTS — considers various concepts and criteria.

Chapter 11. EXCURSIONS — visits areas of concern peripheral to actual dancemaking.

Two hundred forty-seven creative projects are suggested throughout the book, each of which can be used in various ways, and there is an attempt to proceed from less to more complex. Yet Body Shapes (page 26), for example, is good for beginners and can also challenge the most advanced and experimental dancemakers.

I hope this book-as-map can serve as a resource for class and studio work, a guide toward creative goals, and a stimulus to those ready to take the lead in their own creative development.

Since with few exceptions I cite only dances and dancemakers with whom I have had personal contact, many of importance are perforce omitted. But then, *A MAP OF MAKING DANCES* is *not* a history. Yet I hope that the dances mentioned can serve as trail markers for those interested in studying the history of this stirring art form.

Finally, in the growing area of dance for nondancers I hope this book encourages some to try out their creative ideas, and that it conveys the welcome and gladness I feel when those in other disciplines, indeed, people in any walk of life, turn to dance.

ACKNOWLEDGMENTS

Throughout *A MAP OF MAKING DANCES*, I cite dances, including many unlikely ever to be seen again. I cite them as examples of the topic at hand, to honor the ephemerality that is dance's inherent attribute, to pay homage to their makers, and because they resonate in my memory.

I am especially indebted to Martha Graham, with whom I danced; to Louis Horst, whose composition classes I took; to Doris Humphrey and William Bales, whose composition classes I audited; to graduate students of the Directing Program at NYU, whose demand for a dance component in their studies resulted in the Director and Choreographer's Workshop; to Laura Foreman's ChoreoConcerts and Critiques at the New School for Social Research; to Dance Theater Workshop, the Weidman Studio Theater, the 92nd Street YM-YWHA; and to all the little theaters and lofts, where I have seen and shown dances, to every choreographer I've worked with, every dance seen over the decades, to the dancemakers who continually refresh the soul of dance, and to my students.

I am beholden to all who assisted me with research, including Don McDonagh; Deborah Jowitt; the Lincoln Center Library Dance Collection and staff members Elly Peck, Lacy McDearmon, and Monica Moseley; photographers Tom Caravaglia, Jay Colton, Ken Cooper, Johan Elbers, Arthur Elgort, Alfred Gescheidt, Eric Stephen Jacobs, James Klosty, André Maier, Nan Melville, Milton Oleaga, Paul Owen, Robert Rauschenburg, Beatriz Schiller, Stephen Speliotis, and every photographer whose name appears alongside a picture; Jane Halsman and the Philipe Halsman Archives; Rick Schussel and the New Dance Group Archives; Kate Flores and the American Dance Festival Archives; Norton Owen and the José Limon and the Jacob's Pillow Foundations; David Vaughan and the Merce Cunningham Foundation; and the many dancers and choreographers who sent me dates, spellings, and other essentials. I owe personal thanks to my daughters, Catherine, for her insights and ideas, and Martha, for her editorial guidance, and to my wife Elizabeth for her support.

A Map of
Making Dances

CHAPTER 1

SETTING
OUT

From atoms to galaxies, the universe dances. When humankind discovered that rhythmic movement engendered magical powers, dance burst the bonds of instinct, growing into unique cultural possessions passed down over generations.

In ancient Europe dances were religious rites. The roots of pre-Christian rituals are still seen in forms like the morris dance and Maypole dances. Classical ballet evolved from secular court dances to become a diversion of seventeenth-century Italian elite, spreading to France, then Russia. *Les Ballets Russe* played Paris in 1909 and caused such a sensation that for the next half-century, ballet was automatically deemed Russian. Alice Marks, a promising English ballerina, changed her name to Alicia Markova. Tap-dance, a hybrid Irish/African form, was considered so typically American that a dancer named Fred Austerlitz changed his name to Fred Astaire.

The seeds of modern dance were sown in Europe and America. Isadora Duncan gave a little-noticed recital in Chicago in 1899, but a year later was a hit in Paris, and in 1907 danced to acclaim in Russia. Ruth St. Denis gave her first recital in New York City in 1906 and, with Ted Shawn, founded the Denishawn School, which produced such greats as Martha Graham, Doris Humphrey, Charles Weidman, and Jack Cole. In the 1920s, Rudolf Von Laban, Mary Wigman, Kurt Jooss, and Harold Kreutzberg, were among the modern dance pioneers in Europe, to be tragically suppressed by the Nazis; yet their discoveries could not be suppressed, nor their dances, nor their inheritors, among whom Hanya Holm and Alwin Nikolais enriched American dance.

Early photograph of (left to right) Charles Weidman, Doris Humphrey, and José Limón.

Thomas Bouchard. Print: Courtesy of American Dance Festival

After World War II, American modern dance flowered, to become a "dance explosion" in the 1960s. Today there are dance companies, dancemakers, and dance audiences all over the world. Creative ideas exploded too. In 1952, John Cage composed *4' 33"*, a piece of music in which no tones were allowed to mask the ambient sounds of the outdoor concert, and in 1957, Paul Taylor made *EPIC*, a dance with minute scraps of everyday movement. In the 1960s, dancers began to speak (Martha Graham and Doris Humphrey already had) and also dance in silence (Helen Tamiris had done that). They began to use "media" and complex lighting, and Dan Wagoner made a dance in which the lighting was a blackout, with the audience hearing the crackle of plastic costumes! Meredith Monk issued an LP record which she termed "dancing for the voice." Meanwhile, dancers kept right on inventing new movement and new ways to invent it.

Modern dance is now worldwide. Is it a form? Perhaps, but it is also a state of mind that rethinks old assumptions and reinvigorates old myths in a process all choreographers can use to link their creative lives with their inherited traditions.

When the universe was created, perhaps in a big bang 15 billion years ago, time and space were created too. When you come right down to it, time, space, and a dancer are all it takes to make a dance.

Paul Taylor in *Epic*.

Robert Rauschenberg

An Atlas of Ideas

When you make a dance, you explore a landscape. When Isadora Duncan and Ruth St. Denis were exploring, much lay undiscovered. Yet the same is true today and will always be true, for dance exists in the infinite landscape of the imagination.

Most maps are printed in two dimensions to represent three-dimensional space. Dance exists in *four* dimensions, the fourth being time. Yet the body/mind, in which all dances form, has infinite dimensions, and the creative imagination, like the universe, can expand forever. Every time a dance is made, it enlarges the *MAP* and creates a new place to explore.

Books start at the beginning, but a map has no beginning. When setting out on a journey, you must start from where you are and follow the path you choose.

Music

You can make a dance with any aural environment including silence, yet music is dance's primary resource. Exploration of *A MAP OF MAKING DANCES* is well accompanied by intense music listening; if you can, work with and seek guidance from musicians. What music you use and how you use it is your choice; yet a piece of advice from Paul Taylor is worth noting: "Use the music. Don't let the music use you."

Projects

Most places on the *MAP* suggest projects. Think of these as territories to explore. Dances are the treasures you uncover and bring back for your personal collection.

Showings

All dancemakers should commit to scheduled showings, which creates the kind of pressure experienced in real life. There may also be spontaneous showings and showings for invited guests. When people first get together to show dances it's natural to feel uneasy, but that passes—to be replaced by the special joy of sharing with colleagues.

Keeping Notes

When working on a dance, keep notes. Your thoughts, ideas, and insights will gradually become a personal and invaluable record, and like Martha Graham's, Merce Cunningham's, Yvonne Rainier's, Carolee Schneeman's, and others, may be published one day.[1]

Dance Watching

The best way to gain an overview of the great landscape of dance is to attend as many performances as possible. But you need to decide if this can happen while working on a dance of your own. Some feel that when in creative throes, they can't attend any performances; others think that seeing dances stimulates their own creativity.

You can watch a dance performance with the casual nonchalance of a window-shopper or with the concentration of an astronomer viewing a rare comet. Depending on the particular concert and your state of mind, chances are you will do both.

If you want to discuss the dance later in any detail, take notes, which can be a problem in a dark theater while keeping eyes glued to the action. If you only want to record a few thoughts, immediately after the dance ends, write a few lines directly on the printed program. Otherwise, using pure touch, try an oversize scrawl on a large pad, limiting yourself to about a dozen lines per page.

Useful too is a performance log. Written immediately afterward, it can be highly personal, like a diary, recording personal and private reactions. I've done this from time to time—and years later, rereading it usually brings the entire dance concert and each dance in it clearly to mind.

If there are printed programs, save them! A young dancer organized enough to file away dance programs carefully will one day have a collection of both personal and historical value. The New York Public Library Dance Collection has collected thousands of dance programs, but has missed far more, and the only records of numberless small theater concerts are programs saved by those who attended.

Teacher or Mystagogue?

Choreography cannot be taught.
    LINCOLN KIRSTEIN, FOUNDER, NEW YORK CITY BALLET

Granting that Kirstein's statement is true, does it mean there is no need for dance composition courses? My predictable answer: no! Making dances is a complex process involving mind and body, intuition and judgment, a sense of proportion, an eye for design, and a feeling for human relationships, to name some, and is learned differently from history or mathematics. Teaching dancemakers is not didactic—taught in lectures—or Socratic—taught through dialogues; nor is it taught by demonstration, imitation, and correction, as one teaches dance technique. It is interactive and mutual, a process that enlists creative intuition as it builds inventive skills. Its objective is to find and develop an individual voice. The interesting word "mystagogue" seems right for teachers of choreography.

MYS-TA-GOGUE   n. [Fr.; Latin, *mystagogus* < Greek, *mystagogos* < *mystes,* one initiated in mysteries + *agogos,* leader.][2]

The mystagogue is a guide, and when exploring it is good to have a guide along. Many will have danced and made dances, although Louis Horst, Martha Graham's mentor, was a pianist, conductor, composer, and dance writer, not a dancer. But he had spent many hours among dancers and understood their experience. Musicians, historians, even critics can be mystagogues, helping dancemakers bridge the gap between theory and practice, precepts and intuition, concepts and action. Mystagogues provoke, stimulate, encourage, respond, and elicit responses. They share their experience and help others to gain experiences of their own.

The Critique

Most experienced choreographers have someone they turn to whose responses they trust. Everyone needs that outside eye. The young dancemaker's first experience of it is often the critique, where the composition teacher, as mystagogue, takes the lead.

Mystagogues can be bluff or benign, coolly analytical or warmly encouraging. Louis Horst and William Bales were crusty, Doris Humphrey and Bessie Schoenberg encouraging; yet all four got dancemakers going.

Robert Dunn, whose choreographic workshops inspired a generation of experimental dancers in the 1960s, said, "People don't come to study with you because of your technique, they want to be around your personality."[3] One of Dunn's contributions was discovering how to direct a critique that was both revealing and nonjudgmental. Rather than simply asking students to react or opine, he helped them anchor their responses in specific qualities, actions, "flavors," and other ways. Instead of pointing out weaknesses, he sought suggestions on how a dance could be strengthened, which is much the same thing, yet easier to take. (For more on Dunn, see page 161.)

Most people are sensitive about both giving and receiving criticism, yet being in a group encourages both and affords a chance to decide just how much outside opinion you want. A very valuable function of the critique is the chance to practice *seeing* dances and to learn to look more deeply into them.

Before showing, some like to explain; yet in-depth discussion should usually wait until after a dance has been performed. Immediately after seeing a study you might discuss:

➤ images and ideas the dance evokes
➤ notable or strongest movements
➤ associations, top-of-the-head responses

After preliminary discussions, the following might ensue.

Q. *What did you intend for this study?*
A. Nothing. I just put together some moves.

That could mean, "Back off. I'm not ready for criticism." You might then discuss the moves, how they were arrived at, and what they evoke. If the dancemaker is drawn into the discussion, things are probably going in the right direction. Here's a condensation of an actual critique in which the comments grew specific:

Q. *"What did you intend for this study?"*
A. "I'm not sure. It came out of an argument with a friend."

Comments:

"I sensed anger in the way you kept your gaze averted."

"Also in the small quick moves of your shoulders."

"You moved your arms and legs as though they belonged to two different people. It was powerful and unsettling."

"You built tension by moving downstage and upstage. After a while it became predictable. Did you intend it to be, or might it be better to vary the pattern, without letting go of the tension?"

Most comments are positive, and where a problem is noted, its solution is left to the dancemaker. You can go on to discuss:

> ➤ images and associations evoked by the movement
> ➤ strong movements, patterns, inventiveness, use of space
> ➤ choices presented and made
> ➤ the intention and how it is expressed or realized
> ➤ accidental or serendipitous elements
> ➤ alternatives that might be tried
> ➤ audience response

Discussions often range away from the dance into general questions. For instance:

> ➤ Is it all right to achieve something entirely different from what was intended?
> ➤ Is it valid to *analyze* dances, that is, to separate them into components and make judgments about those components?
> ➤ Is there a best way to interpret a dance, that is, discuss what it means?[4]

The Inner Critic

When a writer chooses a word—a composer, a note—a choreographer, a move—the choice is mediated by an inner critic. If a time comes when inventing grinds to a halt, it can seem as though there is nothing to choose from, but that's not it! There is always plenty, except that whatever comes to mind seems wrong: a leap, too ordinary; a fall, too arbitrary; a twitch, too goofy. You stand seemingly empty when actually ideas are trapped like a genie in a bottle. The creative artist tries to choose, but an inner voice squawks, "Ugh! No! Terrible!" One must temporarily squelch that inner critic. Ways to do that are revealed in studies to come.

How Long Should a Dance Be?

A complete dance may be short: in James Waring's *Imperceptible Elongation #1,* a dancer emerged from behind a curtain, did a few clear curving moves, tossed up a handful of confetti, and with a celebratory sweep, slid out of sight, all in about twenty seconds. Doris Humphrey's admonition that "all dances are too long" warns those with a tendency to ramble, but a dance that doesn't take time to develop its ideas is too short.

Morality and Aesthetics

Moral decisions have real-life consequences; the deeds of thieves, cheats, and tyrants cause pain and suffering, whereas honest, generous, loving behavior enhances life. Aesthetic decisions seem to refract moral ones. What we regard as beautiful and ugly seems akin to how we define good and evil. That is why art that breaks aesthetic rules seems to question society itself and why artists are suppressed by despotic regimes. Yet all societies can be shaken by works of art. Recently, New York newspapers carried a story of two women whose visual work used an image of a crucified woman. The headline: ABORTION EXHIBIT SPLITS CAMPUS IN QUEENS.[5]

Conscience commands moral judgments and something just as profound commands aesthetic judgment. Both lie deep within, in our very genes some say. But both need to be exercised! Making dances puts aesthetics to work immediately, and, I believe, engages morality as well.

Art and Belief

Works of art can strike at the heart of belief. If ever you find yourself at the edge, you must decide whether to stop or go on. You may have to question an old assumption or break an aesthetic rule. But breaking aesthetic rules is really an attempt to discover new ones. People who succeed open the way for others.

You can make a dance with detailed plans, building one move upon another as a house is built, or spin it out like a spider spins a web in a spontaneous revelation of order and beauty. Whichever is your way, making dances serves the spirit that put us into this universe and endowed us with the need to dance. Making a dance is a sacred act.

A dance is pure pattern; we trace it with our bodies, but its existence is wholly of the mind. Making a dance is an abiding and direct response to the creative principle, which virtually all define as good, and some as God.

A KINETIC INTRODUCTION

A group that gets together to make dances is like any group that meets for a common purpose. People begin by introducing themselves.

$\mathcal{P}$ROJECT 1 INTRODUCE YOURSELF IN MOVEMENT.

Make a dance statement about yourself, a minute long or less. It can be carefully worked out, or improvised, or parts of both. It can include speech. Preparation should take no more than fifteen minutes. Here are some ways to work:

1. *Intuitively.* Let your body tell you. Try not to censor or criticize yourself as you seek moves.

2. *Situationally.* Imagine yourself at a meeting which begins with introductions all around. Speak your name aloud; then, instead of continuing, "I'm from San Francisco, work in the arts, and my hobby is winetasting," say something about yourself *in pure movement.*

3. *Cerebrally.* Decide how you want to represent yourself, and select moves that do so to your satisfaction. If this sounds calculated, well, why not?

4. *Narratively.* Translate a verbal idea into moves—for example—

   • Hi!
   • I'm okay, you're okay!
   • I like surfing, swimming, painting, pizza.
   • I wonder if we will like each other?
   • (Any other statement.) ∎

ENDNOTES

1. Martha Graham, *The Notebooks of Martha Graham* (New York, Harcourt Brace Jovanovich, 1973). Merce Cunningham, *Notes on Choreography,* ed. Frances Starr (New York, Something Else Press, 1969). Yvonne Rainer, *Work 1961–73* (Halifax, Press of Nova Scotia College, and New York, New York University, 1974). Carolee Schneeman, *More Than Meat Joy,* ed. Bruce McPherson (Kingston, NY, McPherson, 1979).

2. *Webster's New World Dictionary*, College Edition (New York, World, 1966).

3. Paul Langland, *Movement Research Performance Journal* 14 (1997): 18

4. For some powerful arguments on one side, see Susan Sontag, *Against Interpretation and Other Essays* (New York: Farrar Strauss & Giroux, 1986), pp. 3–14.

5. *New York Times,* 15 August 1991, p. B1.

$\mathcal{C}$HAPTER 2

$\mathcal{A}$VAILABLE MOVEMENT

People ask, "How do you make a dance?" My answer is simple.
"Put yourself in motion."[1]
TWYLA THARP

Dance can come from anywhere; but whatever the source, it must be transformed into movement. Happily for dancemakers, life is suffused with movement. The projects of this section draw upon movement that is close at hand.

When you find moves, what then? Twyla Tharp asked herself: "Why did this note, this color, this word follow that one? Why were we here? Where did we come from? What did it all mean?"[2]

Tharp's questions extend far beyond making dances. The amazing fact is, when you make a dance, you answer every question.

BODY SHAPES

All bodies have the same basic shape; yet each body is unique and can be arranged in an infinite number of ways. Choreography springs from this counterpoise of sameness and difference. I once saw a stop-motion film of a man sleeping—six hours reduced to three minutes. The sleeper seemed to jerk continuously from position to position, shape to shape, in a frenetic spontaneous dance. One day I saw this on a stage:

> Upon a bedlike platform lay a woman whose body shifted as though in troubled sleep, going from one broken position to the next, to evoke someone tormented by nightmares. The dance, *Talking in Her Sleep*, choreographed by Wang Mei, was danced by Ying Xiaorong of China's Guangdong Modern Dance Company.

*P*ROJECT 2   A SEQUENCE OF BODY SHAPES.

You may use large shapes made by your whole body or small shapes for only a part: microshapes.

1. Make up five to a dozen shapes. (The mirror is a useful tool.)
2. Repeat one after another. If you have trouble getting from, say, a crumpled heap on the floor to standing on one leg, include some of the shapes your body passes through.
3. Once you have shapes you like, learn them, and put them in some order.
4. Perform them to counts, to a piece of music, a poem, a text, or in silence. ■

Other ways to arrange these shapes and various moves are the subjects of other parts of the *MAP* (page 177). Go there now if you wish, although the goal here is simply to find interesting moves from body shapes.

Alfred Gescheidt

Bodies as shapes. *Hieros,* by Stuart Hodes. Top to bottom: Stuart Hodes, Mariano Garcia, Teresa Hill.

GESTURES

Gesture is movement with such clear meaning that it can enhance or substitute for speech. A shrug says: "I don't know," "Who cares?" or "It's not my problem." Doris Humphrey's "ritualization of gesture" first brought this resource to the attention of the dance world.

Like language, gesture is culture-specific. Many components of sign language are gestures evolved into language. The art of mime is profoundly gestural, and the *mudras* of East Indian dance turn gesture into pure dance.

The Emperor in Command, a gem of a solo I saw in the 1950s, with haughty postures and demanding gestures, revealed a pompous busybody ordering people about. In *American Genesis,* Paul Taylor, who speaks American sign language, created an eloquent gesture dance in which a Native American at Plymouth Rock welcomes uncomprehending Pilgrims, who reply by bonking him on the head and walking over his supine body.

Although cultural, gesture is less symbolic than words. The smile (a facial gesture) is universal. Nodding "yes," and turning the head side-to-side for "no," are widely understood; open hands is an ancient ritual gesture, the "high five" a modern one. "Thumbs up" is a winning gesture, whereas a forefinger drawn across the throat, which means "Cut!" in sound studios, descended from a more ominous meaning. There is no shortage of unmentionable gestures.

$\mathcal{P}$ROJECT 3   GESTURE STUDY.

Make one or more gestures for some or all of the following:

begging	flirting	obeying	rejecting
commanding	hinting	pleading	snubbing
defying	imploring	questioning	soothing
demanding	inciting	quitting	spying
dismissing	inviting	refusing	starving ∎

$\mathcal{P}$ROJECT 4   A GESTURE MONOLOGUE.

Arrange some gestures of Project 3 into a monologue.   ∎

$\mathcal{P}$ROJECT 5   A GESTURE DIALOGUE.

Two or more dancers have a gesture conversation. Improvise, or make up gestures and "speak."   ∎

*P*ROJECT 6   ADDING GESTURES TO OTHER MOVEMENT.

Try enriching another dance study with gestures.   ■

All physical action is a rich source of dance movement.[3] A stunning example is Sybil Shearer's dramatic solo, *Every Nook and Cranny.* Shearer portrayed a woman cleaning house. Wielding broom and dustpan, she gathered every speck of dust, scooped it up in triumph and … let it fall. An important feature of Shearer's dance was her brilliant realization of the many small, precise house-cleaning moves.

   The art of mime is rich with recognizable acts, although over the years, some moves have become more like symbols for acts than veritable actions. Mime also exaggerates for artistic purposes, as expressions of doleful sorrow or antic glee.

Some Actions to Physicalize

Plant a tree. Sculpt a statue. Paint a portrait. Cook breakfast. Peel a banana, an apple, a grape. Go bowling, play pool, baseball, tennis. Clean the bathroom. Pump up a bicycle tire. Change an automobile tire. Set the table. Arrange flowers. Iron a shirt. Carve a turkey. Think of others. Most people wouldn't iron a turkey or carve a shirt, but is that any reason why a dancer can't?

*P*ROJECT 7   MOVEMENT FROM ACTION: PHYSICALIZING.

1. Select one or more physical acts, extract movement, make a study.
2. Manipulate by repeating, changing direction, or level, etc.
3. Show and decide if the study has the seed of a dance. If so:
   a. Develop it from the physical act; develop its consequences, variations, implications.
   b. Develop it as pure form (page 177).   ■

Can anyone invent a truly new move? A long time ago, a prehistoric hunter crouched behind a tree, body tensed in a perfect *contraction.* He dashed out, made his kill, and triumphantly leapt into the air flailing his legs—the first *changement de pieds!*

André Maier

Spontaneous group movement is ancient yet ever new: dancers toss one of their number into the air at the 25th anniversary Woodstock concert.

Even if something like that really happened, it doesn't make the movement discoveries of Martha Graham or classical ballet less original. Many forms of dance require skills obtained only in technique class, yet a good dance is more than just a string of classroom sequences.

Dance historians trace some classical ballet moves directly to individuals and credit Martha Graham, Merce Cunningham, Katherine Dunham, and others with having created enough new movement to constitute a whole technique; but it is almost impossible to know who created the traditional dances of India, Africa, Spain, and other places whose dance forms are centuries old. Yet each move must have done first by somebody!

If you decide to use a lurch, a wiggle, a scamper, and someone says, "That's not dancing!" don't believe it! Any move can be danced. A brand new move is thrilling; so is a new use for an old one, as when making a dance out of moves not usually danced. Paul Taylor's *Esplanade* (page 27) is made of walking, running, and falling. A wonderful thing about making dances is that it frees you to define dance with your own body, which is literally alive with possibilities.

$\mathcal{P}$ROJECT 8   NEW MOVEMENT.

- Make a dance using only three parts of your body.
- Make a dance in which you move as if for the first time.

- Make a dance capturing the quality of an animal: amoeba, eagle, earthworm, dinosaur, or another.

- Make a dance solely for your face, fingers, arms, feet, etc.

- Find a move from a sport and make it into a phrase. (You'll see the word **phrase** often: a brief succession of moves that yields a sense of unity. A **motor fragment** is less; it just hangs there.)

- Find a move from a nondance activity; expand it into a phrase.

- Find a move you rarely see in a dance.

- Invent a move that you have never done before.

- Invent a move you have never seen anyone do.

- Search for ways to limit or trick your body into discovering new moves. ■

ABSTRACTION: PURE MOVEMENT

In the Random House Unabridged Dictionary, a definition of *abstract* reads: "expressing a quality or characteristic apart from any specific object or instance." Many of Martha Graham's early dances fit this definition—like *Lamentation,* a dance of grief, and *Celebration,* a dance of joy. Today dances that depict emotion are not deemed abstract, for dance has reached a deeper level of abstraction—movement for movement's sake.

Merce Cunningham is both a pioneer and preeminent choreographer of pure movement dances, but because dance is made with human bodies, the least abstract of all entities, dances can be both abstract and eloquently human. Cunningham taught me that to some extent this is true of all art. After peering at an abstract painting that hung on the studio wall, he said, "It's very joyous!" That painting has been joyous to me ever since.

Keeping a dance abstract is not always easy. I recall a time that Linda Hodes, then in Paul Taylor's company, emerged from rehearsal to say, "Paul tossed out a whole section because it had started to tell a story." Taylor makes vivid story dances but wanted pure movement that day. That his moves were telling a story anyway is a clue to the nature of dance.

It's liberating to make pure movement, knowing that if a move suddenly takes on character or begins to tell a story, you've been offered a choice. It keeps you constantly poised for discovery. Can this be why so many who danced with Merce Cunningham went on to make important discoveries of their own?

*P*ROJECT 9   MOVEMENT FOR MOVEMENT'S SAKE.

1. Create a series of moves that do not try to tell a story, impart a dramatic message, or have any representational aims.

2. Vary the sound background.

3. Try different titles for the study. See if different titles change the way people perceive the dance, or how you perceive it. ■

FLOOR PATTERNS

In most dances, movement generates floor patterns; but patterns can also generate movement. The circle dance harks back to ancient rites. Squares and lines are sober, formal, or martial. Verticals—toward and away from the audience—can be pounding or threatening, whereas horizontals sweep through the action: once Martha Graham remarked, "Now I must sweep the stage," and gave the men a leaping crossover that swept it clean. Floor patterns have importance in ballroom dancing, particularly in competitions in which certain patterns are required, as in ice dancing, in which some figures are specified.

In "Cerebrals," a topic in Louis Horst and Carroll Russell's book, *Modern Dance Forms in Relation to the Other Modern Arts,* four students decide on a floor pattern for its intellectual resonance, like a star for a dance about the Sun or the number one for a study of someone with a big ego. Playing upon

Philippe Halsman

Dancers in single file carry burdens of sorrow as they cross the stage in the "Exodus" section of Sophie Maslow's stirring dance *The Village I Knew.*

the fact that all Horst's students called him "Louie," Bertram Ross made a study titled, "L for Louie," in which he moved on an L-shaped pattern while parodying Horst's teaching mannerisms. It brought a smile to Louie's face.

The Leningrad Institute in Russia gives great importance to floor patterns. Zhanar Sadyrova, a student of choreography in her sixth and final year there, said she'd studied floor patterns for a whole year.

PROJECT 10 FLOOR PATTERNS AS MOVEMENT SOURCES

Transfer a pattern.

1. Imagine a pattern or extract one from sports, a rug, wallpaper, nature, mathematics, wave forms, or something else.
2. Draw the pattern on paper. (You may have to simplify it.)
3. Imagine it on the floor or chalk it there.
4. Make a dance study using this pattern.
   - Use a clear floor pattern as a recurring figure in a study.
   - Find a competition ballroom dancer and learn more about ballroom patterns. Can they generate studies?
   - Obtain the Horst/Russell book and look up "Cerebrals." ■

Picture Collection, The Branch Libraries, The New York Public Library

Ballroom dancing, circa 1925.

Making dances comes down, finally, to moves. The concept, relationship, image, or any other seed will always be expressed in movement. A great chess master, asked how many moves he thought ahead, answered, "One. The best." In dance there is no best; there is, perhaps, an infinite number. Yet we can make a dance by thinking just one move ahead.

IT'S YOUR MOVE

PROJECT 11 YOUR MOVE.

1. Find a move your body likes. Do it. Memorize it. Keep it where you can get at it. Make notes, if they help.

2. Start exactly where the first move left off and make another move. Take time. Don't try to relate the second to the first. Just find that second move and do it until it feels comfortable. You now have two moves.

3. Do them: one-two. They are just moves. No evoking or relating, just moving. Make a third move . . .

4. When you have five or ten moves, play them back one after the other. Don't get critical or seek meaning.

5. Seek sequence. If you want to alter or adjust the way they fit together, do so. Maybe you'll think of other moves in some places.

6. Find music. Do the moves to the music.

7. Give the moves a title. Perform your dance. ■

FOUND MOVEMENT: PEOPLE WATCHING

The French anatomist and teacher, Françoise Delsarte, watched funerals and mine disasters to study the moves of people in extremes of emotion. If that seems icy and unfeeling, it was nevertheless born of profound interest in people and their modes of expression.

One of the most moving studies I've ever seen was by Anne Stevens, a trained nurse. She drew upon memory of movements made by a dying patient. Her dance, an expression of abiding love and deep empathy, revealed the feeling human being within the trained health professional.

Doris Humphrey's "ritualization of gesture" is an example of found movement, although she adapted the gestures in inventive ways. In his absorbing autobiography, *Private Domain*, Paul Taylor describes how he roamed the streets of New York City seeking moves for a new dance.

There is movement to be found in children at play, spectator sports, birthday parties, weddings, parades, beaches, sidewalks, restaurants. Watch actors in old films: the rolling swagger of John Wayne, the prowling slink of Peter Lorre, the aggressive strut of James Cagney, the debonair sashay of Fred Astaire.

$\mathcal{P}$ROJECT 12 FOUND MOVEMENT: PEOPLE.

1. *Found positions.*

   a. Observe and capture body positions and postures.

   b. Make a study of three or more in any order.

   c. Expand using your own variations on the found positions.

2. *Found motion.* Watch someone directing traffic, moving furniture, cooking dinner, etc.

3. *Found emotion* à la Delsarte. Watch people who are happy, surprised, excited, angry, confused, etc. Capture their moves.

4. *Emotion underlying motion.* Pick a person at random and try to sense the emotion underlying his or her moves.

When showing moves found out-of-doors, it's nice if you can meet out-of-doors for showings. ■

MECHANICALS

Although the body is a mechanical miracle, we think of it as the antithesis of the machine. A mechanical human suggests robots or zombies. An astonishing spectacle sometimes seen at carnivals is a mechanical human— a person imitating a mechanized dummy imitating a person. One of the first and best mechanical movement studies is by Charlie Chaplin in *Modern Times.* He plays an assembly-line worker whose entire job is tightening bolts; even when off work, he can't stop. Sybil Shearer's *In a Vacuum* abstracts and extends this idea in a dance of small repeated moves for her head, hands, arms, and legs to create an appalling portrait of a person as a machine.

*P*ROJECT 13   FOUND MOVEMENT: MECHANICAL.

1. *Mechanical motion.* Observe a lawn sprinkler, locomotive, pencil eraser, windshield wiper, waving flag, soft-drink machine, clothes washer, stop watch, record player, or any moving machine. You might want to show the moves before you work them into a study. Perhaps others can identify the device or machine, although that is not particularly the point.

2. *Mechanical stillness.* Observe an artifact that works without motion: a nail, wall, chimney, hole in the ground, etc. Seek body moves from the *implied* action, the force beneath the stillness:

   a. the squeezing insertion of a nail in wood

   b. the way a wall cleaves space

   c. how a wall projects itself between you and beyond

   d. the power of a chimney to contain heat or smoke and to eject it into the air

   e. the emptiness of a hole

   f. the pseudolife within a computer

Be thoughtful when you title this study. The titles "Wall," "Outside," "Inside," "Escape," "Safety" can all deal with a wall, yet each offers a different perspective. ■

SKILLS, TRICKS

This is in the spirit of, "If you got it, flaunt it!" The key is a skill or trick around which to build a dance. If you can juggle, walk on stilts, balance a stick on your chin, ride a skateboard or unicycle, twirl a baton, run with a book on your head or between your knees, play the piccolo or harmonica, type 90 words per minute, recite the "Gettysburg Address," draw a face on a blackboard, tap-dance barefoot, pare an apple so the skin stays in one piece, perform a magic trick, walk on your hands, play the kazoo, play the piano wearing mittens, make hand shadows in a spotlight thrown on a screen, blow balloons into animal shapes, make an origami butterfly, jump into the air and click your heels twice, or do anything else that takes skill, you can make it into a dance.

Although tricks are eye-grabbing, you do need more than the trick. It can serve as an opening (page 46), a climax (page 197), an ending, finale, recurring motif (page 193), theme (page 194), or simply as one in a bag of tricks.

*P*ROJECT 14   MAKE A DANCE USING A SKILL, TRICK, OR FEAT.

The skill can open, close, be repeated, used like bookends, continue throughout, be a climax, casually "thrown away," or used in some other way. Enjoy. ■

ILLUSORY SKILLS: A CON GAME

In the preceding section, Skills, Tricks, we flaunt skill. In Virtuosity (page 24), we engage it with modesty and grace. Here we fake it! But fake doesn't mean phony, just as imitation doesn't mean counterfeit. Classical ballet's illusion of effortlessness is grounded in effort. *Balon*, the airy elevation that makes jumpers seem suspended in space, is pure illusion. Performance is a kind of con game in which the audience is a willing player.

A dancer carefully takes a position, then "pirouettes" by twirling one finger. A circus clown blows up and pops a paper bag with the aplomb of a magician pulling a rabbit from a hat. A dancer walks a "high wire" taped to the stage floor. Jacques Heim "danced" a sequence of virtuoso foot moves by reading a description of them while sitting in a chair. Mime Marcel Marceau's *Walking against the Wind* is a brilliant illusion; so too is its flamboyant cousin, Michael Jackson's *Moon Walk*.

$\mathcal{P}$ROJECT 15   FABULOUS FAKE FEAT.

1. Decide upon some brilliant feat.
2. Prepare to execute it and at the moment of truth, *evoke* it.
3. Observe another's brilliant antics, then evoke them by doing most everything but the antics, which you evoke with moves and flourishes. ■

FUNDAMENTAL UNITS

Science tells us that microstructure determines macrostructure, which only means that glass looks and feels different from rubber because of its molecules. Molecules are fundamental units of matter. Atoms are fundamental units of molecules, subatomic particles form atoms, and quarks are hypothetical units of subatomic particles. At each level, the fundamental unit is the one from which the next larger unit forms.

What is a fundamental unit of dance? There are different answers, and what a dancemaker views as fundamental will effect the dance.

Music and dance correspond in many ways, but where fundamental units are concerned, they part company. In much of music, the beat is fundamental; however, in Western classical music, says Edward T. Cone, "it is the measure, rather than the beat, which is the fundamental unit."[5] Music of India, however, has a complex rhythmic base, the *tala*, composed of different beats, a fundamental that is equivalent to several measures. Dance also uses rhythmic fundamentals, yet as a corporeal art, it has movement fundamentals as well.

1. There is the contraction of a single muscle.
2. There are the moves by a group of muscles to form a *plié,* a step, or to raise an arm.
3. There is a series of moves to make a motor fragment like *glissade assemblé* or fall-and-recovery.
4. There is a group of motor fragments comprising a combination or phrase.

$\mathcal{P}$ROJECT 16   KINETIC FUNDAMENTALS.

Decide what constitutes your fundamental unit. Build a short study based upon that fundamental. Show it. Discuss how the choice of a fundamental shapes the dance. ■

Note. It is interesting to compare studies based upon different ideas about what constitutes a fundamental unit.

STEPS

After Gregory Hines made the movie *White Knights,* a TV talk-show host asked him how he'd liked working with Twyla Tharp. His reply, "She can make a step," was high praise. Musical theater dancers have great respect for choreographers who can make good steps.

A good step feels good, works in the dance, and sells itself. (**Selling** is show-biz lingo for making a step look good by using energy and personality.) A dance that works after a show is running for years and when dancers may not be selling is called **dancer proof.** In long-running musicals, such dances are pearls beyond price.

Steps imply footwork, yet use the whole body. The difference between rumba and mambo, for instance, is less in the feet than how torso and weight are used. Steps can be both original and within a style; in Bob Fosse's *Rich Kids Rag,* there's no Charleston, Suzy-Q, or other traditional rag step, yet it's clearly a rag. Fosse thought about being stuck-up and snooty, and invented bitingly humorous steps to portray this. Lee Theodore made a hit on TV in the 1960s with *Kabuki Mambo,* a mix of Japanese and Latin steps. Fred Astaire's film dances have great steps.

Musical theater choreographers with whom I've often worked began by making up steps which they put into combinations and then arranged as dance numbers.[6]

*P*ROJECT 17   STEP STUDY.

Traditional: A gold mine! All the dances ever danced are available to use as you wish or be mixed together, as in *Kabuki Mambo.* The following list was gleaned from many sources. Add to it!

ball change	dipsy doodle	hop
bison	do-si-do	hornpipe
black bottom	falling off a log	hucklebuck
boogaloo	fancy steps	hustle
brisé	fish	jerk
bourrée	foxtrot	jig
buck and wing	French kicks	Lambeth walk
cakewalk	frug	lindy hop
chain step	funky chicken	mazurka
Charleston	gagliarde	nautch
chassé	galop	one-step
clog	grand right-and-left	pas de bourrée
coffee grinder	grinders	paso doble
coupé	hokey pokey	peabody

American couples dancing the polka, 1848.

polka

pony

punk

quickstep

ritmo svelto

rumba

samba

sashay

scamper

shag

shim sham

shorty George

shuffle

sidestep

sidle

skip

slop

soft shoe

stride

strut

Suzy-Q

swing

time step

trenches

trucking

twist

two-step

voguing

waltz

waltz clog

wings

(And many more!)

Free-form: Mostly legs and feet. The result may be fleet, as in "fancy feet," mechanical, as in precision drill, rhythmic, like tap or Flamenco, or eccentric, as in "rubber legs." ■

La Rumba, Ernestina Day and Ted Shawn.

DANCES FROM TECHNIQUE

The beginning choreographer often turns to classroom moves, reasoning, perhaps, that you cannot go far wrong with movement lovingly preserved and taught for generations. That is true, although it takes imagination to be original using classroom movement. Here are three dances that succeed:

1. In *Études*, Harold Lander presented the exultant joy of classical ballet class. The drudgery disappeared in the triumph over physical limits that is the dancer's ultimate reward.

2. In *Class*, Robert Cohan did the same for modern dance technique. Cohan was one of Martha Graham's partners before he went to England to head the London Contemporary Dance Company. Never has Graham-based movement been more proudly uttered than in this brilliant technique-based work.

3. The quintessential technique dance is Martha Graham's *Acts of Light*. It begins with floor work, then standing in center, finally traveling moves, and like any Graham work, exceeds its materials, to reveal joy, pain, reverence and transcendence.

One can also use technique to reach beyond technique. I'll talk about one of my own dances now, not because it ranks with the great works cited elsewhere, but because it illustrates this point. I wanted to make a ballet from "The Abyss," a short story by Leonid Andreyev, in which a young couple are attacked by three brutal assailants. The pair are romantic innocents in love. What technique but classical ballet? The assailants were brutish yet beautiful, and each had an animal image: a lion, a bear, and a monkey. What technique but Graham-based modern?

*P*ROJECT 18   TECHNIQUE TO TRANSCEND TECHNIQUE.

Take time alone in the studio. Start with class moves, then gradually shift from technical exercises to freer moves. Dance for pleasure. Don't *set* anything at first. The goal is to let the technique tell you what to do. If moves start going together well, especially in odd and unexpected ways, you are onto something! ■

VIRTUOSITY

Virtuosity is technical skill ennobled with taste, character, and yes, *virtue*, in order to reveal artistry. The virtuoso shuns vainglory, that mix of self-consciousness and arrogance that trivializes the most spectacular skills.

Classical ballet seeks virtuosity as it conceals the effort behind its formidable skills.

We speak of virtuoso dancers and violinists, but not often of virtuoso jugglers, probably because juggling is most often an honest exhibition of pure skill. A notable exception is Michael Moschen, whose skill is only one element of his artistry, making him a true virtuoso.

Why some skilled practitioners become virtuosos, others only showoffs, is hard to explain. It takes character to gain great skills, and character is revealed in virtuoso performance. But a showoff at heart will probably come across as one. You figure it out.

A mysterious component of virtuosity is charisma. Imitating someone who possesses it can be a useful exercise, but doesn't guarantee that you will develop your own. If you achieve a sure sense of yourself, you will be as close to charisma as you need to be for your own virtuosity to shine.

$\mathcal{P}$ROJECT 19   A VIRTUOSIC ATOM.

Build a dance around something you love to do, and do well. Find your virtuosic atom—a move, footwork, a fall, a gliding walk, a bounding leap, fast or slow turns. Perhaps you can recite a poem, sing a song, can produce a special rhythmic sound by hands, feet, or on a drum. Maybe you're brilliant with a soufflé, ironing a shirt, packing a suitcase, knitting socks. Nestle that atom of virtuosity within a dance. ■

**REINVENTING
THE WHEEL**

Engineers don't need to reinvent the wheel, but in dance it's done all the time. A walk is basic, but can be done in infinitely many ways, with original variations constantly being found. Breathing is basic, but Martha Graham reinvented it in "contraction and release." Falling is basic, but Doris Humphrey reinvented it in "fall and recovery." We rise to virtue, fall into sin; yet Alwin Nikolais reinvented rising and falling by removing all moral attachments. "Projecting" is basic for performers, but Erick Hawkins reinvented it by *projecting receptiveness*.

$\mathcal{P}$ROJECT 20   REINVENTING MOVES.

- Reinvent a jump, a run, a walk, or any basic movement element.
- Reinvent moving through space in some other way.
- Reinvent movement above the hips.

- Reinvent your extremities: arms, legs, neck/head.
- Reinvent the floor. ■

PROJECT 21   *(TOUGH)* REINVENTING MOVEMENT SOURCES.

- Reinvent the joints in your body.
- Reinvent articulation.
- Reinvent comfort, discomfort, and other feelings and reactions to feelings. ■

PROJECT 22   *(TOUGHER)* REINVENTING CONCEPTS.

What are your basic assumptions? Explore their movement consequences. Explore the movement consequences of questioning or denying your basic assumptions. ■

WRONG MOVEMENT

My definition of wrong movement: a move that injures your body. AVOID SUCH MOVEMENT! As for flexed feet, flailing arms, twitches, wobbles, lurches, etc., that's technique or lack of it. Go for technique in technique class, but ease off when exploring the *MAP*.

PROJECT 23   A STUDY IN "WRONG" MOVEMENT.

- *"Wrong" arms:* a study using arms jerkily, grabbily, unconnectedly, etc.
- *"Wrong" weight:* lurching, staggering, stumbling, tripping, leaning, spilling, tilting.
- Some dancers *lose their center.* (Bad!) Make an off-center study exploring the possibilities of being off-center.
- *Wobbling* is only permitted to tight-rope walkers, who sometimes do it on purpose to emphasize the difficulty of their art. Make a wobbling dance.
- A dancer who *puts a foot down twice* to get it on the floor once is a tender-foot. Try a study in "antisurefootedness."
- *Control.* All techniques strive for control. Without it, any move can be dangerous. Yet we can become obsessed with it. Make a study in giving up control.
- *"Antitechnique."* If you're trained in a technique, try to discover assumptions you carry from technique into your creative work. Make a study consciously abandoning such assumptions.
- What other "wrong" movement can you think of to make a dance? ■

Caution! Any of the movements in Project 23 can be dangerous. Use all your skill and training to avoid the truly wrong move leading to injury.

When Paul Taylor decided to use nondance moves like walking, running, jumping, and falling down, the result was *Esplanade,* a thrilling dance. Using nondance moves is challenging and a good tonic if you want to escape from well-worn dance technique.

$\mathcal{P}$ROJECT 24 NONDANCE MOVES.

1. List activities where nondance moves are seen in sports, work, recreation, and chores, and are done in home, yard, street, and workplace.
2. Extract and list moves. *Examples:* kicking, digging, exercising, climbing, dodging.
3. Make a study out of those moves. ■

Nondance moves: Dancers crouching as if to begin a race. From Alice Teirstein's *Walking Shoes.*

Ken Cooper

INTERIORS: THE MIND'S EYE

A song begins: "The greatest story ever told is here inside my head." Why not the greatest dance?

Martha Graham said, "The body learns first"; but she also said that you don't know a dance until it's firmly in the mind. She instructed me to lie on my back and mentally dance without moving a muscle, and was delighted to hear that as a U.S. Army air cadet, I was instructed to practice aerobatics in exactly the same way.

Have you ever walked through a junk-littered lot, hiked a mountain trail, or forded a stream by leaping from rock to rock? You visualize each step just before you take it. In dance too, you can visualize moves just before you make them. This study draws out moves formed in your mind.

𝒫ROJECT 25   FROM THE MIND'S EYE.

Interior Dancer. Stand quietly. Close your eyes. Allow the image of a dancer to enter your mind. Watch the dancer move. Open your eyes and do the move. If you don't particularly like the move, wait for something else. If you miss it, replay it. The interior dancer will oblige. When you have it, open your eyes and try that new move. When you have two moves, fit them together. Repeat, returning to the interior dancer for ideas. Make that dance.

Interior Dance. Visualize a dance in your mind. It can be a solo, or group, a dance you know or have seen, or one you imagine. You don't have to catch it exactly. The object is to find kernels upon which to develop moves or the whole dance. Stop anywhere to try a move. "Replay" anything you want to see again. Get on your feet and do it. Learn it. Make the dance. ■

ENDNOTES

1. Twyla Tharp, *Push Comes to Shove* (New York: Bantam, 1992), p. 1.

2. Ibid., p. 45.

3. Physicalization as an actor's exercise is described in Viola Spolin, *Improvisation for the Theater* (Evanston, IL: Northwestern University Press, 1963), p.227.

4. Louis Horst and Carroll Russell, *Modern Dance Forms in Relation to the Other Modern Arts* (Brooklyn: Dance Horizons, 1967), p.101.

5. Edward T. Cone, *Musical Form and Musical Performance* (New York: W. W. Norton, 1968), p. 72.

6. The choreographers are Rod Alexander, Edith Barstow, Valerie Bettis, John Butler, Marc Breaux, Jack Cole, Felissa Conde, Joe Layton, Jonathan Lucas, Agnes DeMille, Ronald Field, Ernest Flatt, Doris Humphrey, Dania Krupska, Jerome Robbins, Herbert Ross, Donald Saddler, Buddy Schwab, Helen Tamiris, and Deedee Woods.

CHAPTER 3

INVENTING MOVEMENT

Movement can flow from perceptions, thoughts, impulses, emotions, and images. This is a transformation—concept to action—and the resulting movement is reasonably deemed invention.

Yet it is important to know that in the preceding chapter, dances fashioned from what we think of as existing moves also demand invention, since any move is transformed when used in a dance.

The projects that follow are meant to elicit physical responses which can be worked into dances. A few, like Project 39, Body Language to

Dance Language, could have been placed in the preceding chapter but are here because they are not often used to make dances.

You will not find music, however, although it is assuredly something to which dancemakers urgently respond. Since music appears in virtually every project and is closely tied to dance, perhaps it's good to liberate dance from it once in a while.

In the projects that follow, dancemakers respond to ideas, to nature and human nature, to sports, tasks, games, chairs, hats, and canes, which are often seen in dances, and also to windshield wipers and floor polishers, not often seen. All these and myriad others can serve to elicit physical responses to be embodied and transformed in dance.

QUALITIES

Qualities can lead directly to movement. A dance can be created expressing the quality of gentleness or dignity or generosity or slyness. Charisma might be more demanding.

A movement has both outer and inner attributes. When walking, for instance, you place one foot after the other—the outer attribute. But a walk can be bold, hesitant, serene, fidgety, or have numberless other inner attributes. We can call the inner attributes **qualities**. Dance is sublimely equipped to communicate the subtlest qualities, and it is impossible to dance without projecting a quality of some kind.

𝒫ROJECT 26   QUALITIES IN CONTRAST.

1. Lyrical and percussive. (The first dance I ever made was based on these two qualities. The title: *Lyric Percussive*.)
    a. Make a single percussive movement.
    b. Make a single lyrical movement.
    c. Do one of these twice, the other three times, in any order.
    d. Manipulate the order until you feel comfortable dancing it as a phrase.
    e. Build more phrases and expand into a study.
2. Try other contrasting qualities: strong/weak, bold/ shy, lighthearted/serious, cold/hot, etc.

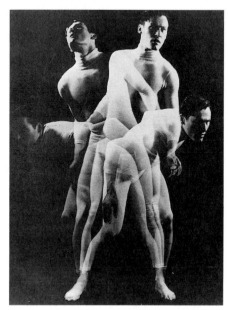

Stuart Hodes in *Lyric Percussive*.

Alfred Gescheidt

3. Choose less related contrasts: empty/hopeful, reluctant/ hungry, etc.

4. Choose unrelated qualities, like delicate/impatient, surprised/silly. ■

PROJECT 27   PROBING QUALITIES.

1. Pick a quality—cruelty, for instance; then seek as many movements in it as you can.

2. Search for the quality of anything or anyone: an apple, a friend, a tyrant, a saint, a skyscraper, shoelaces.

3. Open any book at random and point to one word. Do it a second time. Make moves based on qualities the words evoke. ■

PROJECT 28   UNCOVERING A QUALITY.

Try to make a dance or phrase with no quality whatsoever.
Caution. Something will be revealed! ■

Earth, Air, Fire, Water

The Four Temperaments, a masterpiece by George Balanchine, deals with pure qualities. Balanchine drew inspiration from the medieval concept of four basic elements:

| earth | air | fire | water |

and four related humors:

| blood | phlegm | yellow bile | black bile |

producing four temperaments:

| sanguine | phlegmatic | choleric | melancholic |

PROJECT 29   EARTH, AIR, FIRE, WATER.

Base a study:

1. on one element, humor, or temperament

2. on a vertical group:

    a. earth—blood—sanguine

    b. air—phlegm—phlegmatic

    c. fire—yellow bile—choleric

    d. water—black bile—melancholic

3. on a horizontal group:
   a. earth—air—fire—water
   b. blood—phlegm—yellow bile—black bile
   c. sanguine—phlegmatic—choleric—melancholic
4. on a contrast between two elements, humors, or temperaments
5. on a different quality that is elemental to you ■

IMAGES

We constantly experience images generated by our senses, feelings, thoughts, dreams. Almost any image can become a dance, and dances themselves generate images.

Image has many meanings: picture, reflection, idea, perception, concept, apprehension, etc. There is not a spot on the *MAP* that does not generate an image. In this next project, we will try to turn that image into movement, thinking of it as a projected essence, the sum and substance of the whole.

*P*ROJECT 30   MOVEMENT FROM AN IMAGE.

- A corporate logo is often the object of a long, costly design project. Collect corporate logos and use them for an image study.
- Automobile advertising aims at specific kinds of people: young professionals, outdoor types, growing families, singles, power trippers, etc. Select one or more automobile ads. Make a dance study capturing the image of the person who might be each ad's target.
- An advertising guru said that when people buy perfume, they buy its advertising. Find a perfume ad; make a dance of that essence.
- Seek the kinetic images projected by: celebrities, political figures, pets, buildings, cities, farms, forms of transportation, kinds of food, clothing styles, gemstones, vacation spots, classmates, teachers, yourself. ■

NATURE

Nature is as powerfully present in a single atom as in the entire universe. Its awesome mysteries generate curiosity, reverence, and creativity, inspiring scientists, saints, and artists.

Ted Shawn looked to St. Francis of Assisi, the nature saint, for a solo, *O Brother Sun and Sister Moon* (page 34). Erick Hawkins based his dance technique upon a sensitive and reverential merging with nature, and many of his dances are made directly from nature images. Nature will always be an endless inspiration and source of new dances.

Jacobs Pillow Archives

Ted Shawn as St. Francis in *O Brother Sun and Sister Moon.*

ᐯROJECT 31   NATURE STUDIES.

Select any four entities of nature—for instance: wind, clouds, water, trees—each student to pick one for a study that is exactly sixteen counts long. Show:

1. individually
2. all the wind studies together, then all cloud studies, tree studies, etc.
3. groups that mix the different nature studies
4. nature variations

   • Three students whose studies are based on the same image learn the 16-count studies of the other two. Show as:

   a. three solos each incorporating all three studies,

   b. three duets by dancers 1 and 2, 1 and 3, 2 and 3,

   c. a trio, cooperatively created by the three.

   • Three who've chosen different nature images combine them to produce an out-of-doors suite, such as wind, trees, clouds, etc.

   • The whole group dance together to evoke a nature landscape. Add music, nature sounds, poetry, speech.   ■

Isadora's Way

At the turn of the century, Isadora Duncan rejected artifice and eclecticism, which had largely dominated American dance, and turned to nature. She found a new place on the *MAP*.

> *My first idea of movement came from the rhythm of the waves. I remember the first time I saw a palm tree, its leaves trembling in the early morning breeze and from them I created in my dance that light fluttering of the arms, hands and fingers that has been so abused by my imitators, for they forget to go to the source and contemplate the palm tree, receiving inwardly before giving it outwardly.*
>
> ISADORA DUNCAN, *My Life*

Duncan was an original—but not her imitators, who turned Duncan's work into conventions. Martha Graham, who rebelled against classical ballet, also rebelled against neo-Duncan artifices. She wrote:

> *Esther Gustafson . . . was what was called a nature dancer. . . . It used to be that when dance was staged, a flurry of the hand meant nothing more than the representation of falling rain. . . . The arm, moved in a certain way, suggested a wildflower or the growth of corn. Why though, should an arm try to be corn, or a hand, rain? The hand is too wonderful a thing to be an imitation of something else.*
>
> MARTHA GRAHAM, *Blood Memory*

Erick Hawkins returned to nature, striving to embody rather than represent it. In a real sense he did what Isadora did—he went to the source. Hawkins rejected the concealed effort of classical ballet, his first technique, and the revealed effort of Graham's technique, his second. Dancer Eva Blasczikova, who heads the Duncan Center in Prague, Czech Republic, considers Erick Hawkins to be the true heir of Isadora.

*P*ROJECT 32 STUDYING NATURE.

1. Closely observe some detail of life.
2. From it, extract a kernel of movement.
3. Decide where in the body you can place this kernel of movement.
4. If limited to, say, an arm, expand it. If more general, focus on it. Develop as a study.
5. Find a title from the same source from which you found the movement.
6. Show the study. ■

SIN STUDY

The seven deadly sins:

avarice, envy, gluttony, jealousy, lust, pride, sloth

Mark Morris made a powerful solo, *Jealousy*, torso twisting, arms snaking as if in vain attempt to embrace the unembraceable. The deadly sins can be a mother lode for dancemakers.

*P*ROJECT 33 SIN STUDY.

Pick one sin as the focus of a study. When you show the study, you may announce the sin or let people guess. Moves that illustrate or suggest the sin come first to mind, but also think about moves resulting from the *consequences* of a sin.

Chances are that your personal opinion will be revealed. Do you consider sloth contemptible, avarice irritating, gluttony nauseating? Studies of jealousy and envy can spark thoughtful discussions on the subtle differences between the two. As for lust, dance studies often reveal vastly differing attitudes toward that particular sin.

After the showing, ask if the sin could be identified, although that isn't necessary for the dance to be interesting. ∎

*P*ROJECT 34 DEEPER IN SIN.

- Combine sins, such as sloth and gluttony, jealousy and lust.
- Find a character from literature who embodies a sin (Charles Dickens created some dandies), and build your sin study around that character.
- Look up mortal and venial sins for studies. ∎

*P*ROJECT 35 VIRTUES.

Use virtues for studies, and also the contrast between virtue and sin. ∎

COMMANDMENTS

1. THOU SHALT HAVE NO OTHER GODS BEFORE ME.
2. THOU SHALT NOT MAKE UNTO THEE ANY GRAVEN IMAGE.
3. THOU SHALT NOT TAKE THE NAME OF THE LORD THY GOD IN VAIN.
4. REMEMBER THE SABBATH DAY TO KEEP IT HOLY.

5. HONOR THY FATHER AND THY MOTHER.

6. THOU SHALT NOT KILL.

7. THOU SHALT NOT COMMIT ADULTERY.

8. THOU SHALT NOT STEAL.

9. THOU SHALT NOT BEAR FALSE WITNESS AGAINST THY NEIGHBOR.

10. THOU SHALT NOT COVET THY NEIGHBOR'S WIFE, THOU SHALT NOT COVET THY NEIGHBOR'S OX, NOR ANY THING THAT IS THY NEIGHBOR'S.

*P*ROJECT 36 COMMANDMENT DANCE STUDY.

Eight Commandments are *shalt nots*. Numbers four and five are positive. In your study you may:

- Use one Commandment, several, or the concept of commandments.
- Expand on a single Commandment.
- React to the idea of having broken a Commandment.
- Explore the essence, turmoil, or tranquility of a Commandment.
- Take a philosophical or ecumenical approach.
- Peruse your own conscience vis-à-vis the Commandments.
- Make up a new commandment. ■

RELATIONSHIPS

We are social beings—so any two people onstage *imply* a relationship—but that doesn't always mean there is one. Two brilliant dancers, Molissa Fenley and Doug Varone, choreographed separate solos and performed them onstage together, although neither had seen the other's dance. The result was provocative because their proximity suggested a relationship which the dancing denied. Yet even solos can evoke relationships. Hamlet's soliloquy, "To be, or not to be . . ." presents his relationship with Death.

In Martha Graham's *Appalachian Spring,* the husbandman and his bride provide the central relationship. But the bride's dances also reveal relationships with her pioneer ancestors, the children she dreams of having, and with God; the husbandman relates to the house he is building and to the land.

Improvisation is useful in developing dance relationships. It draws on right-brain knowledge often hidden from the rational left brain.

PROJECT 37 RELATIONSHIP STUDY (PAIRS OF DANCERS).

- Create a pure-movement relationship.
- Evoke a famous fictional relationship.
- Explore your relationship with your dance partner.
- Rework any two solos into one relational duet.
- Respond to the flash-word list presented on page 85 to obtain pure movement; then make that movement relational. ■

PROJECT 38 IMPLIED RELATIONSHIP (ONE DANCER).

Make a solo that evokes an absent partner. ■

BODY LANGUAGE

The term **body language** began to show up in articles on pop psychology in the 1970s when it was realized that the whole body communicates feelings and attitudes, just as do gestures and facial expressions.

Girlfriends, a work by Jawole Willa Jo Zollar, is a gabfest. Four friends talk, argue, and tell stories, *completely in body language.* In the last seconds, one tells a joke, and as the lights fade, real laughter springs from their throats.

PROJECT 39 BODY LANGUAGE TO DANCE LANGUAGE.

1. Extend facial expressions into the whole body—for instance, a frown into rejection or disapproval, a Mona Lisa smile into a seductive mystery. Try expressions from wide-eyed delight to slit-eyed suspicion, from puzzlement to I-told-you-so.
2. Start with body language to create: a quiet conversation between two friends, a theoretical dispute between two scientists, a fight between lovers, a proud mama or papa with a newborn.
3. Improvise in body language: Find a monologue from a speech, a play, etc. Speak it into a tape recorder, then play it as you translate it into body language. Develop it into a dance.
4. Two people try item 3 as a dialogue.
5. Mix body language with verbal speech. ■

VISUALS

Visual artists and dancers inspire one another and often collaborate. An extreme example is the Peruvian painter Oscar Naters who liked to sketch dancers in action; when his sketches inspired them to try new moves, he realized it was a way to make dances. Today Naters has his own dance company and begins dances by making drawings to which his dancers react with movement. Naters then edits and shapes the moves, often making more drawings, until the dance is done.

Postcards

Picture postcards are available on just about any subject, and are excellent for visual studies.

$\mathcal{P}$ROJECT 40   PICTURES TO STIMULATE STUDIES AND IMPROVISATIONS.

Each dancemaker can contribute three or four picture postcards to a pool.

- Select a picture you like or find stimulating, or else draw or photograph one yourself.
- If this picture is of people, use the positions, their action, their relationships, or their character.
- If it is an animal, be the animal, relate to it, sense its life.
- If it is of a landscape, inhabit it, try to escape from it, react with or against it.
- If it is abstract, find moves in its patterns, colors, and shapes. ■

Fine Art

Here's what Martha Graham wrote of the first abstract painting that she ever saw:

> It was by Wassily Kandinsky, and had a streak of red going from one end to the other. I said, "I will do that someday, I will make a dance like that." And I did. I didn't know it at the time, but it had such a great influence on me; that shaft of intimacy. The dance was *Diversion of Angels*.[1]

Graham was also stirred by Pablo Picasso's *Guernica,* which inspired her solo *Deep Song.* Anna Sokolow created *Magritte–Magritte* from the surrealist paintings of René Magritte. Herbert Ross, a dancer and choreographer before he became a movie director, created a powerful ballet, *Caprichos,* from Goya etchings. Choreographer Lynda Gudde created many dances after the paintings of Egon Schiele.

You can seek inspiration in the nearest art museum or in art books. Find an art professor or art student or take an art course. Best, get to know an artist whose work interests you.

$\mathcal{P}$ROJECT 41   FROM A WORK OF FINE ART.

Concentrate on one work of art you admire. Acquire a reproduction if you can. Live with it. Make a dance study. Make a dance.   ■

Expressionism

In the mid-1950s, when Ballet Russe de Monte Carlo brought Leonide Massine's *Mad Tristan* to New York City, many thought it steamy and over-wrought. It was simply influenced by Expressionism, a movement concerned with suffering, death, and doomed humanity.

In its general sense expressionism (lower case "e"), is a somber outgrowth of romanticism. As a movement in Western art, Expressionism, which was centered in Germany, exploded after World War I, and was accompanied by a visionary yet pessimistic socio-political ideal. It influenced music, literature, theater, filmmaking, and dance, to produce dark, brooding, highly charged works. Mary Wigman, Harald Kreutzberg, and Kurt Jooss, are prominent dance exemplars.

The Green Table, Kurt Jooss's fierce anti-war ballet with its characterization of avaricious politicians whose evil machinations succeed in summoning a terrifying figure of Death, is certainly the best-known example of Expressionism in dance. Pearl Primus's *Strange Fruit,* a powerful condemnation of lynching, in its macabre subject matter and searing social statement, projects Expressionist affinities, as does Anna Sokolow's dramatic *Rooms,* a stark portrait of people driven mad by loneliness and isolation.

Pola Nirenska, who danced in Germany with Mary Wigman, fled to the United States when the Nazis took power; in the last decade of her life she made vividly Expressionist dances about the Holocaust.

Dance flows naturally toward Expressionism, for it can deal with sweeping ideas and still remain a passionate personal expression.

$\mathcal{P}$ROJECT 42   EXPRESSIONISM IN MOVEMENT.

- Peruse Expressionist art. Find a painting that interests you. Seek movement in it for a study or a whole dance.
- With no specific subject in mind, develop movement that is Expressionistic in nature. If the movement suggests an idea, follow it. Or develop as a study in Expressionist movement; when you show it, ask your colleagues what ideas it evokes.   ■

Duet 1976, an "Air Mail Dance," by Remy Charlip.

Picture Score or Dance Storyboard

Ruth St. Denis, the story goes, was inspired to make *Radha,* her first big success, by a picture of the goddess Isis that she spotted on a poster advertising cigarettes. Many of her later dances were based on cultures she could not have experienced; so she certainly drew from pictures again, as did her partner, Ted Shawn, who collected drawings, woodcuts, and photographs of statues of saints before he created *O Brother Sun and Sister Moon,* a solo portrait of St. Francis of Assisi.

In the early 1960s, Remy Charlip made a set of drawings for Barbara Dilly, who used them to fashion a dance. Steve Paxton pasted up newspaper photos of athletes for his dancers to use in generating moves. Carolyn Brown used female athletes to inspire *Bunkered for a Bogie,* subtitled, (*Steve Paxton Did It First*).

Remy Charlip expanded the concept with *Air Mail Dances,* sets of pictures he assembles or draws and sends to dancemakers, who take it from there. In one, *39 Chinese Attitudes,* realized and performed by Nancy Lewis, the pictures were displayed in the theater lobby, mostly silhouette cutouts of classical Chinese dance, together with some pictures of Martha Graham, Isadora Duncan, Barbara Bush, and athletes in action—along with Charlip's brief instructions. From this material Lewis fashioned a dance whose success owed much to her own skill and charm, yet sprang from Charlip's idea of bringing all that extravagant, melodramatic action together.

Air Mail Dances has a fascinating genesis. Charlip had gone to Australia to choreograph for the New South Wales Dance Company. However, he had neglected to bring his yellow fever inoculation certificate, so he was sent to a quarantine station. It was there that he made the drawings for *Duet 1976,* mailed them off, and *Air Mail Dances* was born! The drawings for *Duet 1976* are on page 41.

*P*ROJECT 43   A PICTURE SCORE OR DANCE STORYBOARD.

- Collect or make five to twenty-five pictures of people. Bring them to class or workshop. Horse-trade if desired. Use one set to make and show a dance.
- Try Paxton's cut-out-and-paste-up idea using contemporary athletes or other action pictures.
- Make a paste-up picture score of animals in action.
- Have a visual artist make a set of drawings for a dance project.
- Borrow or buy one of Charlip's books: *Arm in Arm* or *Fortunately.* Use his drawings to make a dance.

A departing gift from dancers of the Guangdong Modern Dance Company. It can be a picture score for dancers who are able to shape their bodies into these extraordinary positions.

- Use Charlip's *Duet 1976* drawings, giving Charlip program credit if the dance is performed.
- Commission Remy Charlip to make a set of *Air Mail Dances* for your group. (He lives in San Francisco.) ■

*P*ROJECT 44   ONE PICTURE SCORE, SEVERAL STUDIES.

Use any of the preceeding methods to obtain a picture score. Make copies so that several dancemakers can work on the same score simultaneously. The object is to see how the same visual material can be variously realized. ■

Dance Photographs As Picture Scores

Dance communities everywhere attract a special breed of photographer with a feel for dance. Their images are a bequest to history and a resource for dancemakers.

Steven Speliotis

Sara Hook and Stuart Hodes in Stephen Koplowitz's *Dirty Old Man.*

The earliest dance photos, made with slow lenses and films, were essentially posed; but by the 1940s, photography could stop action. Barbara Morgan's famous pictures of Martha Graham were really performances for the camera. When Philippe Halsman photographed Graham's *Cave of the Heart,* the cast, costumed and in makeup, started the dance from the top. When Halsman said, "Stop! Do that again," the action was repeated, and he took pictures. This remains a favored method for making impeccable photos of finished works. Stephen Speliotis's photos of Stephan Koplowitz's *Dirty Old Man* and *There Were Three Men,* were made using this process.

Some prefer to shoot dress rehearsals or performances, which are less controllable but more spontaneous. In the 1950s, Fred Fehl would show up at everything from studio concerts to Broadway musicals. Many of the photographers whose pictures appear in this book take such an approach, and their work constitutes an invaluable record of New York City's dance scene. Happily, I've seen their counterparts all over the United States, also in China and Russia.

An improvisational approach, pioneered by Max Waldman, was extended by Lois Greenfield, who tells dancers to "leave their choreography outside the door." Improvising for a still camera is different from other improvisation. Since the camera captures dynamic instants, dancers focus upon the instant, which is quite unlike improvising for continuity.

In 1952, Alfred Gescheidt photographed my unfinished solo *Flak*. One image so powerfully extracted a particular move that it sent me back to the dance to rework and strengthen that move. It did not occur to me that this could be a way to create dances until I read about Elisa Monte's *Volkmann Suite,* directly inspired by photographs Roy Volkmann had made of two of Monte's dancers, as they improvised for the camera. Monte used Volkmann's photos as a picture score. About turning those captured instants into a dance, Monte said: "It's how you arrive somewhere and come out of it that makes the movement so important."[2]

Vitali Pustovalov

Gus Solomons jr dancing for the camera.

𝒫ROJECT 45   PHOTOGRAPHS AS PICTURE SCORES.

- Improvise for a photographer. Use the resulting photos to make a solo for yourself.
- Have another dancer improvise for the camera. Use the pictures to make a dance for that dancer, someone else, or yourself.
- Obtain one or more photographs of a dance you have never seen. Use them for your own original study.
- Obtain photos of three or more different dances and use them to make a new dance. Your having seen the dances should not be a problem since you will mix the images.
- Find dance photos from a distant time and place. Recycle and transform into a new dance. ■

NONDANCER DANCES

When Johanna Boyce began, she worked not with dancers but architects. Why architects? Because, like dancers, they are deeply concerned with space.

Stephan Koplowitz's *I'm Growing* uses sixth- to eighth- grade school boys, not dance-trained. Koplowitz drew moves from the dancers, from their sport activities to the way they pose and preen before a mirror.

In the mid-1970s, New York University School of the Arts hosted a dance festival. One of the first pieces shown was by a small upstate New York college. Lacking even a minor in dance, they wowed everyone with an alphabet suite from something like, "A is for Athlete," to "Z is for Zen," scintillating with kinetic puns and punch lines, each segment managing to top the one before! They showed that creative miracles, and every good dance is a bit of a miracle, can spring from anywhere.

*P*ROJECT 46   A NONDANCER DANCE.

1. If you are a trained dancer:
   a. Find a nondancer to work with on a study that one or both of you will perform. Be sure to find moves in which the nondance-trained dancer is comfortable.
   b. Enlist a nondancer as a creative collaborator and make a dance together.
2. If you are a nontrained dancer, try your dance ideas on trained dancers or nontrained dancers or on both. Dance training is sublime, but lack of it allowed Pilobolus to reach an entirely new place on the *MAP*. ■

OPENINGS

There's nothing particularly difficult about beginning a dance, yet it is a special moment that sets up everything to come. It can be explosive, dramatic, cute, funny, or ominous, and some openings work fine without being anything in particular.

Jerome Robbins's *Les Noces* begins with an eye-grabber; a woman lets down her "hair," whose coils shoot out ten feet to each side. Pilobolus often opens dances with intricate body constructions that defy you to tell one person from another. Manual Alum opened a dance with dancers standing on their heads to create a forest of waving legs.

Quiet openings can be memorable. In Martha Graham's *Appalachian Spring,* we see a partly built house, then a serene procession: pioneering woman, a young couple, a preacher, his flock.

Merce Cunningham sometimes seems to omit openings; his dances begin as though we are being permitted to look in on an event that had begun long before the curtain rose and will go on long after it comes down.

Just what constitutes an opening? How long is an opening? You can answer these questions for yourself in this project.

$\mathcal{P}$ROJECT 47   OPENINGS STUDY.

Make one or more studies that consist only of opening moves. Show and ask your watchers what kind of dance the opening implies, and if they want to see more. Pick one opening and add to it. Sometimes an entire dance springs from an opening. ■

ENTRANCES

In a gala performance by American Ballet Theater, as each celebrated ballerina or duo appeared to make their grand entrance, fans screamed. Something like that inspired Antony Tudor to make a hilarious ballet, *Gala Performance.*

There are many kinds of entrances:

➤ *The grand entrance:* "Here I am!"
➤ *The virtuoso entrance:* stunning leaps or other feats.
➤ *The unnoticed entrance:* gets the performer on without distracting from other action.
➤ *The discovered entrance,* in which the character is revealed after an unnoticed entrance.
➤ *The shocking entrance,* as in Herbert Ross's *Caprichos,* where an inert woman falls from offstage into a man's arms.
➤ *The character entrance,* in which something about the character is immediately revealed.

What other kinds of entrances can there be?

$\mathcal{P}$ROJECT 48   ENTRANCE STUDY.

Enter audaciously, boldly, grandly, happily, sadly, shyly, sneakily, stealthily, surprisingly, unwillingly, or in character, so that the entrance propels the dance to follow. ■

DANCING "ABOUT"

Dance is an art form whose basic palette consists of live human beings. Individuals can never be abstractions; each person has a story—and if the choreographer doesn't tell it, the audience will likely make it up for themselves.

All Martha Graham's dances are patently about something. Her final work, *Maple Leaf Rag*, pokes fun at her own stormy heroines. Linda Hodes drew from John Steinbeck's *Of Mice and Men* to make *Curley's Wife*, a dance about a lonely woman whose flirtation leads to tragedy. In Glen Tetley's *Anatomy Lesson*, a group of medical students gather around a cadaver as the soul who had once inhabited it rises for a last dance. *Kiss*, by Susan Marshall, explodes into a spinning, reeling, whirling, maelstrom of every devastating first kiss. *Talking in Her Sleep*, by Wang Mei, deals with abortion; *Strange Fruit*, by Pearl Primus, with racism and murder. *Day on Earth*, by Doris Humphrey, chronicles a peasant family's life. Alvin Ailey's *Cry* is a paean to mother love and pride. *The Moor's Pavane*, by José

Nicolas Gunn and Sally Trammel in *Curley's Wife*, by Linda Hodes.

Alfred Gescheidt

Tom Caravaglia

Left to right: Carla Maxwell, Gabriella Agranat-Getz, and Jonathan Leinbach in Doris Humphrey's *Day on Earth*.

Limon, presents the dramatic core of Shakespeare's *Othello* (page 51). *Le Combat Antique,* by Etienne DeCroux, encapsulates the generation gap. *Cave of the Heart,* by Martha Graham, plumbs destroying jealousy and rage, whereas *Clytemnestra* treats sin and redemption. George Balanchine, credited with perfecting the pure classical ballet, a dance about dancing, said, "Every *pas de deux* is a love dance."

Starting a dance, not knowing what it is about, allowing the choreography to lead the way, can be an exciting adventure.

*P*ROJECT 49 "ABOUT" STUDY.

- *From movement to idea.* You are not bound by any subject matter, so begin gloriously free. Hold off using music in order to let that freedom reign. Begin to dance by letting the moves come from wherever they will. If you improvise, do so with no plan but discovery. When you encounter a sensation, a move, a sequence you enjoy, it's pay dirt! Make your discovery into a phrase or study and present it to your colleagues. Ask what they see, but decide for yourself what you are dancing about.

- *From idea to movement.* Begin with an image, pattern, emotion, dilemma, character, relationship, or setting. Keep it strongly in mind as you begin to move. When you feel the moves have begun to encounter that subject, dig deeper, but, and this is important, do not make judgments. Continue to explore in movement alone, letting your body make the judgments. When you have developed a phrase or study you can repeat, show it to your colleagues. Ask what they see. If it is not what you had in mind, consider it as a new option, something to use any way you please as you further develop your dance. ■

RITE, RITUAL, CEREMONY

One characteristic of rites, rituals, and ceremonies is *purpose*. The purpose can be solemn: coronations, elections, and funerals, or joyous: fêtes, graduations, and parades. There are also intimate rituals: family dinners, baking bread, feeding pets, watering plants, going to the theater, going to bed, rising, washing, asking for a raise, taking an exam, or taking a dance class.

Dances in a ritual mode include Martha Graham's *Primitive Mysteries,* which draws on religious passion, Sukarji Sriman's *Circle of Bliss,* a lyrical ritual honoring death, Paul Taylor's *Runes,* which evokes a vanished people from their mysterious writings, and Barbara Roan's *October Parade,* which expands on the merrymaking and high jinks of a small-town celebration. Many dances by Erick Hawkins draw on the ritual majesty of nature; Laura Dean's dances plumb the hypnotic power of geometric forms; Lucinda Childs magnifies her dances with rituallike use of movement; dances of Anne Teresa De Keersmaeker project the imperative people feel to ritualize their very lives.

Dance was a ritual observance long before the dawn of civilization and still is among dervishes of the Middle East, Hasidic Jews, who follow the teachings of the Baal Shem-Tov, trance dancers of Africa and the Caribbean, and others. At proms and weddings, dance is a modern ritual.

Dancing on Christmas Eve, by Hartmann Schedel, a woodcut from the Nuremberg Chronicle, 1493.

Courtesy of the Pierpont Morgan Library

Tom Caravaglia

Left to right: Carla Maxwell, Clay Taliaferro, Jennifer Scanlon, and Lutz Förster in José Limón's classic *The Moor's Pavane*.

*P*ROJECT 50   RITUAL STUDY.

Find the ritual aspect in

1. *Growth or health:* bodybuilding, jogging, fitness
2. *Warding off evil:* saying "God Bless You!" after a sneeze, knocking on wood, whistling in the dark, and other quasi-magical rituals
3. *Self-help:* EST, Yoga, martial arts, power lunches
4. *Education:* registration, lectures, studying
5. *Crowd rituals:* confrontation, parades, protests, theater openings

When you've chosen a ritual, extract its dance material and make a study ■

TASKS

A task has a short-term objective. It can be burdensome, and like a chore, it is sometimes assigned—clean the apartment, take attendance, wash the windows, weed the garden, deliver a package, alphabetize a list.

In Trisha Brown's *Line Up,* the task is to get all the dancers into line. Visual puns flash as the dancers line up along the back of the stage, become people waiting patiently in line, and form a police lineup. Often, just as the task seems done, someone gets "out of line" and they must start it over—a fascinating dance that grows from its task like a snowflake from its nucleus of dust.

Almost anything can be assigned as a task; yet it takes some thinking to find one as elegant as just forming a line. Following are some tasks I've heard about:

1. Individual tasks
    a. Measure out the dance floor in paces.
    b. Lay out a checkerboard of newspapers or plastic floor tiles.
    c. Wrap your feet and do a "soft shoe" dance.
    d. Block, then unblock, every entrance to the performing space.
    e. Try on shirts, tie on bowties.
    f. Chalk a poem or prose on a large blackboard.
    g. Walk turned in, run turned out.
2. Group tasks
    a. Link all the dancers together with red ribbon.
    b. All take hands and form numbers, from one to ten.
    c. Exchange handshakes, hugs, and kisses on both cheeks.
    d. Signal "How do you do?" with semaphore arms.
    e. Run a footrace, make a clean sweep, erect a fence.
    f. Spell "Happy Birthday."
    g. Make a tight pack in the center of the stage, blow up like a balloon to the limits of space, then deflate.

*P*ROJECT 51   TASK STUDY.

Devise a task and make it the seed of a dance. Build the dance to achieve the task. Divert it with barriers and deflections, challenge it with obstacles, hewing to the task until the task and the dance are done. ■

GAMES

Games are competitions with rules in which tasks are embedded—hit a ball over a net, toss a horseshoe at a stake. In solitary games you compete with the task itself, as in walking on the sidewalk but not stepping on the cracks, or in the card game solitaire.

Games have winners and losers, yet, like dances, can be interesting in themselves. Most games are metaphors for war, from American football, which has real physical combat, to chess, a symbolic battlefield in which each player sets out to capture the other's king. Businesses, the manufacturing game, the real estate game, and so on, contain a powerful element of combat. Games are primal.

Donald McKayle and Jeff Duncan were early explorers of game-based dances. McKayle's classic, *Games*, uses children's street games as a metaphor for their lives. Duncan abstracted the idea of tasks, rules, and competing to create *Three Fictitious Games*. Any task or activity can become a game: trying on clothes, baking bread, making faces, shifting weight, etc. Marlene Pennison made an eerie solo titled, *Don't Step on the Pavement Cracks*. The core of a game is an objective with rules. It's easy to create a wholly new game.

*P*ROJECT 52 GAME STUDY.

1. Recall a game played as a child: tag, hide-and-seek, red light, giant steps, capture the flag, hopscotch, jacks. Identify its objectives and rules. Adapt it into a dance. Try changing a rule to see how it changes the dance.
2. Make a dance from chess, checkers, Parcheesi, riddles, crosswords, mah-jongg, bingo, Monopoly. Try baby games: peek-a-boo, this little piggy.
3. Create a new or imaginary game. ■

DOFFIT! A Nonsense Game, or Rules Run Amok.

DOFFIT! requires three or more players.
Objective: to doff (remove) 6 doffing items.

BASIC RULES (for which any others may be substituted)

Each player needs one sturdy chair and wears 6 doffing items: for example, a glove, sock, hat, tie, necklace, sunglasses.

Each player has an ally who watches an opposing player. Conversely, each player has a watcher, who is the ally of an opposing player. The ally/watcher keeps track of a player's windings and doffs, and sees that all rules are followed. A win is credited to both the player and ally.

Players begin sitting on their chairs wearing their 6 doffing items. Watchers stand near the chair they are watching and are free to move around it. They may not block the moves of that chair's player, however.

At the signal, which can be the start of music or the word "GO!" given by a nonplayer, all players begin to wind. Winding is always clockwise. **1st phase winding** is around one's own chair, **2nd phase**, around an opponent's chair. A **full winding** consists of circling one's own chair 5 times (1st phase), then any opponent's chair 5 times (2nd phase).

A player who completes a full winding may make a doff. When this happens the watcher yells, "DOFFIT ONE!" Then the player returns to his/her own chair to begin another winding. This continues until the call of "DOFFIT SIX! WE HAVE A WINNER!" The game ends and the victory conga begins.

EXTENDED RULES (for which any others may be substituted)

Each winding must be done in a different *gait,* which may be a dance step, like a waltz, chassé, assemblé, samba, or Charleston, or a character move, like a duck walk, waddle, hop, sidestep, etc., or any John Cleese–type silly walk (page 58). Before beginning each winding, the player picks a gait and yells it to his/her watcher, as, for example, "Suzy-Q!" or "Silly Walk!" or "Shuffle Off to Buffalo!"

Doffing is done while sitting in an opposing player's chair. When a chair is *occupied for doffing,* the player at that chair enters involuntary *hiatus.* All winding at that chair stops. The doffed item is placed under the chair, at which point involuntary hiatus ends and winding may resume.

TACTICAL RULES (for which any others may be substituted)

Storing: Upon completing a winding, a player may elect *not* to doff but to store the doff. The watcher keeps track of stored doffs. A maximum of 3 doffs may be stored.

Featherbedding: The doffer removes the doffed item and tosses it to any opposing player's watcher, who must toss it back. A game of catch ensues. This forces the opposing player at that chair into extended involuntary hiatus. Featherbedding may continue for a maximum of 10 back-and-forth tosses.

ADVANCED TACTICAL RULES (for which any others may be substituted)

Rhythm Bumping: The purpose is to cut down the lead of players who are ahead. Only one player may rhythm bump at a time. Rhythm bumping starts when a player begins conga drumming on the seat of his/her own chair. The watcher at that chair yells, "RHYTHM BUMPING!" All players who are in 2nd phase winding (that is, at an opponent's chair) must "de-wind," that is, begin circling counterclockwise. Whatever gait is used to wind must be done backwards to de-wind.

During de-winding, watchers subtract from the number of full windings completed. For example, if a player has completed 4 full windings, each "de-wind" reduces the number by one. On reaching zero, any player who has already doffed, must undoff, or don, that is, put one item back on, except those who have stored their doffs.

De-winds cannot exceed the number of full windings. If a player de-winds to zero, the player dons, then is free to wind again, and is thenceforth immune to all rhythm bumping.

INCOMPREHENSIBLY COMPLEX RULES (for which any other incomprehensibly complex rules may be substituted)

Rest Mode. Rest mode begins when any player takes a *voluntary hiatus.* All players must sit down on the chair at which they are winding or doffing. There are two types of voluntary hiatus—major and minor. Players are allowed one major voluntary and one minor voluntary hiatus in each game.

Minor Voluntary Hiatus. A player stands on the seat of any chair in the game, sings "*Row, row, row your boat, Gently down the stream, Merrily, merrily, merrily, merrily, Life is but a dream.*" All other players must stand on one foot and sing along. A minor voluntary hiatus ends when the player who had initiated it jumps down and starts winding.

Major Voluntary Hiatus. A player lies on his or her back, and begins bicycling, legs in the air, while singing "A Bicycle Built for Two":

> Daisy, Daisy, give me your answer, do.
> I'm half crazy, all for the love of you.
> We won't have a fancy marriage, I can't afford a carriage,
> But you'll look sweet, upon the seat of a bicycle built for two.

All players lie on their backs and begin bicycling in time to the music. At the end of the song the player who had initiated the major voluntary hiatus is allowed to go back to winding, while all the others must sing another full stanza.

WINNING

When a player doffs all 6 items, the player's watcher yells, "DOFFIT SIX! WE HAVE A WINNER!"—grabs the winner by the hand and forms a *victory conga line* that picks up all players and watchers, weaves through the chairs, into the audience, out of the studio, and into the world.

*P*ROJECT 53   ORGANIZE A GAME OF DOFFIT!

Now you know the "rules"; work out how they play. ■

Surprises can add excitement to a dance, and more. In Paul Taylor's *Esplanade*, a woman leaps into empty space, to be caught by a man who suddenly appears, epitomizing the trusting wildness of youth. In Martha Graham's *Diversion of Angels*, each flashing crossover of the "woman in red" presents the breathless surprise of romantic love. In James Sutton's

Steven Speliotis

Rising over the toes from a crouch, as demonstrated here by Steven Speliotis, is still a virtuoso move. When done by José Limón in *Lament for Ignacio Sanchez Mejias*, it shocked, not only for its virtuosity, but because it was the perfect move to show the slain bullfighter rising to heaven.

Gambol, a dancer preparing for a ballet pas is jolted out of his reverie when a bowling ball rolls by. In Doris Humphrey's *Lament for Ignacio Sanchez Mejias,* after a bullfighter has been fatally gored, he rises from a fetal crouch right up onto his toes, as if being lifted toward heaven. Surprises seem to be pure inspiration, yet you can seek them thoughtfully, alert for the unexpected.

ℙROJECT 54   KINETIC SURPRISES.

You can recycle a previously made study if you are willing to subject it to mayhem. The study should be rational enough so the audience thinks it knows what to expect. Then shatter those expectations.

- If there is continuity, break it.
- If there is a steady tempo, unsteady it.
- If there is a clear dynamic or intensity, change it.
- If there is a discernable style, violate it.
- If a dance-in-progress suddenly veers from your plan, go with it.
- If there's a clear statement, add a contradictory one.

At first, don't worry about results. Regard your study like a bug under glass. If something catches your interest, draw it out. This is not an easy project, but even modest success can make it worthwhile. ■

THE CUTES

In 1950s musical theater, "cute" was kudos. Cute numbers were staples of Broadway musicals and movies. Cute TV dances were made by Mata and Hari, the Hamilton Trio, and Alwin Nikolais, among others. I performed in a cute nightclub act: *Beatrice Kraft and Dancers.* Kraft was a stunning dancer who did India's *Bharata Natya* skillfully, if not authentically, in a style once known as "Broadway Hindu," which lies at the root of the jazz styles developed by Jack Cole and Bob Fosse. Kraft's routines were cute, yet she was a class act. Cute is popular in ballet: all those tutus and angel wings. And don't forget the cute cowgirl in Agnes DeMille's *Rodeo*. With television, cute boomed because it comes across well on screens.

Cute is not automatically trivial; Charles Moulton's *Nine-Person Precision Ball Passing* is cute and thought-provoking. There's cute in almost every dance by Pilobolus, and some, like *Walklyndon,* are pure cute. Martha Graham's own role in *Acrobats of God* and much of the rest of the dance is cute.

Cute is adroit, bright, smiling, nimble, heartfelt, quirky, even a bit flaky, like Lucille Ball in *I Love Lucy,* but not quite zany and never psycho. Cute can have scatterbrain charm or the harmless cleverness of a crossword puzzle; it can be feisty but not heroic. Virtuosity is okay, like cute juggling acts, as long as there is no challenge or threat. Even a hint of anger obliterates cute.

Cute is babies; windup toys; dog acts; theme parks; Barbie dolls; miniature golf; pillow fights; innocent showing off, like a kid in a space suit; Walt Disney; boy/girl stuff that's not sensual; dance steps, like pecking and Suzy-Q; Michael Jackson's Moon Walk; and some Charleston steps, although not the wild ones; but not the elegant waltz or aggressive 1940s lindy or 1990s hip-hop. There will always be a market for cute. But beware! Dances that try for cute and fail are sorry sights.

𝒫ROJECT 55   A CUTE DANCE.

1. Make a cute motor fragment.
2. Develop a cute phrase.
3. If it works, you're on a roll; make a cute dance. ■

COMIC MOVEMENT

Humor is serious. Comic actor Phil Silvers was always searching for the exact facial expression, tone of voice, gesture, and timing that brought laughter. During the run of the Broadway musical *Do Re Mi,* he said to the cast, "When you find out exactly what gets the laugh, lock it in!" When comic Buddy Hackett was preparing to shoot a TV commercial that showed him in bed asleep, he asked, "Do you want me to sleep funny?"

Theories of humor describe funny components: non sequitur, surprise, exaggeration, skewed focus, skewed context, misdirection, etc. You can try such things, or having found something humorous, try to figure out why it's funny. Yet humor seems resistant to deep analysis. The following project derives from a showing at New York City's Neighborhood Playhouse School of Theater, where students train in comic movement.

$\mathcal{P}$ROJECT 56   COMIC MOVEMENT: A FUNNY WALK.

Because walks reveal so much, modern dance spends a lot of time on them, but never, in my experience, on funny ones. Some funny walks are famous: the crouching walk of Groucho Marx, the feisty saunter of Chaplin's little tramp, the turned-in stumble of Jerry Lewis. The English actor John Cleese created a TV sketch on the premise that a government agency gave grants to develop "silly walks." His own were side-splitting. Here are some suggestions on developing funny walks:

- *Exaggeration.* Overdo or underdo how high you lift your feet, the length of your stride, the bend of one or both knees, the arm swing, the turn of the head, the carriage of the torso. Exaggerate ballet walks or modern dance walks learned in technique classes.
- *Surprise.* Change direction, focus, or tempo. Start, stop, hesitate, lurch, add a hop, a shoulder shake, a kick, etc.
- *Context.* While your legs walk, give your arms something other than swinging: scratch, point, sew on a button, type a letter, send a semaphore.

When you have a funny walk, add moves, comic or not, for other parts of the body. If you start to sense a character or situation, you're closing in on a comic dance.

Caution: the line between a funny and a demeaning move is subtle. Sensitivity is needed here. ■

ROOTS

In *Blues Suite,* Alvin Ailey evokes the Texas town of his childhood; *Revelations* is drawn from his religious upbringing; and *Cry,* dedicated to "all black women everywhere, especially our mothers," was a birthday gift to his own mother. Rudy Perez knows about construction work; in his dances he carves up space, lays down strips of masking tape the way builders mark out foundations, and performs in a hard hat. Sophie Maslow's creation *The Village I Knew,* from Sholom Aleichem's stories, and Pearl Lang's dance *The Possessed,* based on the legend of the *dybbuk,* draw

Paul Owen

Marlene Pennison in *The Hurricane,* a dance about growing up in the Deep South.

Paul Owen

Marlene Pennison and Peter Bass in Pennison's *Mother and Child.*

on their cultural backgrounds; Charles Weidman's *On My Mother's Side* and *And Daddy Was A Fireman* are autobiographical. Marlene Pennison created an entire body of works based on growing up in the Deep South.

*P*ROJECT 57   A DANCE FROM YOUR ROOTS.

Ponder aspects of your life that could make a dance:

- a parent, grandparent, great grandparent, great aunt, or other relative
- a family ritual
- a black sheep

- a family story, triumph, or tragedy
- a childhood dream or obsession
- a real or imaginary playmate
- a neighborhood character or event
- a coming of age
- a reunion, meeting, or farewell ■

POLITICS: MAKING STATEMENTS

At a press conference in Calcutta, held in 1956, a reporter asked Martha Graham, "Why are there no dances in your repertory based on equality and the brotherhood of man?" Graham replied: "If I did not believe in equality and the brotherhood of man, I could not have made a single dance. But I want my dances to be works of art, not propaganda!"

Some say art and politics don't mix, others that art is inescapably political. But all might agree that a work of art can be politically inspired, as are Pablo Picasso's *Guernica,* Martha Graham's *Deep Song,* Bertold Brecht's *Good Woman of Setzuan,* much poetry by Langston Hughes, and centuries of painting and music when art's mission was deemed to be propagating the faith. Even Leni Reifenstahl's film *The Triumph of the Will,* although made as Nazi propaganda, is today regarded as a cinematic work of art. The key ingredient seems to be passionate belief—and political belief, even if misplaced, can serve. A work unsupported by belief, whatever its skill and cleverness, is hack, not art.

At the American Dance Festival in 1990, Leonid Lebedev, a young Russian choreographer, turned every study into a political statement. In a study on props (page 96), his prop was a broom; he entered as an old peasant leaning on a cane, became a cossack swinging a sword, then a soldier shouldering a rifle, finally a gravedigger with a shovel burying all the others. American choreographer Jane Comfort encapsulates political issues in pure movement; in "Bites," a dozen dancers rise from chairs at the blast of a factory whistle, to work beset by political sound bites and bureaucrats, who remove their seats, one by one, until all twelve are struggling for the only chair left.

Those who know little about dancers are often unaware of how concerned they are with ideas and issues like environment, race, culture, gender, health, hunger, homelessness, equality, education, drugs, crime, and censorship, to name a few. A political dance need not be a harangue, nor, if you have convictions, propaganda. As for satire and comedy, they take conviction too.

Arthur Elgort

"Bites," one of the *Three Bagatelles of the Righteous,* by
Jane Comfort.

*P*ROJECT 58   POLITICAL STUDY.

Make a dance based on an idea or issue in which you believe and that
means a lot to you. ∎

**CHARACTER
STUDY**

Modern dance began with and continues to produce character studies.
Some examples: Ruth St. Denis: *Jeptha's Daughter, Sappho, Salome;* Ted
Shawn: *Diana and Endymion, Pierrot and the Butterfly, Cowboy;* Martha
Graham: *Judith, Clytemnestra, Phaedre;* Helen Tamiris: *Portrait of a Lady;*
Nina Fonaroff: *Little Theodolina;* Pauline Koner: *Portrait of a Child;*
William Bales: *Peon Portraits;* Valerie Bettis: *The Desperate Heart;* Pearl
Lang: *Song of Deborah;* Jane Dudley: *Family Portrait;* Jean Erdman:
Ophelia; John Butler: *Portrait of Billie;* Jeff Duncan: *Winesburg Portraits;*
Alvin Ailey: *Cry;* and many more.

*P*ROJECT 59 MOVEMENT FROM CHARACTER.

1. Beside each of the categories below jot down the name of an individual who could spark a character study:

   a. a relative

   b. a friend

   c. a teacher

   d. a celebrity

   e. a political figure

   f. a historical figure

   g. a fictional character

   h. a film or TV personality

   i. an imaginary character

2. Find a move for each character. Decide which character yields the most interesting moves.

3. Develop that character with more movement or by developing the situation the character is in or both. ▪

*P*ROJECT 60 CHARACTER FROM MOVEMENT.

Begin improvising or choreographing and look to the moves for ideas about the character. From these ideas generate more moves. Continue this cross-fertilization, letting moves and character stimulate each other as you build the dance. ▪

DANCING IN ANOTHER PERSON'S SKIN

Because dance uses the body as its instrument, dance is a highly personal art. Every dance must pass through the persona of the dancemaker, which embodies a lifetime aggregation of behaviors and responses constituting a personal style. Audiences don't mind; they even seek it out. In fact, a personal style that audiences like is one of the most precious assets a dancemaker can have. And yet, sometimes the dancemaker longs to escape.

A writer, remotely manipulating words, is free to present the undiluted voice of a hero or villain or a person of the opposite sex or an impersonal all-seeing eye, knowing that readers can flesh out the characters for themselves, whereas in dance, the connection between artist and subject is immediate and inescapable. Martha Graham acknowledged that her great character roles, Medea, Jocasta, Clytemnestra and others, drew on aspects of herself. Is there no way to make dances, then, except by draping them on one's own persona?

In *Cosimo's Dream of the Adults*, a picture of grownups as seen by a child, choreographer Valerie Striar, dancing with Patti Bradshaw, evoked eerily exotic beings hard to identify with either of the performers. The performers were right there, of course, but their personas were so far in the background that the characterizations were starkly revealed.

Just how did Striar manage to dance as if in another person's skin? Her source was a character from Italo Calvino's novel *The Baron in the Trees*—yet it could have been something else. Her secret, I believe, is a double leap of the imagination. After conceiving one character, an alienated boy, she went on to imagine how that character would conceive yet another character. The moves she found, twice separated from herself, strongly gestural, deftly sculpted, coming together in unexpected and disturbing ways, created a portrait of impersonal, unpredictable, not-to-be-trusted adulthood, as a sensitive child might perceive it.

That second leap seemed to have been the catalyst. One's persona and personal style is so deep that if one cannot escape it, one can try to evade it, confuse it, work around it, at least for one dance. By infusing one's self with another, then using that other's imagination, the dancemaker enters a new realm of possibilities.

PROJECT 61   A DANCE STUDY FROM ANOTHER'S POINT OF VIEW.

Build a dance by imagining how another person sees yet a third person. Some possibilities:

- an employer through the mind of an employee
- a passenger through the mind of a flight attendant
- a diner through the mind of a waiter
- a teenager through the mind of a parent
- an unruly student or teacher's pet as seen by a teacher
- a consumer as seen by a huckster
- a voter as seen by a candidate
- a choreographer as seen by a dancer

Reverse any of these possibilities, and dream up others. Another challenge is a dance portrait of yourself as seen by someone you like or dislike. ■

DANCING HISTORY

Dance may be the only art form whose styles never go out of style. A contemporary artist who paints an Impressionist or surrealist painting, no matter how well, will likely be dubbed derivative; but a dancer who produces a fine waltz, minuet, or mazurka will be appreciated—even acclaimed.

At Princeton University, Ze'eva Cohen teaches a course that includes dance technique, improvisation, composition, dance history, and aesthetic appreciation. Students not intending to become dancers gain a broad perspective and feeling for dance in this one course. Yet dancemakers can also gain from such studies because every corner of dance history is ripe for rediscovery and reanimation.

𝒫ROJECT 62   A DANCE FROM DANCE HISTORY.

Dig into dance history; take a course or just read. You're seeking glimpses to be used as a jumping-off place for a new dance. Peruse material on cultural dances, biographies, and autobiographies. Look over dance criticism, especially by critics who try to descibe movement. How-to-dance books are useful because it is so difficult to make sense of them; whatever you come up with will probably be wrong enough to be right for an original dance. Dance videos and films can work too, but you'll want to do more than copy or adapt moving images.

When you find a dance style or form, some music, a cultural trait, social custom, costume, reason or occasion for dancing, or anything else that intrigues you, there are two different ways to proceed:

1. Thoroughly research the dance, music, period, or culture, etc., and make a dance using your research.
2. Use pure imagination. Imagine a dance in the context or to the music that interests you. Make that dance. ■

ABUSING THE AUDIENCE

Show biz expressions like "knock 'em dead" and "lay 'em in the aisles" reveal the performer's drive to conquer the audience. The usual way is with charm, seductiveness, humor, virtuosity, or intellect. In the 1960s, many tried abuse.

➤ In *The Blacks*, by Jean Genet, abuse is verbal.
➤ A performer named Brother Theodore offered an unceasing tirade and sometimes challenged the biggest man in the audience to a fight.

➤ In Anna Halprin's *Parades and Changes,* the dancers silently stripped bare, glowering at the audience as if to say, "Prurient creeps! We all have bodies. These are ours!"

➤ Jeff Duncan's *View* began with jack-booted storm troopers who hurled "latecomers" into their seats.

➤ The most devilish: in *The Rehearsal,* by Paul Taylor, danced to Stravinsky's *Rite of Spring,* a young couple and their baby, a lovingly handled doll, struggle to survive. Following an orgy of comic mayhem, a gun-moll character stabs the doll, which pops out of the mother's cradling grasp, invariably provoking laughter. Then Taylor strikes with a wrenching, desperate dance of grief that makes everyone who had laughed feel like a fiend.

There are endless ways to convey malediction in movement, some symbolic, like thumbing the nose, some suggestive, like the extended middle finger. Martha Graham took a well-known obscene gesture—one hand caught in the crook of the elbow—and magnified it in *Night Journey,* in which Oedipus catches his leg in the crook of his elbow.

*P*ROJECT 63   A KINETIC CURSE.

Make a move or phrase that projects pure invective. Show individually, then in groups. Exchange kinetic curses, each dancer learning three or more, to set up a kinetic cussing match. Can kinetic cussing be extended into a dance? ■

CHANCE

In the early 1950s, I had the luck to see a preview of Merce Cunningham's *Suite by Chance,* and was astonished to learn that hats placed offstage on the floor contained numbered slips of paper which dancers picked, read, then went onstage to dance the moves that the numbers indicated. *Suite by Chance* is a landmark and chance will always be associated with Cunningham, who was influenced by the *I Ching,* The Book of Changes. But beneath Cunningham's chance numbers was a planned and charted process.[3] Cunningham not only made a fascinating dance but alerted us to the role chance plays in life. (Once, when making a dance, I heard the telephone ring, spun around, and realized that a sudden turn exactly there would work. Later, I thought, what if the phone had not rung?)

*P*ROJECT 64   CHANCE STUDY.

1. Recap Merce Cunningham's process.

   a. Jot down ten moves on small slips of paper—for instance, hop, jump, kick, bend, slither, tilt, squat, chug, run, contract. Extract the slips one at a time, and make a dance in that exact order. If you have to go from *slither* to *jump,* give it your best shot or devise a rule for transitions.

b. Devise six to ten motor fragments, combinations, or phrases. Learn them all. Give each move a number and devise a chance method of selection. Use a hat if you wish.

2. Seek other ways to bring chance into your dances.

$\mathcal{P}$ROJECT 65   CHAOS.

Read about the scientific theory of chaos in *Chaos,* by James Gleick.[4] How might it be used in making a dance? ■

SHTICK AND KITSCH

Shtick is a vaudeville term for diverting but meaningless business:

> A man enters a room and trips on the rug. He bends to straighten the rug and his hat falls off. He reaches for his hat and his eyeglasses fall out of his shirt pocket. As he reaches toward the eyeglasses, he steps on his hat.

"Kitsch" is an anagram of shtick; it once applied only to objects: souvenir-shop kewpie dolls, a lamp in the form of a fire hydrant, paintings on black velvet of big-eyed, tearful children. Kitsch now extends to greeting-card sentiments, soap-opera dialogue, and choreography.

Kitsch is corny, cluttered, saccharine, and maudlin, but also whole-hearted, sincere, unself-conscious, and unashamed. A kitschy classical pas de deux has a supercilious cavalier parading a coy ballerina through pretentious promenades and pompous poses. Modern dance kitsch includes dying falls, agonized contractions, macho jumps, dramatic confrontations, and cute capers.

A great kitschy duet by Agnes DeMille is *Summer Day.* DeMille and George Church enter carrying a picnic basket; they spread a blanket and set out plates. She's hot for romance, but all he wants to do is eat.

If you succeed in combining kitsch with exuberance, you may produce what critic Clive Barnes terms a "good bad dance" (page 247), which can be a high or low road to popular success.

$\mathcal{P}$ROJECT 66   USING SHTICK AND KITSCH.

Make a dance involving:

- a sweet senior citizen and a lost child
- a boy scout helping someone retrieve contents of a burst shopping bag

- feeding pigeons in the park
- any saccharine, overly sentimental action

Make a dance to the accompaniment of:
- a cartoon soundtrack
- a sci-fi movie score
- a speech by your favorite or least favorite politico   ■

Begin with a somewhat bland move; make it strong; make it stronger; make it still stronger!

GOING TOO FAR

Agnes DeMille, alone in my experience of Broadway choreographers, would allow dancers to suggest moves. Working on the musical *Paint Your Wagon,* she began a cancan by having the men and women kick between each other's legs. As the dance got wilder, she needed something stronger. My partner, a fireball named Ilona Murai, showed me how to flip her over my head so that she came to rest sitting on my shoulders facing backward, her skirt covering my head. "That's really vulgar!" said another dancer admiringly. "Show it to DeMille!" We did. DeMille shuddered and waved us away. We'd gone too far!

I still like the lift DeMille nixed, but a censor lives inside every dancemaker. In this project we will engage it and then *override* it. The objective is to bypass that sometimes too-proper gatekeeper.

𝒫ROJECT 67   A DANCE TOO FAR.

By going too far, we learn our own sense of limits. You benefit greatly by showing since others are often able to help you push beyond the point where your inner censor says, "Stop!" Some typical intensifications follow:

SNIT → TANTRUM → RAGE

AMUSEMENT → PLEASURE → ECSTASY

RUE → REGRET → SORROW

NERVOUSNESS → FEAR → TERROR

DISTASTE → REPUGNANCE → HORROR

GIGGLE → LAUGH → SIDESPLITTER

SATISFACTION → JOY → HAPPINESS

You can also extend pure movement. It is a form of variation.

MOVE → MORE OF THE MOVE → THE MOST OF THE MOVE   ■

NON SEQUITUR

The Oxford English Dictionary lists the Latin word *sequitur* as meaning "an inference or conclusion following from the premises," or "a determination arrived at by reasoning."[5] People ordinarily speak in *sequiturs:* words and sentences reasonably follow what had come before. The kinetic equivalent is defined by the body with movement that flows easily out of other movement.

Choreographers like *sequiturs* because they make dances flow rather than flit, sweep rather than zigzag. Dance techniques whose moves fit neatly together, like ballet, jazz, and *Bharata Natya*, encourage *sequiturs*. But if moves do not fit together neatly, as Martha Graham's often do not, dancemakers tend to smooth them out since bodies like the feeling of flow. For a kinetic jolt, then, consider the non sequitur. Depending on where and how used, it can be dramatic or comic and can often jar a dance out of blandness or unstick a stuck dancemaker.

Many dancemakers cultivate their instinct for flowing movement, so a kinetic non sequitur is more easily produced by reason than intuition. To find non sequiturs, we can use deliberate stratagems to foil that feeling for flow. You can use an existing study for the following project.

$\mathcal{P}$ROJECT 68   NON SEQUITUR STUDY.

1. Break into any movement sequence with a deliberately disruptive move. (Wrong Movement, page 26)
2. Insert a move or phrase from a different technique.
3. Make or use two contrasting studies—for instance, one serene, another stormy. Break each into parts and recombine.
   a. Begin dancing one of the studies. At a point where the movement flows well, stop abruptly, and then begin to dance the other study. Now make the two into one.
   b. Two dancemakers do separate studies. Divide each study into two sections and show the sections alternately. The non sequitur will be where the separate studies, are joined. If one person dances both studies the non sequitur should be more obvious since it will result solely from the moves. ■

AFTERMATHS

In the aftermath of any stirring event lies a dance. It may be welcome: the birth of a child, winning a lottery, winning a Bessie—or unwelcome: an IRS audit, losing an election, losing your house keys.

In *Dromenon,* Merce Cunningham evoked the aftermath of a ritual in which a group of people summoned a spirit into their midst. In *After Eden,* John Butler portrayed Adam and Eve after expulsion from the Garden of Eden. In *Pandora,* Tao Strong imagined the moment after Pandora had opened her infamous box. My own aftermath dance is *Orison,* from the Greek myth of the flood, whose survivors, Deucalion and Pira, faced a drowned world.

$\mathcal{P}$ROJECT 69   A DANCE FROM AN AFTERMATH.

It can be:

- a personal event: a victory, defeat, birth, bereavement, milestone, mistake, accident, bit of luck, or anything else
- an internal event: insight, observation, change of heart
- a historical or current event
- a fictional, mythical, or imagined event   ■

"Control freak" is a disapproving term for someone who seeks to manipulate others. But isn't that exactly what choreographers do when they direct dancers through precise actions in space and time?

If you demand absolute control over your creative work, this study may unsettle you because it sets up mischances to make your designs slip off the path you planned. The payoff comes when you find that what happened accidentally is even better. Keep in mind that it takes sensitivity to recognize and self-confidence to accept the superiority of accidental discoveries.

$\mathcal{P}$ROJECT 70   TRANSFORMING VALUABLE ACCIDENTS.

1. To exciting music, make up a dance phrase long and complex enough to take more than one demonstration to learn.
2. Get the dancers on their feet and tell them to learn the phrase you will demonstrate. Show it once, cleanly and forcefully.
3. Now instruct them to dance to the music, remembering the phrase as best they can, and *not to stop even if they forget or make mistakes.*

Dancers can be told to dance together, so they can't copy from one another, or individually, so they can. Either way, except for the rare dancer with a steel-trap movement memory, most will make mistakes—which is the idea. Try to spot moves that are better than the original.

This is a kind of trick, so it may not be repeatable. On the other hand, if the dancers know why you are encouraging mistakes, they may hand you some beauts! ■

AMBIGUITY: A RORSCHACH STUDY

The Rorschach ink-blot test depends on ambiguity. The ink blots summon buried thoughts. In a book worth perusing, William Empson defines ambiguity as "any verbal nuance, however slight, which gives room for alternative reactions to the same piece of language."[6] In dance it has much the same meaning. An ambiguous dance leaves room for the imagination.

> The curtain rises; a dancer stands, gaze lifted, one hand reaching into space. We sense exaltation, but is it with love, longing, defiance? Will her next move be an approach, a retreat, a fall?

Antony Tudor said, "I want my ballets to be so clear that the dumbest person in the last row of the third balcony understands everything."[7] Tudor, a strong storyteller, wanted audiences to know what was going on, and yet his ballets leave much to the imagination: In *Lilac Garden,* a woman appears, sees her secret lover gazing into the distance, runs, leaps at his back—and he catches her foot in his hand, a strange lift that reveals their fear of exposure and their agony at her approaching forced marriage to another.

Ambiguity is said to be inherent in our very thought processes. Since there's no avoiding it, make it work for you.

𝒫ROJECT 71 RORSCHACH STUDY.

Borrow a set of Rorschach cards from a library or psych lab. If it is easier, make your own. Fold a dozen or more slips of paper in half, then open. Put a few drops of liquid ink or watercolor paint on each. Fold in half, squeeze, open, and let dry. Use as follows:

1. In-class improvisation: Respond to the blots with moves. Work intuitively (right brain). Then analyze (left brain) to decide what your moves mean. Get outside reactions, remembering that a dance is itself a kind of ink blot. Encourage people to see different things in it.

2. Choreograph a deliberately ambiguous dance. Show and ask for interpretations. Welcome disagreement.

3. Make up some *ink-blot moves.* Present them to the group and ask each person to write down what the moves suggest. Read all the responses aloud. ■

The fourth wall is the barrier between audience and performer. In modern proscenium theaters it is the invisible wall that rises from the footlights. But it was also there for the ancient Greeks in their circular outdoor amphitheaters, for the Romans who had a sort of "backstage," although not like ours, and in Shakespeare's Globe Theatre, which is different from a modern theater. It is there too, in studios and black boxes, however mingled audiences and actors seem to be, and even between villagers and the dancers who travel through rural India. Performers need this wall because it allows each member of the audience the privacy to co-create an inner fantasy as they watch. It is gone only when no distinction is made between those who watch and those who dance, as in social dancing and in celebrations or rituals where all join.

Well, why knock it down? Because reaching out to the audience is a challenge, because performers long to go one-on-one, because theater audiences are real, not virtual, because if you touch an audience, you transcend yourself, and finally, because it is there. Beyond that, who knows? Anyway, it's not easy to knock down the fourth wall.

James Cunningham successfully destroyed it in *The First Family: Isadora Duncan and Donald Duck*, performed outdoors at New York City's Chase Manhattan Plaza;[8] when he removed the police barriers and invited the audience to dance with the dancers, in they poured! Broadway's *Cats* does something like that in reverse; the show starts with performers in fiery-eyed cat costumes among the audience in every part of the theater. In the 1950s, Judy Garland at Broadway's Palace Theater wiped out the wall. She called for a drink of water and out popped her hairdresser (whom she introduced) with a brimming glass. Glass in hand she sat on the edge of the stage, chatting and singing, legs dangling down, everyone visiting with dear Judy. The fourth wall was gone!

*P*ROJECT 72   BANISH THE FOURTH WALL.

1. Perform in the audience's space.
2. Bring the audience into the performing space.
3. Talk to someone in the audience.
4. Have the audience contribute something: clapping, counting, singing, an object, etc.
5. Use an audience member in the performance.
6. Do something with which the audience can identify. ■

PROBLEMS AS OPPORTUNITIES

In a lecture at the North Carolina Museum of Art, visual artist Alex Katz described a set he had designed for Paul Taylor. "Paul does most of his choreography in the center of the stage, so I put a large piece there just to see what he would do." Then he added, "Paul is a strong choreographer or it wouldn't have worked." The large piece was an open cube and in the dance, *Polaris,* Taylor used it for the dancers to lurk in, hide behind, skulk around and what have you. Taylor evidently enjoyed the challenge, for he commissioned Katz again. This time, the problem covered the entire stage, thirty-six sharp-edged metal cutouts of Taylor's dog, Dee Dee, an unavoidable obstacle course for racing dancers. On a bare stage *Diggity* would be a sprightly romp; in a field of dogs it becomes a daring enigma.

Johan Elbers

Alex Katz's set center stage was no problem to Paul Taylor in *Polaris*. Left to right: Lila York, Monica Morris, Ruth Andrien, Robert Kahn, and Thomas Evert.

Johan Elbers

In *Diggity*, Alex Katz's metal cutouts were no problem to Paul Taylor, though the dancers, left to right, David Parsons, Victoria Uris, Linda Kent, Kenneth Tosti, and Monica Morris, may have felt differently.

PROJECT 73   CREATE AND SOLVE A PROBLEM.

1. Start in an uncomfortable position. Consider it your theme.
2. Use music you dislike.
3. Dance to poetry you don't understand.
4. Carry an object that has nothing to do with the dance.
5. Eliminate part of the stage area (Paul Taylor's challenge).
6. Make a combination that feels awkward, clumsy, lumbering.
7. Make a combination that feels great; then dance it too fast or too slow.
8. Devise other problems. ■

ENDNOTES

1. Martha Graham, *Blood Memory* (New York: Doubleday, 1992), p. 98.
2. *New York Times,* 18 May 1997, p. H44.
3. Remy Charlip describes the process in an essay, "Composing by Chance," *Merce Cunningham,* Richard Kostelanetz, ed. (Pennington, NJ: a cappella, 1992) p. 40.
4. James Gleick, *Chaos*: Making a New Science (New York: Penguin, 1987)
5. *Note:* Perhaps this subject belongs with *Dance and Rhetorical Forms* (pages, 206–34); but it is too important to be tucked away with asyndeton—to which it is related, chiasmus, ellipsis, and other less immediately useful devices.
6. William Empson, *7 Types of Ambiguity* (New York: New Directions, 1966), p. 1.
7. Said to the author in a casual conversation in the 1950s.
8. Hereafter, New York City venues will generally not be so identified.

CHAPTER 4

IMPROVISATION

We improvise every day of our lives: One day, when my daughters, aged two and four, were eating breakfast, I stepped away for a moment and returned to see oatmeal on the table, floor, TV set, and both children, who were laughing with joy at the lively designs produced by warm oatmeal pitched with a spoon. I contracted my torso, scrunched my shoulders, crooked my arms, clawed my hands, lifted my head, closed my eyes, and said, "Ohhhh Noooo!"

> **Kinesthetics: the link between perception and movement.**
> **kin'es-the'sia** or **kin'es-the'sis** n. [Gr. *keinen,* TO MOVE and *aisthesis,*
> PERCEPTION.] The sensation of position, movement, tension, etc.,
> of parts of the body perceived through nerves and organs in muscles,
> tendons, and joints.

A perception is always followed by a response, even if it is only an attempt to hide the perception. Dance improvisation, however, attempts to reveal that response—to seek a spontaneous and coherent movement response to perception. When that happens, we dance; it is the instant critic Marcia Siegel terms "the vanishing point." Yet dancers experience it as a *flash point*, a springing to life.

The moves we make each day in ordinary life contain a full range of gestures, facial expressions, body language, sounds, speech, even dance moves. Yet it is not at a level of lyrical intensity that dance is expected to reach. Were you asked to converse in melody, it might offer a challenge comparable to the act of dance improvisation.

In the 1950s, as a young professional dancer, I was never asked to improvise, not by Martha Graham or any other choreographer. Yet when we performed in colleges, I learned that improvisation—the dance students called them "improvs"—were enthusiastically done by all.

Improvisation fits educational goals because it is self-expressive and often individual-centered. But how did it get into academe? Research through old college catalogs and course proposals might shed light on this intriguing question.

Some attribute improvisation to Hanya Holm and Alwin Nikolais. Are they, then, the source of all improv courses everywhere? Whatever the source, improvisation may well be a major contribution of academe to American dance; on campuses many, including nondancers, find it a fulfilling form of personal enrichment.

REASONS FOR IMPROVISING

There are three basic reasons to improvise:

1. *For Personal Enrichment.* Once inhibitions are shed, which is easier among kindred spirits, improvising is sheer joy. The constraints of spoken language disappear. One can "say" anything without revealing secrets, and any number can speak with no one interrupted. There's a feeling of oneness with the group along with an increase in personal integrity. All of which makes improvising great fun to do, but not necessarily fun to watch.

2. *For Performance.* Improvising for audiences demands sufficient coherence and intensity to hold interest. It became popular in the 1960s when compelling artists emerged, including Margaret Beals, who improvises as she recites poetry, Richard Bull, and Cynthia Novak

all of whom have a theatrical approach, and Steve Paxton, who is the originator of Contact Improvisation©, which teaches participants to trust one another and draws on that trust for often surprising results. These are studies in their own right, and if you wish to explore further, interesting books are available, although the best way, surely, is to work with a master.[1]

3. *As a Creative Tool.* When you start a dance, even if you begin by thinking up moves, the instant you engage your body there is an act of improvisation. Every dance thus has its improvisatory seed, which must be recognized and captured. This form of improvising is the ground beneath your feet, no matter where you roam on the *MAP*.

Before venturing into improvisation as a tool, I must mention yet one other form, the subtle variation that makes each performance, no matter how carefully choreographed, unique. We may call what results "interpretation," but in its spontaneity and response to the moment, it is an act of improvisation.

Charles Weidman is said to have been a brilliant spontaneous improviser, whereas Martha Graham never improvised in that way. Yet when searching for moves, Graham drew directly on her body. The great seminal modern dance techniques with their vast number of original moves were all generated in one or another kind of improvisation before being carefully and rigorously codified.

Improvisation can stimulate the mind, generate creative energy, point in new directions, encourage happy accidents, and spill out ideas before your inner censor can say no. To some, improvisation is effortless. If you utter moves like the birds sing, they may be as fleeting as dreams and as hard to remember. But there are ways to capture them.

If you are in thrall to an inner critic whose doubts suppress your flash point, there are ways to overcome that watchful censor.

Improvising in the presence of others stimulates some and inhibits others. If you are in the second group, try improvising alone. Yet in all the exercises that follow, concentrate on the process rather than on the results.

American Dance Festival Archive

Martha Graham on lawn at Bennington College, circa 1940.

PEOPLESCAPES

Early German modern dance invented the "movement choir." Dancers stood shoulder-to-shoulder, every eye focused on the same point, arms reaching, hands clutching. In rare photos they look like giant sea anemones. Peoplescapes are inspired by those photos.

$\mathcal{P}$ROJECT 74   PEOPLESCAPES (FOR ANY NUMBER).

Dancers move, chant, sing, speak, with music or in silence. What touches one, touches all. Interaction is the goal.

Each peoplescape begins as a cluster, then seeks other forms. It shifts internally, changes shape, travels, spreads into the studio space or beyond. But whatever it does, it stays closely interrelated.

A theme helps focus the peoplescape. It can come from nature, city life, people, relationships, images, pure movement, etc. When using text, words and movement interact. If someone says "Tomorrow, and tomorrow, and tomorrow," there is both movement response and repetition of the words until another says "Creeps in this petty pace. . . ." No rules are fixed; peoplescapes are wide open for original adaptions.

One dancer is the conductor. Select a theme. Dancers gather about the conductor, with each dancer placed so as to see as many others as possible. Those in the center of the cluster face out, those on the perimeter, face in. If there is music or sound, it begins. The first response is by the conductor. Others respond by reflecting or slightly varying the action. Action travels through the peoplescape like a breeze through a grainfield. After each action peaks and fades, there is another. By pressing outward, the conductor initiates expansion of the entire peoplescape. There is no set time limit; each peoplescape goes on as long as it is interesting. All take turns as conductor. ■

LIVING STATUES

Both statues and dance use bodies, space, and time. In September 1992, I was conducting a choreography workshop with superbly trained 16-year-olds in Voronezh, Russia. About to graduate as professionals, they breezed through technique class but could not comprehend improvisation. "What should we improvise?" they asked. I suggested they limit themselves to steps (Step study," pages 22 and 103). "But what steps?" they asked. When I answered, "Any!" they seemed baffled. Russia is filled with statues, so I suggested they make a living one. The result was magical. They made statues inspired by their school, the city of Voronezh, undersea life, and a whole series poking fun at their teachers.

The author's collection

Living statue improvs,
Voronezh, Russia

*P*ROJECT 75   STATUES: A GROUP IMPROV.

1. *Still statues.* The group decides on a theme and names its statue, for
   instance: "The Coral Reef," "Revenge of the Nerds," "Thanksgiving
   Day," "Disneyland," "Atop Mount Everest," and so on. Each dancer
   receives a number. Then:

   a. Dancer #1 enters and takes a statuesque position.

   b. Dancer #2 joins, relating to #1.

   c. Then dancers #3, #4, etc., join.

   d. Repeat until each dancer has been in every numerical position.

2. *Moving statues.* Same as *still statues*, except that each dancer moves in
   position and each dancer adds to the movement.

3. *Traveling statues.* The whole statue moves about in the dancing space. ■

DANCE PORTRAITS

Sybil Shearer can characterize anything in movement. Once, trying to describe the male dancer she needed, she "danced him," giving an impression of earthiness, friendliness, intelligence, sensitivity, and strength. She danced a portrait of New York City a-go-go, as it was in the late 1950s, then contrasted it with the New York City she remembered in the late 1940s. She danced her native Midwest with serene moves that evoked a spacious, agreeable landscape. She danced Erick Hawkins, Charles Weidman, and then Charles Weidman doing a dance characterization of Erick Hawkins!

Beginning each improvised characterization, she would stand in deep concentration until moves came. Watching, one was sure anyone who wanted to could do it. And anyone can!

$\mathcal{P}$ROJECT 76   A PORTRAIT IN MOVEMENT.

Think deeply about someone. Keep her in mind until moves come. You are not imitating, but instead, seeking an interior character who comes to life in your moves. Seek moves in the character of places too, places you love, or loathe, or dream about. ■

TWENTY-TWO IMPROVS

1. *Self-Portrait:* Even if you've done it at the start (A Kinetic Introduction, page 8), draw more deeply on your inner self for an extended improvisation.

2. *Say Goodbye:* In movement, express sweet sorrow, good riddance, or something else. Respond to: *Adios; Auf wiedersehein; Au revoir; Beat it!; Bye bye; Ciao; Farewell; Get outta my face; Go fly a kite; Goodbye now; Hasta la vista; On your way; Safe journey; Sayonara; Scram; See you later, alligator; Shalom; So long; Take care; Ta ta; Toodle ooh; Zai jian.*

3. *Music:* Dance to the music! There are three stages:

   a. The first flush when the music is new.

   b. When you have mostly danced yourself out. Stop, but keep listening.

   c. When you get the urge to dance again, new moves will happen.

4. *Sound effects* (From recordings or made to order): Sounds can have personal associations. To some, dancing to the sound of heavy traffic would be like dancing their daily lives. To others, sounds of nature or the sea reflect their daily experience.

5. *TV takes:* Use a tape recorder to record segments of television sounds. Stripped of image, TV sound can be a surreal mix of the banal and bizarre.

6. *Vis-à-vis:* Face another person. Make eye contact. Clear the mind. On a slow beat, step together, then step back. Have no expectations. See only the other, toward and back. Relinquish control. Make no plans. Let the relationship and the moves happen.

7. *Conversations* (for two or more): One is Speaker, other(s) Listener(s). Speaker reasons, prattles, babbles, orates, declaims, rants, and raves. Listener(s) react(s) with agreement, disagreement, sympathy, impatience, disgust, understanding, incredulity, amazement, pooh-poohing, and in other ways. Take turns as Speaker.

8. *Questions & answers:* Dancers work in pairs. The counts give a rhythmic footing and freedom to concentrate on the moves. You can use other counts, or none.

    Dancer #1: *Ask a question* in movement, using the following counts:

One and-a/	two and-a/	three and-a/	four
1 – 2 – 3,	2 – 2 – 3,	3 – 2 – 3,	4

    Dancer #2: *Answer the question* in movement using the same counts:

One and-a/	two and-a/	three and-a/	four
1 – 2 – 3,	2 – 2 – 3,	3 – 2 – 3,	4

    Repeat as dialogue. Variations:

    a. Mine the the improv by repeating cogent moves until they become a sequence you can repeat.

    b. After you have mined the improv, work individually or collaboratively to make it into a choreographed dance.

9. *Go kinetic; group speak* (for three to ten dancers): There are special dynamics when people converse in groups. Think of dinner conversations and parties. Seldom do all hold silent for one, and if they do, the silence is momentary. Some tend to dominate, some listen, some speak over others, some hold cross-conversations. Sometimes one just listens or does something else entirely.

    Pick a topic from gossip to philosophy. Begin the discussion with words. Presently, someone comments, wholly or partly, in movement. As others begin to go kinetic, moves and voices together make an interesting mix. Eventually, all are completely kinetic. From there the discussion can go back to voices until it comes to a natural conclusion.

10. *Big bang/big crunch* (for groups): Try New Age music. Start in a tight mass. Begin to expand. At the limits of the space, rebound toward the center. Nearing others, sense their gravity. If their gravity is strong, go into orbit; engage as stars, planets, moons, comets, or black holes—until your kinetic universe ends, with a bang or a whimper.

11. *Cosmic evolution* (for a group): Split into two groups. Mark one group with headbands. Each group stands on opposite sides of the studio. In silence, the groups move toward one another and *pass through*. Turn and pass through again. Repeat. Introduce music, rhythm, chanting, sounds, to which any dancer can respond while passing. Dancers begin to seek eye contact. Presently, through eye contact, each one settles on a partner from the other group and continues with that partner. Now pairs may join to become a quartet. Concentrate on the newly formed unit and seek internal relationships. Continue as long as the dance keeps evolving.

12. *Role-playing* (for pairs): Moves here are shaped by roles. *Suggestions:* seller/buyer; parent/child; palm reader/fortune seeker; expert/novice; teacher/eager learner; teacher/reluctant learner; artist/critic; orator/listener; orator/heckler; confessor/confessee. Devise more.

13. *Snapshots:* Respond—bang!—like a reflex, to a word, a short phrase, a picture, a sound, a movement.

14. *Situations* (probes deeper than snapshots): *Suggestions:* about to fall; fear of flying; owing money; a new toy; meeting a rival; lost; warm hello; chance encounter; unwanted encounter; being nice to one you loathe; can't remember his/her name; coming out of orbit; back from vacation; what time is it?; tornado on the horizon; longing for a hug; stuck in traffic; slowly sinking; what's that smell in the kitchen? Add more.

15. *Reflections* (for two, several, or a group): There is one initiator. The initiator does a move and the others reflect it. Decide first on the kind of reflection: faint, distorted, enlarged, or some other kind. Vary initiators and the kinds of reflections.

16. *Cadenzas:* In music, a **cadenza** is an ornamental phrase. In the Classic period, cadenzas had grown into lengthy variations, in a stipulated place and usually improvised. They are rarely improvised today. The improvised cadenza is perfectly suited to dance. You may listen to musical cadenzas, which these days are usually notated in the scores of violin or piano concertos. Then use a dance you know, made by yourself or another; find a junction or climactic nub within it, and improvise a kinetic cadenza there. This can be an

interesting group project in which the group learns a dance or uses one they know, giving individuals and subgroups turns to improvise cadenzas.

17. *Identities* (for pairs): Make two decisions.

   a. You are neighbors, rivals, siblings, business partners, comrades in arms, or in some other relationship.

   b. (This can be kept secret from the other partner.) You are ambitious, distracted, jealous, nervous, scared, bored, secretly in love, resentful, eager to please, trying to impress, desperate to escape, afraid to be alone, or are in some other frame of mind.

   Stand facing your partner and make eye contact. Begin to move, at first without touching. Build the relationship based on your identity and frame of mind.

18. *Embryos* (for two or more): The embryo is a physical act from which the improv grows. *Examples:* shrug, hug, salute, handshake, arms akimbo, aiming, shielding, or any other gesture or kinetic signal. People can have the same or different embryos, building upon them in response to the other(s).

19. *Inflecting* (introduced to me by Stephan Koplowitz): Two or more people *using only one set of moves,* hold a conversation. Begin by selecting from three to five moves which don't have to be dance moves. Koplowitz gave something like:

   a. Stand at attention.

   b. Slap thighs.

   c. Slide hands up and down on the hips.

   d. Place arms akimbo.

   e. Signal "Safe!" like a baseball umpire.

   Then, by inflecting *this one set of moves* done in any order, you can whisper, shout, laugh, cry, agree, argue, contradict, get angry, etc. You can use any set of moves including dance moves.

20. *Galloping canon* (for three or more dancers):

   Dancer #1 begins a repeating 4-count improv done in a moderate $\frac{4}{4}$ or a slow $\frac{3}{4}$ time. Dance to counts or to music. Repeat the 4-count sequence eight times for eight measures of 4.

   Dancer #2 joins after four measures of 4, copying dancer #1 for four measures. On the fifth measure, dancer #2 is free to change the sequence in any way while keeping the established rhythm. Dancer #1 may:

a. continue the original sequence

b. pick up dancer #2's sequence, or

c. improvise new moves.

Dancer #3 joins after dancer #2 has done four measure of 4, and for the first four measures picks up dancer #2's moves. On the fifth measure, dancer #3 is free to change the sequence in any way while keeping the established rhythm. Dancers #1 and #2 may:

a. continue the original sequence

b. pick up dancer #3's sequence

c. use any moves already done and feed them into the continuing canon, or

d. improvise new moves.

Dancers #4, #5, #6, etc., build the galloping canon, as indicated.

21. *Fishing:* One dances, the other(s) extract(s) move(s) and make(s) them into a dance. Work in teams of two or three. One is the fish who just swims to whatever bait and lures the fisher(s) have to offer: music, words, phrases, props. When the fish responds, the fisher(s) attempt to catch movements, which they can store or cook up immediately. All take turns being fish and fishers.

22. *Riffs:* A **riff** in jazz is a strong, repeated melodic phrase that provides a theme for an improvising soloist. Turning it around, we can adapt it for an interesting dance improv. The natural music for this is jazz, but you can use any music you enjoy.

a. Before starting, everybody gets a number.

b. Play the music.

c. Dancer #1 begins by dancing a two-bar phrase (one eight in dancers' counts). It can be improvised or carefully crafted.

d. The others pick it up, repeat it, then take off from the moves, using them as the basis for individual improvisations.

e. After thirty-two bars (sixteen eights in dancers' counts) dancer #2 a phrase, and all improvise on that.

f. Continue until all have presented phrases, going around and around as long as each phrase stays fresh.

MISCELLANEOUS IMPROVS

Broadcast Takes

These are short segments recorded from radio and television. The sounds accompanying TV commercials, which many obliterate with the mute button, are great for improvisation just because they can be so obtrusive and annoying.

Outdoor Improvs

There is literally a world of opportunity in the great outdoors. Improvs can flower from the earth; they can branch from or bloom beside trees, reflect clouds, bubble like brooks. Contrasting improvs refract rather than reflect—for example, a stormy improv on a sunny day. Improvs can seek beneath the surface in the domain of earthworms and moles. Improvs in the rain or wind (*not* in lightning) offer unusual opportunities.

Aural Improvs

Tannis Hugill made a fascinating dance to sounds captured while walking on the beach. The idea can work for any kind of environmental sounds. Take a cassette recorder on a walk in the city, in a park or zoo, to a lecture, a dinner, a party, etc.

Flash Words and Phrases

They should be short and punchy and are found everywhere, from advertising to the Bible. Each participant brings in a few to form a pool. When called out, dancers respond with movement. There can be a caller who reads each *clearly and loudly,* several times. On a call, all move.

FLASH PHRASE SAMPLER

Abie's Irish Rose. Across the river and into the trees. A kiss is still a kiss. Alive and kicking. All's fair in love and war. Ante up! A rolling stone gathers no moss. Arthur Murray taught me dancing in a hurry. Artsy-fartsy. Bad day at Black Rock. Beer-barrel polka. Be fruitful and multiply. Black belt. Blowhard. Board of Education. Breaking the sound barrier. Carry me back to old Virginny. Catch 22. Chanel No. 5. Chattanooga choo-choo. Chocolates for breakfast. Come and get it! Come up and see me some time. Do it my way. Eager beaver! Flow gently, sweet Afton. Flying down to Rio. Follow the yellow brick road. Footprints in the sands of time. For me and my gal. Fuzz buster. Give us this day our daily bread. Go and catch a falling star. Godzilla! Gone with the wind. Handsome is as handsome does. Have your palm read? Here kitty, kitty, kitty. High noon. Hold that tiger! Home in Indiana. Home sweet home. How now, brown cow? How to dance forever. Hurry up and wait. Hush little baby, don't say a word. I dare you! I dreamt I dwelt in marble halls. If a body meet a body. If I were king. If you got it, flaunt it! I led three lives. It's not what you do, it's the way that you do it. It's only make believe. Just in time. King's English. Kitten on the keys. Ladies and gentlemen, our president! Lassie come home. Let's do it! Life of the party. Lose ten pounds in two weeks! Louisville slugger. Love me, love my cat. Madam, I'm Adam. Madame Butterfly. Mirror, mirror, on the wall. Moon walk! My cup runneth over. My name is Tondelayo. My psychiatrist hates me. No deposit, no return. No news is good news. Nude descending a staircase. Oh, yeah? Ole buttermilk sky. Ole man river. Open-ended. Or would you rather be a fish? O say, can you see? Palsy-walsy. Peel me a grape. Play it again, Sam! Polly wanna cracker? Practice makes perfect. Prime time. Private domain. Problem child. Quit your bellyaching! Rambo mambo. Read all about it! Rimsky-Korsakov. Robin Hood. Romeo and Juliet. Rorshach test. Safe sex. Save the Earth! Save the last dance for me. Sentimental journey. Shake it, but don't break it. Shall we dance? Sign on the dotted line. Sock it to me! Speak low, when you speak love. Standing room only. Star-spangled banner. Stop—look—and listen! Stuff and nonsense. Sweet and low. Take me to your leader. Tea for two. Teenage mutant ninja turtles. The razor's edge. Thus spake Zarathustra! Try and stop me! Up the creek without a paddle. Up your ante! User-friendly. Violets are blue. Walking on air! Watch it, buster! Who washes galoshes? Would you like to swing on a star? X-ray eyes. You must remember this. Young at heart. Zorba the Greek.

STUCK—AND UNSTUCK

Choreographers get the equivalent of writer's block. Every move seems insipid or insufferable or no movement comes. Writers use tricks to break blocks. So can dancemakers.

- ➤ *Crash.* Accept the first move that comes. Suspend all self-criticism to crash into movement. Eventually, you will break through with a move you like.
- ➤ *Do the wrong thing.* Deliberately try things you know won't work. You'll get going fast. Keep doing wrong things because it keeps you moving—so the right thing is bound to come. When it does, you're not stuck anymore.
- ➤ *Be a critic.* Imagine that your dance was choreographed by someone else. How would you critique it? How would you improve it? Do it!
- ➤ *Thought dances.* Sit or lie prone. Empty your mind. Don't hurry. Let pictures of movement flow, and gradually direct them to the problem. When you see something interesting, get on your feet and try it.
- ➤ *Find the fallacy (Martha Graham's way).* Run the dance from the top. Long before the stuck place, look for the move that heads in the wrong direction.

It you don't find it, change any move that comes before the stuck place. This can get you onto a new track that keeps going.

➢ *Literals*. Write out a list of movements you haven't used. Read over the list to see if anything you've written might break the impasse.

➢ *Change Contexts*. Put the dance out of your mind. Now start a different dance. When you have something else, tack it onto the place where you're blocked.

➢ *Chance*. Chance (page 65) can get you unstuck; and is also a whole territory to explore.

Freeze Frames

Freeze Frames are a form of crashing. They force you to do something, which gets you unstuck. Freeze frames are also interesting in their own right.

*P*ROJECT 77   FREEZE-FRAME STUDY.

The moves in this study will be body shapes (page 11). A **freeze frame** is a kinetic instant—what you see on a single frame of a video or movie film. Make up fifteen, twenty, or more freeze frames. Don't go for originality at first—just keep moving and changing. As you work, count out loud: "Number one!" Do a freeze frame. "Number two," another frame, etc. After a time most dancers run out of familiar moves. When that happens, look for frames that feel different, strange, uncomfortable. When you start getting interested in them, go back to the stuck place in the dance and try one of the interesting freeze frames. If it's not quite right, chances are you can get going anyway. ■

Floor Study

This is useful if you are not used to working on the floor; it is good for classically trained dancers who find it hard to come up with moves not learned in technique class. You can work on your knees, crawl like a crab, stand on your hands, do anything not on your feet. It is very limiting and can annoy some people—summoning movements that say: "Such a preposterous idea deserves preposterous dancing!" In that frame of mind surprising things happen!

*P*ROJECT 78   AN ON-THE-FLOOR DANCE.

Make a dance entirely on the floor. ■

IMPROVS WITH VIDEO

Viewing with a Fresh Eye

Set up an improv problem, and do it for the camera. Keep the camera running only as long as the improv feels fresh or you'll have to sit through a lot of dull viewing. Before viewing, do something else for a while so you can see it afresh.

Iterative Enhancement

This is a fancy term for an old process; automobiles are improved with each new model, computer software with each new version. You can improvise moves, then improve them.

1. Do a good warm-up. Think about a two-to-five minute improv, but don't actually do it until the camera is running. Then give it all you've got.
2. View the video, pick out a move or phrase you like, *and make it the core of the next improv*. Repeat, as long as it keeps improving or until you have what you want.

Chaining

The trigger, an image, word, or other stimulus, should be short and the response short. For instance, "Open Sesame!" and you respond with a move. One move is easy to remember. If you like it, commit it to memory. Then do another, and another. When you have a few, chain them together. Memorize the chain. When you have enough material, work it into a dance.

Group chaining can be done with two or more dancers. Use triggers with an element of surprise—for instance, a sheaf of postcards. Exhibit one, and all dancers respond with a move. Each dancer then memorizes his or her move. Then show each move successively. In a largish group even one go-around will produce a store of movement material.

FINDING, CAPTURING, AND TAMING THE WILD IMPROV

Finding the Wild Improv

The great move is what most improvs are about. You can use any stratagem on the *MAP*, or any of the exciting improvs that dance composition teachers are always inventing.

Capturing the Wild Improv

After one magical appearance, the great move refuses to return. How can it be captured?

1. *Collaborate.* I learned an exciting process from Linda Boyd, an American Dance Fesitval associate in the summer of 1991. A bountiful and spontaneous improviser, she had trouble remembering her moves. So we made a dance together, she responding to images and ideas, me remembering moves and reminding her of what she had done. Try both sides of this collaboration.

2. *Get an assistant.* I had the pleasure of assisting Broadway choreographer Donald Saddler on several musicals. Saddler is a fine improviser and I'd stand by, grabbing his gems. But I was never good at letting others grab my moves, stopping instead, to learn them myself. Once I was making a dance with Allen Tung; he did a move and I said, "That's nice, where did it come from?" He looked puzzled, and said, "You just did it."

3. *Use video.* You can pop in a tape, switch on, and dance. But remember, you have to watch the whole tape afterward; so it's good to prepare mentally, and concentrate as though you were improvising for an audience. When you're primed, hit the record button.

Taming the Wild Improv

Once you've captured—can remember—the move, you can put it to work immediately, or if you're sure it won't escape—be forgotten—wait until later. You "tame" it by harnessing it into a dance, using any choreographic maneuver or stratagem, many of which are described in Chapter 9 on Form (pages 177–236), where you encounter ways in which a dance can be constructed from a core of basic moves.

ENDNOTES

1. Lynne Anne Blom and L. Tarin Chaplin, *The Moment of Improvisation* (Pittsburgh: University of Pittsburgh Press, 1988); Eric Franklin, *Dance Imagery for Technique and Performance* (Champaign, IL: Human Kinetics, 1996); Joyce Morganroth, *Dance Improvisations* (Pittsburgh: University of Pittsburgh Press, 1987); Daniel Nagrin, *Dance and the Specific Image* (Pittsburgh: University of Pittsburgh Press, 1994); Georgette Schneer, *Movement Improvisation* (Champaign, IL: Human Kinetics, 1994); Viola Spolin, *Improvisation for the Theater* (Evanston, IL: Northwestern University Press, 1963).

CHAPTER 5

DANCE ENVIRONMENTS

The ultimate dance environment is space-time, within which the whole universe dances. People, however, experience space and time separately. Time itself can be thought of as a dance environment, yet one that defies us to do much about it, although dances mark the passage of time and lend it shape.

Music also marks time, although that is its lesser attribute. But in its ability to surround and penetrate movement, it becomes an important element of the dance environment.

As to space, we have many choices. Stages and black boxes are protean because audiences, eager to suspend disbelief, allow the dancemaker to make all of them what they wish. We can also dance in streets, parks, railroad stations, museum galleries, cemeteries, on rooftops and factory floors.

Philosopher George O. Wilson believes that because dance has existed in every human society of which we have any knowledge, even those without music or language, it is programmed into the human genome. If so, then dance environments are all of those in which humanity has ever existed.

Fifteen or twenty billion years ago, says science, a big bang created space and time. Space and time are all a dancer needs to make a dance. Scientists say space and time may be a single entity—space-time—but we experience each differently. We feel time through rhythm and tempo; we perceive space when we move through it.

Louis Horst credits Mary Wigman with early space awareness: "The Wigman dance . . . was concerned principally with the relationship of man to his universe. Mary Wigman conceived of space as a factor, like time, with which to compose."[1] Wigman's followers, Hanya Holm, Alwin Nikolais, Murray Louis, and others, continued to explore the bond between space and dance.[2]

We usually separate *dance space* from *audience space*. Theaters have a fourth wall, the proscenium, whereas in black boxes and lofts, the audience is assigned to space. Some artists try to erase this by moving through the audience. Reijo Kela, in a dance titled *Keskiverto (Everyman)*, put the audience onstage, into the set, and amidst the action.

Dance space is shaped by the dancers in it. Isn't this in some way like Einstein's discovery that outer space is curved by the stars in it?

Limbo is blind space created by surrounding darkness; it can evoke anything from outer space to the secret spaces of the heart.

*P*ROJECT 79   USES OF SPACE.

1. *Fill space.* Make a study that reaches into every part of the studio.

2. *Divide space.* Imagine a straight line crossing the dance space in any direction:

   - Make a study staying on that line.
   - Use all the space, but make the audience aware of the divide.

- Use a curved line, a wavy line, a broken line, a branching line, a line that rises and falls, or several lines.
- Make all your moves on top of the line or lines.
- Take a new look at a dance you know, and consider how it uses space.

3. *Define space.* Make a study that uses different spaces for different actions. For instance: fast here, slow there; jumping here, crawling there. Find variations on this idea.   ■

$\mathcal{P}$ROJECT 80   PATTERNS IN SPACE.

Pattern is the track dancers make as they move. How does the pattern affect the space? How does the space affect the pattern? Does movement change when a pattern changes, for instance, from circular to zigzag? Can you work against a pattern, that is, force movement into it that seems not to want to fit? Can a pattern expand space, shrink space, ignore space?

1. Design a floor pattern. It can be circular, square, zigzag, branching, etc., or shaped like a letter of the alphabet, a number, or a logo. If you know Chinese or Japanese, you have thousands of calligraphic patterns to choose from!
2. Use your pattern for the floor patterns of a dance.   ■

$\mathcal{P}$ROJECT 81   THE RELATIVITY OF SPACE.

1. Try simple or very small moves in a large space.
2. Cram large or complex moves into a small space.
3. Imagine that the space is broken by invisible barriers or marked with zigzags, spirals, or polka dots.   ■

$\mathcal{P}$ROJECT 82   SPACE LEVELS.

You ordinarily dance on your feet, but you can also get down on the floor or jump into the air. This yields three levels: level one—down on the floor; level two—on your feet; level three—up in the air.

1. Make a level-one study, i.e., completely on the floor. This is good for dancers who tend to assemble classroom technique. (A compelling solo, *Crash!* came out of this assignment, by classically trained Jennifer Peebles.)

2. Make a study using any two levels. Falls and jumps are inherently passes between levels. Find other ways to pass between levels.

3. Start a study on one level, end on another.

4. Start a study on one level, proceed through the others, and end on the level on which you began.

5. Make three phrases, one for each level. Dance them in different orders.

6. Think of other ways to use levels.   ■

*P*ROJECT 83   CREATE SPACE.

This can be tricky and also fun. Use movement to evoke:

1. space that is thick, or resistant, as mime Marcel Marceau did in *Walking against the Wind*

2. space that is hostile or dangerous

3. space that is liberating or exhilarating

4. space that might explode or collapse

5. space that can't be entered, or space that can't be exited   ■

SOUND SCORES

Dances performed in "silence" are accompanied by the ambient sounds of the space where they are danced. Even if the space could be silenced, there would still be the interior music within each mind.

In the movie *Tonight and Every Night,* Marc Platt danced to the crazed rantings of an amok tyrant. Platt's dictator dance brought an expanded aural environment to a vast new audience.

*P*ROJECT 84   MAKE A SOUND SCORE.

1. *Go prospecting.* Take a cassette recorder to a beach, construction site, dentist, dog kennel, family meal, food store, hotel cashier, lecture, museum, rehearsal, restaurant, shopping mall, sports event, street fair, traffic light, or record the sounds from radio or TV. For more sophisticated prospecting, enlist a composer familiar with the electronic wizardry called "sampling." Composers-cum-sound engineers can produce *The Rite of Spring* for chain saws, *My Gal Sal* on a whistling tea kettle.

2. *Make the sound score.* Having found sounds, play them for your group. Compare, exchange ideas, do some trading. To connect sounds from

several tapes, you need two tape recorders. The simplest way is by "air coupling," playing one while the other records. This can yield a usable rehearsal tape. Patching together with cables give cleaner recordings. A multitrack recorder allows you to blend and manipulate sounds, which takes some know-how. Computer digital processing opens more options and takes much more know-how. If you can, go for it. But keep in mind that the great photographer Richard Avedon made his first stunning photographs with a Brownie box camera. You can make a sound score using a cheap cassette recorder.

3. *Use your sound score for a dance.*   ■

THE BEAT

To many, a good beat is an irresistible summons to movement. It also serves dancers as a marker; they count beats to keep exactly where they need to be in the music. Dancers tend to count eights, a practice that trained musicians, who count measures, call "dancers' counts." Sure enough, when dancing, I count eights; when I play my violin, I count measures like a musician.

Every piece of music has a time signature, which indicates the number of beats per measure and the duration of each beat. This is its meter. Simple meters have two, three, or four beats per measure, with an accent on the first beat, and have time signatures like $\frac{2}{2}$, $\frac{3}{4}$, and $\frac{4}{4}$, respectively, duple, triple, and quadruple meters. Music writer and teacher George A. Wedge relates these meters to breathing:

> As we breathe, the inhalation corresponds to the unaccented pulse in music, the exhalation to the accented pulse. When exercising, the periods occupied in inhaling and exhaling are of approximately equal duration. This corresponds to duple meter. When we are relaxed or asleep the exhalation is from twice to three times as long as the inhalation. This corresponds to triple or quadruple meter . . . breathing begins with the unaccented beat, or up-beat. This accounts for the fact that it is more natural to begin a composition on the up-beat.[3]

Musicologist Cecil Smith, who taught music for dancers at the Martha Graham School, sparked a discussion when he said that anything beyond four beats was compound meter—a combination of simple meters. "What about a five?" I challenged, and he shot back, "Do you mean two and three, or three and two?" Years later, working with a score in $\frac{5}{4}$ time by Henry Cowell, I attempted to treat fives as simple meter. Yet mostly we do break fives down. Dancer and musician Ted Dalbotten teaches his students to combine triplets and duplets in $\frac{4}{4}$ time by saying "Pineapple grapefruit," alotting each *word* the same amount of time. Alice Teirstein adapted it to teach a $\frac{5}{4}$

compound meter by giving each *syllable* the same amount of time as, "Pine-ap-ple grape-fruit," (1-2-3, 1-2) or "Grape-fruit pine-ap-ple" (1-2, 1-2-3).

Compound meters have time signatures like $\frac{5}{4}$, $\frac{5}{8}$, $\frac{6}{2}$, $\frac{6}{4}$, $\frac{6}{8}$, $\frac{7}{8}$, and $\frac{9}{8}$, which can all be broken down into combinations of simple meters. Leonard Bernstein's driving, "America," from *West Side Story*, in $\frac{12}{8}$ time, actually consists of two threes and three twos. The last movement of Sergei Prokofiev's Second Piano Sonata is in a breathless $\frac{7}{8}$ time, like boogie-woogie eight-to-the-bar, with the last beat missing. *Syncopation* shifts the accent away from its normal place and opens up a whole new world. Time signatures give music a useful rhythmic framework; yet when modern composers feel too confined by them, they simply leave them out.

Percussionists can play one beat against another. Here's an easy one: a slow beat with the right foot, doubled with the left, redoubled with the right hand, redoubled again with the left hand. Try it! Ravi Shankar, the Indian sitarist, demonstrated astonishing virtuosity by playing 3 against 4, then 4 against 5, and if you can believe it, 10 against 11, counting out loud to help his awed audience follow.

A good beat energizes dances, but total domination by the beat weakens them (Mickey mousing, page 151). Sophisticated choreographers weave in and out of the beat, and a few, notably Merce Cunningham, make deeply rhythmic yet beat-independent dances. To get the beat into your bones, study hand drumming: tom-toms, conga, bongo, African, or mid-Eastern. Indian tabla are superb but very difficult.

The kinetic excitement of a powerful beat is reflected in the performance of Hélène Grand dancing in *From Vegas with Love*.

*P*ROJECT 85 BEAT STUDY.

1. Make a dance with:

   a. *A beat different from the music*—a "counterbeat."

   b. *Contrasting beats*—different meters used successively.

   c. *Multiple beats*—pitting one beat against another.

   d. *Syncopation*—shifting the accented beat.

   e. *Eccentric beats*—$\frac{5}{4}$ or $\frac{7}{8}$ time. Try contemporary music, or have a composer write a piece for you.

   f. *Moves against the beat*—slower or faster than the music.

   g. *Moves above the beat*—create long phrases that start and end on the beat but are free in the middle.

2. Can the beat, like beauty, be in the eye of the beholder? ■

*P*ROJECT 86 BEATLESS STUDY.

Make a study with *no beat*. Show it and ask if anyone picks up a beat in it. ■

PROPS

Physical objects can be used symbolically, the way a flag is used, or for their associations: a hat can signal pride or despair; a cane can impart insouciance or decrepitude; a flower can evoke one's soul.

➤ In *People and Things*, Mark Ryder and Emily Frankel used props to portray a couple whose possessions meant more to them than they meant to each other.

➤ In *Deaths and Entrances*, Martha Graham offered a chalice to her beloved. When he rejected it, it was she who was spurned.

➤ In *Nevada*, Douglas Dunn deftly manipulated a three-foot plywood cut-out of the state of Nevada, a kind of kinetic pun with some dexterous prop handling.

➤ In *Wood*, Cliff Keuter entered with an armload of kindling, dropped it to the floor with a clatter, saying "I would, if I could," then danced an imaginative verbal/kinetic pun.

Chairs

After telling a class that I'd seen every possible chair dance, Melanie Slater promptly made a dance that took place entirely beneath one. Anne Teresa De Keersmaeker littered the stage with chairs in her mysterious *Elena's*

Alice Teirstein

Dancers on a park bench. From Alice Teirstein's *Walking Shoes*.

Aria, and in *Vespers,* Ulysses Dove made a *tour de force* for women and chairs. And Alice Teirstein used a park bench for a pivotal moment in *Walking Shoes.* Chairs and benches are frequently used props, but originality can prevail. If an object intrigues or has meaning for you, use it.

𝒫ROJECT 87   PROP STUDY.

Make a study using:

- a common object found around the house
- a personal object or one associated with your own person
- an object associated with sports
- an object associated with food
- an exotic object
- a mysterious or unrecognizable object
- a balloon, or a bunch of flowers

- boxes of corn flakes, or some other cereal
- Post-it™ paper, stick-on labels, or children's stick-on toys
- a musical instrument
- something you can turn on and off
- something you can get into and out of
- any object you find interesting ∎

FABRIC

Fabric can be turned into costumes, props, and stage sets; its ability to re-veal movement and make it linger in space makes it appealing to choreographers. In many paintings by old masters, large areas are simply draped fabric. Once very costly, fabric appealed to painters because of its luxury and the way it reflected light.

In her 1893 Paris debut, the American modern dancer Loie Fuller used voluminous silken scarves and dramatic lighting to score a huge success at the *Folies Bergère*. She became the toast of Europe and did essentially that same dance for the rest of her life, an entire career pretty much out of whole cloth.

Doris Humphrey in *Day on Earth*, made a sweet, solemn ritual out of folding a large piece of fabric.

In the opening of *Eye of Anguish*, from Shakespeare's *King Lear*, Martha Graham put Lear and his two wicked daughters, Goneril and Regan, in-side a giant tube of fabric, where they literally had a tug-of-war for their father's affection.

In China, wanting to give the Guangdong dancers a fabric study, I asked for some fabric and got a dozen thirty-foot lengths of pure silk!

*P*ROJECT 88   FABRIC STUDY.

Obtain any piece of fabric except a bed sheet. Handle it until you compre-hend its feel and "fall," which depend on how soft, stiff, stretchy, crisp, crinkly, light, heavy, sheer, and so forth, it is. Make a dance using:

- pure movement and pure fabric
- movement between people transmitted by the fabric
- fabric to conceal, reveal, or disguise
- fabric to create images or characters
- fabric added to a costume or as the costume itself
- fabric as a door, a path, a barrier, an environment ∎

Speaking during a dance was experimental as late as the 1950s. Although there were successes, like Martha Graham's *Letter to the World* and Doris Humphrey's *Lament for Ignacio Sanchez Mejias*, most attempts were clumsy. Today fine dances with speech are common.

Text can be spoken live by the dancer or by another person, can be pre-recorded and played, accompanied by music or other sound. It can be text or poetry or a recipe for potato pancakes, spoken ad lib or in conversation with the audience.

$\mathcal{P}$ROJECT 89   TEXT AND MOVEMENT.

Movement first. Create a short study in silence or use a study already made. Look for text accompaniment: poetry, a passage from a novel or nonfiction work, a scene from a play, a news article, a taped conversation, a TV soap opera, a radio call-in show, a weather report, a perfume commercial, or text written especially for the dance.

Try something you think can't possibly work: a recipe for baked Alaska, computer documentation, a medical text—you name it. If you don't much like it, try something else. But if you really hate it, forbear. Anything powerful enough to evoke a strong response is worth a closer listen.

Text first. Find a textual passage you like. Tape it, recite it live, or have another person recite it. Make a dance to it.

Caution: If your dance idea came from a text, you might feel pressured to illustrate that idea. Paul Taylor's advice about music applies equally here: use the text, but don't let the text use you!   ■

Writing poems and making dances have much in common, and poetry brims with dance ideas. Reading poetry, especially aloud, can yield aesthetic, emotional, and intellectual insights. Like all art, poetry offers most to those who give it the most. Browse through poems to find the image, metaphor, or wordplay that strikes a spark.

$\mathcal{P}$ROJECT 90   USING POETRY IN DANCES.

Individual project. Find a poem or passage to be spoken before, during, or after the dance. The speaker may dance, speak only, or be on tape. There may or may not be music. Add moves.

Group projects.

1. Everyone find a few lines of poetry, write them on index cards, and bring to class. Exchange cards. Make studies to someone else's selection.

2. Begin as in item 1. From all the contributions, select one, two, or three which are then assigned so that each selection is danced several times. ■

TITLES AS IDEAS

A title sets up a mental image and thus becomes a kind of environment. When the title comes early in the creative process, it influences the dance itself. Dances can even be generated by titles. In 1969, in a preperformance introduction at the New School for Social Research, moderator Laura Foreman discussed Marshall McLuhan's book, *Understanding Media,* and its famous dictum, "The medium is the message." A title popped into my head: *Audio Visual.* I made the dance using movement, sound, text, and projections; but when I finally read McLuhan's book, I realized that my dance had nothing to do with it.

In some cultures, names have power; learn a person's true name and you control them. Gertrude Stein said she wrote "A rose is a rose is a rose," in order to return meaning to the word "rose" after centuries of use as a metaphor. A title frames a dance. It may box it in but can also magnify it.

*P*ROJECT 91   TITLE BECOMES DANCE.

Use any process (Title Searches, page 261) to find a title.

1. Make a study for the title you found.

2. Two or more people each find one title. Exchange titles. Each then makes studies to another's title.

3. Each member of a group write five titles on separate slips of paper. Put all the titles into a hat, then each member draw one and make a study for the title drawn.

4. Collect many titles. Each participant contribute five or more, neatly printed out.

   a. Each participant pick one title, let it suggest moves, and then make the moves into a study.

   b. Show the studies and consider whether the titles fit. If not, make up new ones. ■

This study is related to Tasks (page 51) and Games (page 52), but is different from each. Tasks have inherent, not arbitrary, rules; for instance, to wash clothes you must soak, soap, scrub, rinse, dry. Games, however, have arbitrary rules; no natural law says baseball must have three strikes for an out or that boxers are out after ten counts. This exercise differs from games in another way: there are no winners or losers. You begin by devising the arbitrary rules which can apply to:

➤ *Space:* rules for specific areas, for example, stage left for allegro, stage right for shaking hands, upstage for hugging, downstage for jumping, proscenium for resting, the aisles for conversation.

➤ *Levels:* for instance, floor for solos, standing for partnering, in the air for competition.

➤ *Action:* what is allowed or required. For example: running moves, laughing out loud, changing socks, blowing up a balloon, giving pennies to the audience.

➤ *Time:* when to start and stop, and how long to continue.

➤ *Rhythm:* kinds of beat and when to speed up and slow down.

➤ *Sequence:* what may follow what.

➤ *Relations:* how dancers behave toward each other, toward the audience, toward stagehands.

➤ *Qualities:* when to be lyrical, percussive, surprised, stoic, nervous, serene, etc.

➤ *Patterns:* traffic, bottlenecks, circles, figure eights.

➤ *Conditions:* actions initiated by other actions. For example: when three dancers occupy center stage, others must lie down.

➤ *Results-orientation:* Laws are passed to assure results: the 55 mph speed limit makes people drive safely. (Right?) Rules can also assure a choreographic result. First think up a result. For example: to collect all tall people on stage left, the rule could be that tall people must take three steps left for every two taken right.

*P*ROJECT 92   A STUDY WITH ARBITRARY RULES.

Make up a set of arbitrary rules and devise a dance using these rules.   ■

*P*ROJECT 93   INTERPRETING RULES.

Give the same set of arbitrary rules to different dancemakers to see how different interpretations generate different studies.   ■

ARBITRARY LIMITS

The moment you begin a work of art, you face its limits. Some are physical: a painting can't extend beyond the painted surface, a dancer can't fly. Some are subtle: a line of poetry or a move generates its own parameters, which limits succeeding lines and moves. Limits can feel restricting, yet they are essential because they define the work of art. This can happen even when we impose completely arbitrary limits.

Clarice Marshall made a dance limited to the color white: costumes, set pieces, and props were white and the floor was painted with white-on-white squares. Dancers drank milk, ate white bread, peeled white eggs, and spoke in whispers because whispers are "white" sound. Their moves were square and measured, until suddenly they stripped off their white jump suits to reveal colorful clothes, leapt off the white checkered stage, and ran off singing! Marshall had set strict limits to make a moving comment about the restrictions life imposes. But she allowed the dancers to escape into a colorful world.

𝒫ROJECT 94   A STUDY WITH ARBITRARY LIMITS.

Some arbitrary limits:

1. A study limited to the head, one hand, vocal sounds, and one word. You can nod, shake, roll your head, blink, squeeze your eyes shut, roll your eyeballs, smile, frown, make funny faces, wiggle your ears, stick out your tongue, puff your cheeks, do one-handed gestures, hum, moan, hiss, yell, and pick the word from any language.

2. One body part must always point at something. Expand on that. For instance, it might suggest a pointer—the hunting dog—and its prey. Or you can point to someone in the audience, "You there!" or yourself, "Who, me?" Don't feel obliged to make too much sense.

3. Some action limits: while dancing, keep one hand hidden, face upstage, carry golf clubs, play with a yo-yo, knit, etc.

4. Choose an arbitrary time limit, for example, a 30-second dance, by the clock. ∎

JUXTAPOSITIONS

Simultaneity to Unity

In the following project, a number of people make individual studies, then juxtapose and rework them into a single dance.

*P*ROJECT 95   JUXTAPOSITION: SOLOS BECOME A GROUP DANCE.

1. Select one or several common points of reference. For instance:

   - *Time:* any agreed number of seconds
   - *Counts:* any agreed counts or measures at a given tempo
   - *Music:* to which all work
   - *Text:* a line of prose or poetry
   - *Other points of reference:* a move, a pattern, an image, etc.

2. Working independently, each dancer or group makes a short solo using the agreed points of reference.

3. Show all the solos individually and if there is time, in pairs. The main showing will be all at the same time. Decide whether:

   a. The common focus can be seen or sensed.

   b. Similar or different movement material is used.

   c. The moves mesh or clash.

   d. Anything unexpected happens when all are danced together.

   e. The studies still make separate statements when shown together, or suggest something that encompasses all.

   f. The whole is more (or less) than the sum of its parts.

Discuss changes that might strengthen or create a new whole. These can include new moves and exchanges of moves between solos, changes of direction, new spacing, different tempos, and anything else.   ■

*P*ROJECT 96   JUXTPOSITION: UNIFYING.

Rework the individual studies to make them into a unified dance.   ■

Confined Step Study

A step study focuses on footwork. Confining it to one square yard restricts movement through space and allows close comparison when two or more studies are performed at the same time.

*P*ROJECT 97   STEPS JUXTAPOSED IN TIME AND SPACE.

Each member of the group creates a sequence of steps to music or counts while keeping within an area of *one square yard.* If danced to music, all use the exact same number of measures. If danced to counts, all use the same counts and tempo. Short studies—30 seconds or so—work well.

1. *Juxtaposition in space.* Half the group performs for the other half, and then the entire group performs simultaneously. When many dance together with all doing different steps, the performance is likely to be chaotic, looking like "a can of worms."

2. *Juxtaposition in time.* Show one after the other to yield a continuous sequence of solos.
   a. A dozen 30-second studies will take six minutes, plus time to leave and enter.
   b. For closer juxtaposition, eliminate time to leave and enter by having dancer #2 stand by as #1 dances. As dancer #1 finishes, #2 begins; and as #1 leaves, #3 enters to stand by, etc.

3. *Juxtaposition in time and space.* Two or three dancers begin. After any set number of measures, add in dancers as others exit, so that two or three dancers are always seen performing together.

4. *Juxtaposition: duets, trios, quartets.* Two, three, or four dancers show their studies together. One way to lessen confusion is to have all dancers learn one other step study and have pairs perform in unison. This increases the number of dancers but not the number of steps. Everybody could learn all the step studies so that all can dance in unison, which is often seen in folk dancing. The objective here, however, is to juxtapose contrasting steps. ■

FRAME OF REFERENCE

Art is limitation. The essence of every picture is the frame.
  G. K. CHESTERTON

Not many artists think of frames as the essence of their work. But if frame includes *frame of reference*, then Chesterton's observation is acute; for every action exists within a frame of reference, whether clear or implied. Martha Myers goes directly for framing in her dance lab. In one study, sounds of slamming doors and footsteps framed the action with urgency; in another, objects the dancers carried implied a subtext, and objects they encountered evoked mysterious surroundings.

A common dance frame is darkness—limbo—created by black drapes and confined lighting. Limbo gives importance to action by isolating it. Other frames set the action against something recognizable:

➤ Tannis Hugill made a dance framed by sounds recorded while taking a seaside walk.

➤ Stephanie Skura danced while carrying a large carved wooden picture frame held in portrait position around her head and shoulders, simultaneously employing and parodying framing.

Here are some kinds of frames:

➤ *Background movement:* A frame seen in every dance that puts a corps behind a soloist.

➤ *Foreground movement:* It can imply that the surrounding area is confining, inviting, threatening, relaxing, etc.

➤ *Sets and props:* Recognizable objects narrow the focus, whereas abstract constructions can broaden it.

➤ *Surreal space:* It is created using real objects in unreal ways—piling up chairs, sitting in a large plastic trash basket, etc.

➤ *Sound:* What we hear always has a framing function. It can be a recognizable sound, like Martha Myers's slamming doors; or sounds transplanted from another context, like Tannis Hugill's beach dance; even pure rhythms, or music of clean character, like the songs of Stephen Foster, which perfectly frame the manners and mannerisms of Elizabeth Keen's *Polite Entertainment for Ladies and Gentlemen.*

➤ *Conceptual frames:* Games, emotions, messages, stories, rituals.

➤ *Psychological frames:* Emotions, obsessions, states of mind.

➤ Also: Changing frames, shifting frames, hidden frames, implied frames, ambiguous frames, and more.

*P*ROJECT 98   FRAMING.

1. Consider any dance you've made. Identify its frame of reference. Might it be enhanced by emphasizing, heightening, or changing that frame?

2. Make a new dance, keeping its frame always in focus. Build both dance and frame at the same time.

3. Create a frame first, then make a dance for it, or fit a dance into it. ■

A subtext is a hidden influence at the core of the action that gives the action meaning. It acts in some ways like a frame, except that where a frame surrounds the action, the subtext lies at its heart. What is the subtext of the following dialogue?

SUBTEXT

Mary: *Bill was my boyfriend before I met you.*

John: I didn't know that.

Mary: *Yes you did. I told you.*

John: When did you tell me?

Mary: *Here, in the kitchen. Six months ago.*

John: You couldn't have because I was painting the kitchen.

Mary: *Of course, dummy! I held your ladder.*

John: I would remember that.

Mary: *Not if you didn't want to.*

John: Why would I not want to?

Mary: *What about Jane?*

This mundane argument can have many subtexts:

1. Each is afraid that the other has a roving eye.
2. John wants to leave Mary or Mary wants to leave John.
3. Each likes to bring up the other's old flames.
4. Both are afraid Aunt Jane will cut them out of her will.
5. Mary's friend Jane is in love with John.
6. Mary's boss, Bill, didn't invite them to a party.
7. John's boss, Jane, invited them to a party.
8. John's best friend, Bill, married Jane.
9. John's ex-wife, Jane, is scheduled to go on a TV talk show.

$\mathcal{P}$ROJECT 99 INVOKE A SUBTEXT.

Use this or another dialogue, and decide upon a strong subtext. Use both dialogue and subtext as the basis of an improv. You may speak the lines or not. In either case, can watchers figure out the subtext? ■

MINIMALISM

In the 1960s, when most Western composers were occupied with twelve-tone music and other variants of harmony, Terry Riley, Steve Reich, and Philip Glass were prominent among those who turned to pure rhythm and melody, using repetition with continuous variation to produce driving music that was also intellectually engaging.

When choreographers began to make dances in a like manner, dance critics, borrowing from other art forms, tagged this genre *minimalism*, perhaps because the thematic materials appear to be minimal. It seems a weak term for such powerfully kinetic, relentlessly formal construction; but call it what you like, the dances can be emotive and powerful.

The first such dance I saw was Laura Dean's *Circle Dance,* which made me think of trance dancing. **Trance dance** predates history, is marked by strong rhythmic moves repeated at length, and is still done in religious rituals.

*P*ROJECT 100 MINIMALIST MOVEMENT STUDIES.

Make an 8-count pattern using four to eight moves in which the last move leads back to the first. Consider this your *plasma.*

1. Dance the pattern four times in a row; change direction; dance it two to four more times.
2. Dance it in reverse *(retrograde)* four to eight times.
3. Create internal variations by changing the order of movement elements within the 8-count pattern. Repeat four to eight times.
4. Invent a new move and add it to the pattern or substitute it for one of the original moves.
5. As you repeat the pattern, substitute new, slightly changed moves for the original ones, until none of the original moves remain.
6. Learn to dance the pattern continuously from the first sequence through each change. You will have from thirty-two to quadruple that number of 8-count patterns. ◼

As described, this is a cerebral process; yet it is best achieved with physical judgments. Your body can tell you if a move is right or wrong, how long it can be repeated, when to change, and when enough is enough.

Minimalist Music

Definitions of minimalism infer restricted materials and structures. Yet a literally minimalist score would also be reticent, modest, discreet, would not demand attention or thrust itself at you, would be more of a presence, like moss or warmth. Thus, I question the term for music as insistent and complex as that of Philip Glass, Steve Reich, and Terry Riley, although it seems to fit some music. In 1968, I saw Merce Cunningham's *RainForest,* with music by David Tudor, a resonant thrumming that gave the dance lush surroundings.

Two decades later, I entered a room in downtown Manhattan to hear a low hum. Fifteen minutes later, it had not changed perceptibly—a sort of aural presence in a clean, bare, brightly lit room that had small drawings on the walls. Another room had other drawings and a hum of a different pitch and timbre. It was the work of La Monte Young, who assuredly regarded the room and all its elements as the *object d'art*. I left his thrumming chambers with the regret I feel for not spending more time contemplating nature or the meaning of life.

Minimalist Dance

By my own restricted definition, there's not much minimalist dance—perhaps Paul Taylor's *Epic*, with its virtual lack of movement, and in a different way, Marcel Marceau's *Ages of Man: Childhood, Adolescence, Maturity, Old Age, and Death*, which stays in one spot as it encapsulates a lifetime. But are Lucinda Childs's ceremonious, multilayered constructions minimal, or Laura Dean's lusty charged articulations of space? But my definition is not a critic's nor is it yours, and yours is the one that counts when you make a dance.

$\mathcal{P}$ROJECT 101   SEEKING MINIMALISM.

Find moves that can be continued while being subtly and constantly varied. A walk, for instance, can be done in different directions, tempos, levels, and styles; its dynamics can be intensified or attenuated.

1. Make a 1-minute study that uses:

   - a single movement concept: walking, falling, jumping, peering, swaying, turning, etc.
   - a single dynamic: soft, loud, slow, fast, accelerating, etc.
   - a single focus
   - a single tempo

2. Extend the study with subtle changes and keep it going for as long as it sustains interest. ■

LAYERING

Our Earth is layered: hot molten core, magma, hard crust, ecolayer, atmosphere, ozone, halo of radiation. And just as every Earth layer is essential to life, in successful dance layering, each layer affects the others and the whole work.

If movement is defined as the core of a dance, lighting and music can be considered layers, although here we seek layers somewhat external to the work to add interest and complexity. Such layers can be quirky. In Lucinda Childs's *Relative Calm*, during one briskly danced passage, curious combinations of words flashed on and off the backdrop. During another, a man entered leading a dog on a leash; they circled the stage, and exited.

Layers can consist of dance or nondance action, projections, sounds, environments, house lights, action in the audience, events from Frames of Reference (page 104), and more. A new layer can lead to a new way of seeing a dance, even new to the one making it. You don't have to limit yourself to logical layers, and even layers that seem to have little bearing on the work can be effective.

How do you distinguish a layer from the work itself? I'm not sure you can or need to. And since you never know how a layer will affect the final dance, take chances.

*P*ROJECT 102   A LAYERED DANCE.

- Add layers to an existing dance.
- Make a dance and give it several layers. ■

➤ Hungarian folk melodies are heard in the music of Béla Bartók.

➤ *Character dance,* which is taught in many ballet schools, is based on Caucasian and Eastern European folk dances.

➤ Sean Curran, of the Bill T. Jones/Arnie Zane Company, created a powerfully dramatic work out of Irish step dancing.

➤ In Aaron Copland's music for *Appalachian Spring,* the theme of the last movement is an old Quaker hymn, *The Gift to Be Simple.*

➤ Russia's renowned Moiseyev Company has turned folk dance into a virtuoso art form.

➤ Twyla Tharp's *Nine Sinatra Songs* is based on ballroom dance, which surely can be deemed a Western folk form.

Use material you know and feel connected to. Do research; knowing that the dance tarantella is named for the tarantula spider, whose bite was thought to cause people to run themselves to death, offers a compelling point of departure!

*P*ROJECT 103   FOLK, CULTURAL, AND POPULAR FORMS.

1. Take inventory of your dance lore; do you know tap, ballroom, folk, Baroque, Scottish, Irish, African, Indian, Native American, Latin, disco, break dancing, hip-hop?
2. Determine the basic moves and mood of one such form.
3. Develop them into a dance. ■

ENVIRONMENTAL AND SITE- SPECIFIC DANCES

There's a challenge in making a dance in places where an audience doesn't expect one. Dances performed outside of performing spaces can be broadly environmental or site-specific, i.e., for one specific place. If the site has beauty, like a golf green or museum gallery, you can make use of that. If it's a parking lot or bowling alley, the dance can add contrast or humanity. If people normally hurry through the space, like a railroad or bus terminal, the dance may tempt them to tarry.

Troupes of Merce Cunningham danced in Grand Central Station, of Jamie Cunningham in Chase Manhattan Plaza, of Gus Solomons jr in the sculpture court of the New School, of Twyla Tharp in the Cloisters, of Stephan Koplowitz in the Museum of Natural History, and of Mark Dendy on the quad at Duke University. Joanna Boyce's *Water Bodies* put naked dancers into the Duke University swimming pool, where they made quite a splash!

I once saw a dance that took place in a stairwell and read about one on a mountain top. That's all right if you are content with a tiny audience. If not, the site should be accessible.

American Dance Festival performance of *Sea Dappled Horse*, performed on Duke University campus by Dai Rakuda Kan Dance Company of Japan.

American Dance Festival Archives

*P*ROJECT 104   A DANCE FOR AN ENVIRONMENT.

Finding a site may take some doing, and you may need permission to use it. When you have a site, feel it out to learn how people behave in it. You can't rehearse in a public site unless you don't mind watchers.

Ways to work in a site:

- Respond and react personally. How does the site affect you?
- Become one with the site: be a branch of the tree, door of the building, lawn of the sprinkler, extension of the bus stop.
- Use the site in some imaginative way: become rain upon the tree, a prisoner in the building, entertainers at the bus stop.
- Defy the space. Do a mechanical dance on a lush sward, a meditative dance in a busy mall, aerobics by a bus stop.
- Pick an aspect of the site that is interesting or overlooked. Stephan Koplowitz set *Fenestrations,* his Grand Central Station dance, in the beautiful windows overlooking the main plaza.
- Ignore the site. Merce Cunningham's Grand Central Station piece was danced on a platform above people rushing to and from trains; it seemed to say, "This rat race isn't all there is to life!" ■

HOSTILE ENVIRONMENTS

A hostile environment can be the crater of a volcano, a dangerous neighborhood, or underwater. The rope-clinging dancers of the Experimental Anti-Gravity Aerodance Group looked stressed, whereas Esther Williams underwater looked as natural as a rainbow, at least on film.

Hostile environments are fascinating partly because they present a stark contrast to fragile bodies. At the American Dance Festival, Maia Heiss made a study on top of the central air-conditioning unit just below the studio's fire exit. She crawled on narrow ledges, hair flying in the breeze of huge fans, which also provided a roaring aural envelope. The contrast between Maia's serene movement and the rackety machinery made a compelling study.

In the Broadway musical *Bye Bye Birdie*, Gower Champion made an exciting opening with dancers hanging in what looked like industrial shelving. The Venezuelan modern dance company Danza Hoya made a stunning dance in what looked like a large jungle gym up which dancers climbed, to tumble down through the bars. Spain's Danat Danza troupe performed on a huge gyrating teetertotter that seemed about to catapult the dancers into the audience.

Some hostile environments: automobile junkyards, a factory production line, a building under construction, a tiny islet in a river or lake, the former prison island of Alcatraz, private property with signs that say "NO TRESPASSING," abandoned buildings, target ranges, mine shafts, missile pads, landfills, trash-filled lots; and anywhere in the pouring rain or in a hurricane. Some hostile environments have wall-to-wall people, like subway platforms and prison compounds; others are likely to be hostile to audiences, which may be where film and video can avail.

$\mathcal{P}$ROJECT 105   A DANCE FOR A HOSTILE ENVIRONMENT.

Over to you! ■

MEDIA/ TECHNOLOGY

A "medium" is a means or an instrument. The body is a dance medium, the voice, a song medium; song and dance are both expressive media. Media today, however, implies technology: film, still projection, video, audio, lighting, computers.

In the late 1960s, Mimi Garrard and her lighting designer, James Seawright, devised a lighting system controlled by computer in which lighting "scores" could be created and played back like music. With composer Emmanuel Ghent they created a sound-and-light score for Garrard's *Phosphones;* although computers are now commonly used to control lights and generate sounds, I've yet to hear of anyone else putting movement, lights, and music together in quite this way.

Twyla Tharp once attached video cameras to dancers so the audience got a dancer's-eye view when they glanced at a screen.

In *Hexa,* Anita Feldman used an ingenious invention, "The Tap Dance Instrument," to amplify and digitally process the dancers' taps.[4]

In the movie *Anchors Aweigh,* Gene Kelly danced a duet with Mickey Mouse, mingling animation with filmed live dance.

We live in an era of burgeoning technology and thus must learn to deal with sensors, switches, lights, microphones, and cameras attached to leaping dancers, to name a few. Technical experts are essential; yet the dance-maker needs expertise too, gained by reading, taking courses, apprenticing, hanging around techies, and just tinkering. Broadway dancer/choreographer Sandra Devlin bought a VCR to help her prepare choreography for summer-stock musicals. One thing led to another, until she had a thriving business, Devlin Videoservice, Inc.

Still Projection

This is a relatively easy technology. You need a slide projector, slides, a surface or surfaces to project onto, and someone to run the projector. Don't worry about dancers dancing through the beam.

$\mathcal{P}$ROJECT 106   DANCE AND STILL PROJECTION.

1. Make your own 35 mm. slides, using color slide (not print) film, have slides made from prints, or buy slides in a museum.
2. Arrange the slides in an order. Project them to get a good sense of sequence, rearranging, as you go.
3. Start making movement. The slides give you a focus; but with media, you never really know what you've got until you put it all together.
4. Some decisions are temporary; for instance, each slide can be arbitrarily allotted 5 seconds on screen. For 30 slides, that's 150 seconds or 2½ minutes. But that can change as the work develops.
5. Play the music, project the slides, dance the dance. ■

Film Projection

It's no harder to project a film than to run slides; but since film projects a *moving* image, there are significant differences:

➤ Whereas still images tend to augment live movement, moving images tend to compete with it.

➤ Slides can be varied in time and sequence; but once a film is made, you have little control over it.

➤ A slide sequence can be assembled as you make the dance, but a film is usually made separately.

➤ Editing film takes more expertise than sequencing slides.

➤ Film is more expensive, even 8-millimeter film.

On the positive side, a film can:

➤ Amplify an idea with parallel or complementary action.

➤ Take the audience deeply into the dance with zooms and close-ups.

➤ Open a window on a different space.

➤ Manipulate time with slow or fast motion.

➤ Echo stage action with footage of the same or similar moves.

➤ Use different or the same dancers seen onstage.

Super 8 is shot in segments, a few minutes per roll. When developed, run the segments, then edit and splice. You need a splicer and a viewing editor to check results. It's time-consuming but not difficult. Incidentally, regular films are *never* made this way. All but a few filmmakers put every shot, angle, scene, background, prop, and word into a script. But this is an intermedia film—a different animal.

$\mathcal{P}$ROJECT 107 DANCE AND FILM PROJECTION.

1. Obtain a short film or segment. You can use films made by a colleague or filmmaker, borrowed from a college film department, or rented.[5] Unless you shoot your own, ask permission before using a film for a dance.
2. Decide whether to run the film before, during, or after the dance, in its entirety or in part, continuously or stop-and-go.
3. Decide whether to project images upon a screen, scrim, hangings, set pieces, or on the dancers.
4. If you want to project the same dance that is performed live, decide whether to film it in rehearsal, shooting as you choreograph, or afterward in other settings. You can also film the dancers doing other things. ■

Onstage Video and TV

Putting a TV set on a stage raises questions in an audience's mind. Is the scene a living room or bedroom? What will the set play when turned on? Would I rather be home watching television?

Video is a personal medium. It doesn't "belong" on a stage and sets up tension when placed there. That tension is one of its objectives. Injecting video into a dance is like doping silicon wafers by injecting an impurity, thus transforming it into a transistor.

> ➤ D. J. MacDonald put a television set onstage and used the raster's glow as a source of lighting in *Grandfather Songs*.
> ➤ Twyla Tharp, at the Brooklyn Academy of Music, put above the stage a TV screen that showed her at work in her studio choreographing the dance while growing more and more pregnant.
> ➤ Robert Streicher, in a 1960s solo, wrestled with a large TV tube, taking a terrible chance since it was not devacuumed.

I have seen dances performed while several onstage monitors each showed something different. At a Hong Kong dance festival, a Phillipine dancer set a moving solo against extended coverage of a bloody street riot. Onstage video is easier to manage than film, but know that video is its own art form. Combining it with dance is still experimental.

$\mathcal{P}$ROJECT 108   DANCE AND ONSTAGE VIDEO.

- Develop a short scenario using video technology and movement together, and present it for discussion with your group.
- Make a dance to be performed with video. The monitors can be onstage with the dance or elsewhere in view. The video can be of the dance or of something else; it can be custom-made, recorded off the air, rented, or piped in from a live video camera, which can be onstage, in the wings, balcony, lobby, roof, or elsewhere. ■

Intermedia

The term **intermedia** is often used interchangeably with multimedia, although intermedia connotes the freedom to range through media and the liberty to take from anywhere. It is a liberating concept as long as the emphasis stays on the creative act rather than on the technology. Intermedia includes: computerized lighting as in "light shows"; projected computer graphics; sound produced by dancers passing through beams of light; sound produced by dancers stepping on floor panels; onstage and offstage microphones into which dancers and others speak; electronic sound combinations of slides, film, and video; projections beamed onto shaped fabric screens; and, with the explosion of computers and the Internet, who knows what next?

Use of such elements demands lots of work outside of a dance studio; with so many variables there are unpredictable consequences. The potential is vast, yet few works transcend the passing interest of their technology. I've seen none that compare with the brilliant intermedialike works of Alwin Nikolais made in the 1950s. The world still awaits a true intermedia genius.

$\mathcal{P}$ROJECT 109   INTERMEDIA.

Devise a work using movement plus two of the following: music, text, sound effects, still-image projections, moving-image projections, active lighting, or something else. ■

ENDNOTES

1. Louis Horst and Carroll Russell, *Modern Dance Forms in Relation to the Other Modern Arts,* (Brooklyn: Dance Horizons, 1967), p. 18.

2. Murray Lewis's video, *Space,* one in a series, *Dance As an Art Form,* is in many libraries. Alwin Nikolais's forthcoming book, *The Unique Gesture,* will certainly have important things to say about space.

3. George A. Wedge, *Ear-Training and Sight Singing* (New York: G. Schirmer, 1921), p. 13.

4. The Tap Dance Instrument was built and is patented by Feldman and Daniel Schmitt, and the choreography-cum-musical score was created collaboratively by Feldman and composer Lois V. Vierk.

5. Film-Makers' Cooperative, 175 Lexington Ave., NY, NY, 10016, 212-889-3820, has films by artist/filmmakers available almost nowhere else. For dance films, try Dance Films Association, 31 West 21 St., NY, NY 10010, 212-727-0764.

$\mathscr{C}$HAPTER 6

$\mathscr{D}$ANCE AT WORK:
"APPLIED DANCE"

In academe, some studies are termed "pure," others "applied." Pure science and pure mathematics are devoted to theory, whereas their applied versions put theory to work making things people can use.

There is also pure music for those who study theory and composition, and applied music for those who sing and play. This seems a bit strange since someone making music would seem to be the very soul of purity. That point aside, the term *applied dance* could be used for dance that is put to work in other art forms, like musicals, movies, television shows, or for dance on ice, as exercise, in recreation, as healing, as ritual, even as sport.

Most dancemakers welcome the idea of applying dance to as much of life as possible.

STAGING A SONG

If you can stage a song swiftly and well, you can make a living at it. Musicals, stock companies, dinner theaters, and rock and rap groups always need staging. Television needs less now than in the golden days of variety shows, but MTV has become virtually its own art form. When staging a song, you can:

➤ Illustrate or act out lyrics.

➤ Set up action peripheral to the song; this can be seen in Astaire films as he sings or just before he starts to dance.

➤ Set up action contrary or unrelated to the lyrics. This is tricky; but if it works, you look like a genius.

➤ Use pure movement, especially if the singer can dance at all. Use moves that the singer does best.

➤ Stage it as a scene, using the song lyric as text, as in Project 110.

➤ Invent business with prop or item of clothing, like blowing up a balloon, tying a bow tie, trying on a hat, etc. With the right business, a song will practically stage itself.

➤ Let the singer sing amid peripheral action—for instance, dancers moving on and off, being careful not to distract from the singing. This is good for singers who don't like to move.

➤ Go bananas. Richard Foreman's *Ontological Hysteric Theater* creates wild action; people dash onstage, string ropes, hang flags, wield canes, wear gas masks, fall down, wave legs and arms in the air, crawl on all fours. If you think it sounds childish, well, some said that of paintings by Pablo Picasso.

*P*ROJECT 110 VOCAL THEATER.

Vocal theater is a concept of Elizabeth Hodes. It combines acting and improvisation to develop staging for a song.

1. Speak the lyrics of the song as a monologue. Repeat until the lyrics make sense to you. If they make little sense, create a subtextual meaning (pages 105 and 156) you can work with.

2. Forgetting lyrics, improvise movement to the melody alone until you have moves you like.

3. With no music, speak the words in rhythm as you try out moves from the improvisation. Repeat until words and moves work together.

4. Now sing the song as you do the moves. The song is staged. ■

PROJECT 111   STAGE A SONG.

Stage: a song you love; a song you loathe; a song you've known since childhood; a ballad; an "up," that is, a fast, happy song; a show tune; a country, rock, Reggae, rap, or other genre song; a standard, a golden oldie, a Top 40 song, a patter song, a comedy song. ■

DANCE OUTREACH

When dancer/choreographer Chuck Davis accepted an invitation to move his African-American Dance Ensemble from New York City to Durham, North Carolina to perform in schools and public spaces as well as theaters, he joined the "dance explosion" that was carrying dance to new audiences everywhere. It could not have happened without a growing appetite for dance, whetted by vigorous dance outreach.

Dancing in the Streets, a New York City-based organization, seeks public spaces for dance. When forty acres of the Hudson River were filled in for a building tract, Dancing in the Streets produced concerts there in the years before construction began.

D. J. MacDonald works with senior citizens in centers and residences, putting his own dance company into works with the seniors, who sometimes evince talent that had lain dormant for years.

Liz Lerman's company of Washington, D.C. and Takoma Park, Maryland, uses community outreach as a creative resource. One of the dances she made at the American Dance Festival used her own dancers plus some twenty-five local residents for an amusingly buoyant takeoff of *Swan Lake*.

At NYU in 1974, a graduate student proposed a thesis project to teach dance to female residents of Riker's Island prison. After convincing a doubtful faculty that she'd be safe, she returned to wow them with a final report that showed warm welcome and an impact.

PROJECT 112   OUTREACH.

Take dance to a new population; you can:

- Seek educational programs willing to piggyback some dance.
- Seek artists of any discipline who involve themselves with the community and who might be glad to include dance.

- Identify populations that can benefit from dance.
- Seek ways to take dance to people who have had little. ■

AQUADANCE, ICE DANCING, GYMNASTICS

Aquadance (also called synchronized swimming), ice dancing (figure skating), and gymnastics share a unique characteristic; they are competitive sports with an aesthetic component. Anyone making routines for these must consider more than technical skills, as a choreographer does when making dances.

Serious gymnasts turn to choreographers for help in assembling their routines, and ice dancers have long enlisted choreographers for competitions and ice shows. I swam beside Esther Williams on TV's "Esther Williams AquaSpectacle," in routines made especially for a doughnut-shaped swimming pool, whose island in the center held the camera. The aqua-choreographer, to whom I wish I'd paid closer attention, came with charts, diagrams, and counts.

The pure dance potential of human beings gliding on ice is being seriously explored by Ice Theatre of New York, founded in 1984 by Moira North, who conceives of ice dancing as art. As of this writing Ice Theatre offers works by Ms. North, Lar Lubovitch, Joanna Mendl Shaw, Elisa

A dramatic scene on ice: *Reflections,* by Laura Dean.

Nan Melville

Monte, Doug Webster, and Beth Woronoff, and past choreographers include Laura Dean, Ann Carlsen, David Dorfman, and Donlin Foreman.

Yet even as competitive sports, choreographers are needed because of the aesthetic component. They offer interesting challenges to dancemakers who can accept and work within their parameters.

ℙROJECT 113 DANCE FOR A SPORT-AS-ART.

1. Locate a gym, ice rink, or natatorium where these activities are taken seriously.
2. Ask permission to watch, and do so long enough to gain a clear sense of what is happening.
3. Try to become acquainted with a participant who will likely be interested in you as a choreographer.
4. If ideas to improve a routine occur to you, offer them. Be open to whatever develops.

Things to consider:

- Whether what you see engages your choreographic instincts.
- Whether any dances you've made have elements that you can translate or transform into the sport.
- Whether anything you see can serve as the basis for a stage dance that captures something of the sport. ■

Jay Colton

Not your usual ice-show look: Beth Woronoff in *Red*, her dramatic solo for Ice Theater of New York.

CHEERLEADING

In the movie *Smile*, a cheerleading troupe hires a choreographer to create its routines. The role was played and the routines were created by choreographer Michael Kidd, famed for his ballet and musical theater choreography, whose portrayal in the film captures the intensity of cheerleading as a choreographic endeavor.

Students in high schools and colleges who go out for cheerleading are auditioned for dance, athletic, acrobatic, and vocal skills, and it can be as tough to become a varsity cheerleader as a varsity athlete.

$\mathcal{P}$ROJECT 114   CHOREOGRAPH A CHEER: CHEER A DANCE.

1. Find a troupe of cheerleaders who might welcome a choreographic contribution.
2. Use the concept of cheerleading to make a dance.
3. Use cheerleading moves to make a dance on any theme.
4. Make a dance based on the relationship of cheerleading
   a. to a sport
   b. to athletes
   c. to the audience. ◼

BUGLE-AND-DRUM CORPS

With roots in military drill, bugle-and-drum corps is a popular halftime feature at football games. The first time I saw a televised competition, I was astonished by its sophistication and power. One team, the Bayonne Chargers, of Bayonne, New Jersey, played the jazziest march music this side of New Orleans.

Bugle-and-drum corps has potent resources: huge performing spaces, huge audiences, performing troupes of fifty and more, fully mobile musical ensembles, a trained drill corps, a tradition of precision, a national presence. Its two basic elements are the band—brasses and drums—and the drill corps, who carry rifles. Forget the square patterns of army drill. One sees stunning kaleidoscopic patterns of inventive beautifully executed choreography. Musicians play while marching, running, even knee-crawling, and the rifle corps can be as skilled as baton twirlers. I've seen two lines toss spinning rifles back and forth as a third line passed between; amazingly, no one was brained.

$\mathcal{P}$ROJECT 115   BUGLE-AND-DRUM CORPS: DANCE POTENTIAL.

Find a local bugle-and-drum corps. Many of these groups are associated with football teams and perform at halftime. Watch them perform and, more important, rehearse. Might something in your experience making dances invigorate their routines? Can anything about their work be adapted for a dance? ◼

Chapter 7

Collaborations

Dancing must have collaboration and help; help is people, and people are trouble.[1]
Agnes DeMille

Dance is inherently collaborative; choreographers work with dancers, composers, designers, writers, directors, stage managers, producers, and other choreographers. In successful collaborations each gives up something to gain more. There are often power struggles; but if anyone wins too big, the collaboration loses.

WITH MUSICAL THEATER DIRECTORS

The choreographer's job is to flesh out the director's vision. Choreographers Herbert Ross, Michael Bennett, and Tommy Tune became directors; but as choreographers, they knew that the director was in charge.

Collaboration begins before rehearsals and includes meetings with composers and authors. It must be decided which songs will be staged, which will be danced, and which will be production numbers. Costume and set designers, production stage managers, and producers all put in their two cents.

When director/choreographer Jerome Robbins told composer Leonard Bernstein that a song written for *West Side Story* would be impossible to stage, Bernstein rewrote it completely. That's collaborating!

Pure dance is the choreographer's turf, pure dialogue is the director's; but it's rarely that simple. The following examples try to show how the functions of choreographer and director can overlap. Italics indicate how the director views the choreographer's task.

- ➤ *Choreographer as dance movement specialist.* "*I want a nightmare ballet in which the villain does a Charleston, but the hero can't—and falls on his face.*" The director knows exactly what he or she wants and even specifies the kind of dance. The choreographer supplies it, subject to the director's approval.

- ➤ *Choreographer objectifies the director's idea.* "*I want a nightmare ballet in which the hero dreams he loses to the villain.*" The director specifies the concept but not exactly the means of working it out. The choreographer may use a Charleston, tango, or some other dance form.

- ➤ *Choreographer supplies the dance idea.* "*I'd like a dance to show that the hero is intimidated by the villain.*" The choreographer is free to flesh out the director's concept.

- ➤ *Choreographer conceives the dance idea.* "*In Act I, we show how the hero feels about the villain. How about a dance number?*" The director supplies the broad overall objective, asking the choreographer to contribute specific ideas.

- ➤ *Choreographer as a full creative partner.* "*Here's the script. Read it, and tell me where you think we should put musical numbers.*"

For the next four projects, you'll need to work with a director.

$\mathcal{P}$ROJECT 116 COLLABORATE WITH A DIRECTOR TO STAGE A SONG.

Directors with little or no dance background often have good staging ideas—so be ready to use them. ∎

$\mathcal{P}$ROJECT 117 COLLABORATE WITH A DIRECTOR TO ADVANCE THE PLOT.

Obtain a musical script (libraries have them), pick a song, discuss and stage the song. ■

For the next two projects you also need a composer and lyricist.

$\mathcal{P}$ROJECT 118 TEAM COLLABORATION: MUSICALIZE A SCENE.

1. Find a play that you think might be adapted as a musical.
2. Decide on a scene that could be a musical number.
3. Write lyrics and melody from the dramatic crux of the scene.
4. Stage it.
5. Do a second song, and you're on your way to a new musical. ■

$\mathcal{P}$ROJECT 119 ADAPT A SCENE FROM A NOVEL.

Read the novel. Select a scene to adapt. Remember that song and dance can reveal depths that take pages of prose. Search for dance potential in:

1. Pivotal scenes between two people for dramatic duets
2. Any of the following for production numbers:

- descriptions of vast landscapes (Western novels)
- sleepy towns full of sleepless people (Southern novels)
- mean streets (urban novels)
- arrivals: newness, strangeness, challenge, fear
- brawls: excitement, bravado, oafishness
- emotions: innocence, first love, daring, danger
- transitions: departures, elopements, gold strikes, harvests, holidays, horse races, house-raisings, kidnappings, parties, picnics. ■

WITH TELEVISION DIRECTORS

Adapting a Dance

TV director Merrill Brockway tells that when he first met Martha Graham to discuss *Clytemnestra* for public television's *Great Performances,* she announced, "I do not collaborate!" Brockway stayed cool. He knew that dance often fared badly on television and that TV directors were often to blame. Once Graham realized that he respected her, understood dance, and was a fine director, she welcomed his expertise and together they created a triumph.

𝒫ROJECT 120 TV COLLABORATION.

Have a short solo or duet ready that you want to adapt for the screen. Finding a video director is the hard part. If there's a TV production course around, start there. There are also small video companies, video artists, and people with cameras who shoot weddings. Someone should welcome a chance to experiment with dance.

1. Show the whole dance to the TV director.
2. Discuss the kinds of shot suited to each section: distance, full figure, close-ups, etc. If the director wants to add special video effects, be tactfully wary; the more effects, the less dance.
3. Since the camera cannot convey the impact of a live performance, certain subtleties, or movement through space, consider how you can compensate by utilizing the camera's ability to zoom, move close, give quick changes of view, multiple views, and (last resort) use electronic tricks.
4. Consider choreographic changes to make the dance better for the screen; view it and decide if it is the same dance, or better, or worse. ■

Making a Dance for the Camera

In 1994, Mark Morris, with director Barbara Sweete, created *Falling Down Stairs*,[2] featuring cellist Yo Yo Ma and Morris's dance company. Conceived as a work for video, when Morris wanted to present it onstage, it required some adaptation.

𝒫ROJECT 121 CONCEIVE AND MAKE A DANCE FOR VIDEO.

Use video to focus, amplify, emphasize, extend, repeat, speed up, and otherwise manipulate human movement and control the viewer's eye. ■

A Video Dance

The foregoing project, although closely tied to video, is not a "video dance," which can be made using images from any source. I saw one titled, "Bridge," about a New York City East River bridge. There were distant shots of the bridge, closeups of bridge traffic, people walking beneath looming towers, views of arching cables, shots of the river with ships passing beneath, the bridge seen from below, etc. It was good, with a bright musical score—but lacking dancers, was of limited interest to me. Video dances can of course include dancers and thus might employ a choreographer. I say "might," because it seems very much a director's medium. The artist Andy Warhol, invited to handle a video camera at a 1960s Harkness Ballet rehearsal, seemed fascinated by the streaks that resulted when he panned rapidly back and forth. He recorded about a half hour of dancing streaks—a video dance—but unfortunately, the tape was not saved. If a choreographer and director can work to a common purpose, video dances offer interesting possibilities.

$\mathcal{P}$ROJECT 122   A VIDEO DANCE.

Make a dance so contingent upon video that it could not be adapted for live performance. ∎

WITH COMPOSERS

There is a special sense of achievement in making a dance with an original score; but before deciding to collaborate, listen to a composer's music. Also, be aware that collaborations are not always serene.

Jean Erdman commissioned a score from composer Morton Feldman, which turned out to be more silence than sound. Erdman had agreed to pay by the minute, but the silences took so much of the time that she said she would pay only for the notes. Feldman sued and won. Erdman took it philosophically. When William Schuman wrote a score for Martha Graham's *Night Journey,* it had a prelude Schuman wanted played before the curtain rose. Graham danced to it. When he wrote *The Triumph of St. Joan,* he gave her a piano reduction on which she worked for months. Two weeks before the premiere, he turned in the orchestration, which included a prelude he wanted played before the curtain rose. By opening night, Graham had choreographed it. Schuman took it philosophically.

$\mathcal{P}$ROJECT 123   COLLABORATE WITH A COMPOSER.

- *From concept:* Offer your idea. Discuss length and the number of dancers, listen to the composer's musical ideas, and respond.
- *From scenario:* Include concept, structure, plot, length of segments, dramatic peaks, casting, etc.

- *From choreographic and musical drafts:* Invite the composer into the studio to see the movement. Listen to her musical ideas.
- *From a finished dance:* Make the dance, count it out, show the dance, giving counts to the composer who writes a score to fit it. Few composers work this way, yet it's how Louis Horst wrote Graham's *Primitive Mysteries.* ■

WITH COSTUME DESIGNERS

Dance costumes must allow dancers to move; so in addition to expertise, a costume designer must have a feeling for movement and respect for dancers. In the Broadway musical *First Impressions*, Raoul Pené DuBois designed skirts with five petticoats, dismissing dancers' complaints that they inhibited movement by saying it was authentic for the period. When dancer/choreographer/director Herbert Ross arrived as show doctor, he had every woman discard four of her five petticoats.

Some choreographers know exactly what they want but can't sew. They only need good costume constructors. Others rely on a designer completely. Some designers ask the choreographer for guidance, whereas others prefer to be left alone. Most fall between. Before working with a designer, discuss working methods. Will the designer want to see rehearsals? Do you want to see sketches and have the right to approve them? Will you need rehearsal costumes? Cost is important and surprises are upsetting, so budgets should be agreed to at the start. Designers who produce good costumes on small budgets are treasures!

$\mathcal{P}$ROJECT 124   COLLABORATE WITH A COSTUME DESIGNER.

1. Show a finished solo to a costume designer. Exchange ideas. Costume the dance.
2. Begin a dance and its costume together. Let the designer's ideas influence your choreography. Work up a rehearsal costume, made with an inexpensive fabric, and show the dance-in-progress to the designer. Complete the dance and costume together. ■

WITH LIGHTING DESIGNERS

Loie Fuller's famous silk dances at Paris' *Folies Bergère* would not have caused a sensation were it not for lighting. One wonders how she did it with the crude arc lights of the time. Unfortunately, Fuller kept her lighting plots secret.

After lighting designer Tom Skelton watched a runthrough of my ballet *Abyss,* he asked, "Am I telling the story of the man or the woman?" A mean voice in my head squeaked, "You, Tom Skelton, are not telling the story, I am!" I stifled it, thank goodness. When a lighting designer tries to get in your head to tell the story as you would, you're in good hands!

Most dancemakers want lighting that enhances the choreography without calling attention to itself. You need a space with lighting equipment, but it does not have to be elaborate or state-of-the-art. Wonders can be wrought with a dozen instruments, color gels, and a dimmer board.

*P*ROJECT 125 COLLABORATE TO LIGHT A FINISHED DANCE.

Show the dance; discuss your lighting ideas, but let the lighting designer do the lighting. If you like it, ask for the lighting plot. Although different designers may have different ideas, there's no law saying you can't ask for what you know works. ■

*P*ROJECT 126 A DANCE FOR LIGHT FANTASTIC.

The lighting takes the spotlight to become part of the choreography. Design movement to enhance the glorious lighting, just as the lighting designer usually enhances the dancing. ■

WITH SET DESIGNERS

If you need a high-backed chair, try a thrift shop. But if you want to suggest a mountain top, deck of a ship, or inner landscape, get a set designer. If the designer is innovative, expect surprises. For the set of *Voyage,* Martha Graham asked Isamu Noguchi for a desert. He gave her a ship.[3] In the Hades scene of Balanchine's *Orpheus,* some Noguchi costumes became set pieces; dancers wearing them could barely walk. Andy Warhol put huge helium-filled mylar pillows into Merce Cunningham's *RainForest.* One floated into the audience, to be batted around until someone whacked it back onto the stage.

Although classic ballet sets often suggest grand ballrooms or sculptured gardens, dance sets are seldom literal locales, as in plays. If you envision a dance beneath a spreading chestnut tree, designer Andrew will produce a spreading chestnut tree, designer Beth a leafy bower, designer Charles a stark bole, designer Doris something not easily describable.

Photo credit: Milton Oleaga

A moment from *Seraphic Dialogue,* one of the great collaborations between Martha Graham and set designer Isamu Noguchi. Left to right: Nancy Stevens, Bertram Ross, Linda Hodes, and Ellen Seigel.

ℙ ROJECT 127   COLLABORATE WITH A SET DESIGNER.

If you have an idea for a set, describe it. Or describe your dance, show it, and let the artist take it from there. If a painter or sculptor is not available, try a lighting or costume designer, who may welcome a chance at a new challenge. ■

WITH DANCERS

There are two general modes of making movement for other dancers.

Dancer As a Reflecting Instrument

The dancer's function is to play back your moves. Prepare alone, then teach. Choreographers in classical ballet tend to work this way. Arnold Spohr, former director of the Royal Winnipeg Ballet, is probably the extreme example.

He made up ballets while vacationing at Banff. Working with the musical score, he wrote out combinations later taught straight from his notes.

In commercial venues—musicals, television, trade shows, etc.—where rehearsal time is tight, the choreographer arrives prepared and dancers are expected to learn rapidly. Ronald Field, the choreographer of *Cabaret, Applause, Barishnikov on Broadway,* and other shows, could make up long combinations in his head and demonstrate them immediately. His dancers had to learn quickly.

Such a process is speedy, with little time to rework moves. If you want dancers to be instruments, you will have to be choosy since what works on your body will not work on everyone's.

PROJECT 128   TEACH YOUR DANCE.

Make a solo for yourself or use one already made. Teach it to someone else. ■

PROJECT 129   EXCHANGE DANCES.

Two dancers work together, each as the instrument of the other.

1. Team up with another dancer/choreographer.
2. Working alone, each makes up a short solo.
3. Each then teaches her solo to the other.
4. Show both solos twice, danced by the choreographer and by the dancer who learned it. ■

Dancer As a Unique Instrument

When Martha Graham was making *Diversion of Angels,* she would get inside a dancer's skin. As Pearl Lang, she became elegant and mysterious, as Helen McGehee, elfin and mercurial, as Natanya Neumann, sensual and serene. When she grew weighty and lumbering, it was the men's turn.

Even when Graham no longer danced, she worked with the innate qualities of each dancer. For her last dance, *Maple Leaf Rag,* made at age 96, she was confined to a chair; although she had a highly codified vocabulary, she constantly sought to enlarge it, using dancers as both an extension of her body and as originators of movement. This way of working allows older choreographers to make dances for young dancers, and technically weak choreographers to make dances for the technically strong.

Handwritten note: Show each versions. Did the adaptions change the dance

PROJECT [...]ER.

1. Find a dance [...] th and ask
   if you can m[...]
2. Make the da[...]
   personality. [...] w moves,
   and put hims[...]

PROJECT [...]

Take another d[...] ....g a dance
with, for, and out of that dancer's moves and ideas. The other dancer will
be listed as a creative collaborator. Pilobolus was the first to list as co-
choreographer every dancer in the original work. ∎

PROJECT 132   RECAST AND REVISE A DANCE.

1. If you made a dance for yourself, teach it to another dancer, revising it
   to engage that other's strengths.
2. Adapt it for a third dancer.
3. Show the versions, one after the other.

Did the adaptions change the dance? You may make a new solo for this
project, but it may also be achieved by using one already made.

This project can also be interesting in reverse; take a solo made for another dancer and (with the choreographer's permission) revise it to fit
your own special strengths. ∎

WITH OTHER CHOREOGRAPHERS

When someone asked Jonathan Wolken, a founder of Pilobolus, why the
group choreographed collectively, he replied, "Why doesn't everybody?"
Actually, there are reasons: a dancemaker with a clear vision may not want
someone else changing it. And, of course, there is ego and power; a choreographer is a sort of puppet master and often likes it that way.

Co-choreography is not all sweet sharing. In Shanghai, I saw a clever
comic ballet credited to two choreographers. Next day, I met one, and
through an interpreter said, "If two Americans tried to choreograph the
same dance, they would fight." He replied, "We fight all the time."

When Austin Hartel was dancing with Pilobolus, he said that after performances of *The Return to Maria La Baja,* jointly choreographed by Robby Barnett and Alison Chase, each demanded different details, like the direction of a gaze or position of a hand. To keep peace, the dancers did whatever the choreographer present in the theater wanted.

Co-choreographed dances are no longer rare. My own two, *White Knight, Black Night,* with Catherine Hodes, and *I Thought You Were Dead,* with Alice Teirstein, were great fun to make despite marked disagreements, and turned out better than most of those I made alone.

Stuart Hodes and Alice Teirstein in *I Thought You Were Dead.*

Paul H. Taylor

$\mathcal{P}$ROJECT 133   TEAM CHOREOGRAPHY.

1. Team up with one other choreographer. Make a duet together.
2. Three dancemakers get together to make themselves a trio.
3. Two people make a duet for two other people.
4. Try any other variations, always being ready for surprises. ∎

P.I.C.K.: A Structured Co-choreographic Workshop

The objective of P. I.C.K. (*Prepare, Improvise, Choreograph, Keep*) is a completed draft of a dance. Working sessions should be two to three hours. Before starting, select one person to be a moderator, who is delegated to settle disagreements that can't be settled by consensus. All must agree to abide by the moderator's decisions.

$\mathcal{P}$ROJECT 134   A P.I.C.K. WORKSHOP.

1. *Prepare:* 20 minutes (all times approximate). Warmup may be individually or together as improvisation, acting exercises, or dance technique.
2. *Improvise:* 20 minutes. The moderator selects improv subjects or takes suggestions from the group.

3. *Choreograph:* 30 minutes. Work individually and in small groups. Extract movement from improvs, assemble as short studies.

4. *Keep:* All remaining time. Select and assemble studies into longer work. Decisions shall be by consensus, with the moderator deciding when consensus is reached. The spirit is collaborative; all credits go to the group.

5. Try dancing the completed study to different music; if none was used, dance it to music at the end. ■

Extended P. I.C.K.: An Experiment in Collaborative Choreography

In April 1992, I traveled to China, the sixth teacher sent there by the American Dance Festival, to encourage the brilliant dancers of the Guangdong Modern Dance Company to make dances for China's first modern company. I arrived to find a two-day choreography competition in progress, the winners to dance in Paris. I saw many tightly knit, clearly focused, dramatic solos, duets, and trios, but most seemed to deal with the same theme—the clash between tradition and change. And every choreographer seemed bent on wowing the audience with virtuosity. Clearly, they were very advanced and needed an advanced challenge, to try something other than their important, yet overworked, theme. I decided on a greatly extended P. I.C.K. workshop.

Extended P. I.C.K. is like many composition workshops, except that the fourth part, *Keep,* connects all the studies and strives for a completed work. In four weeks, the Guangdong dancers took it all the way.

The morning technique class was used to *Prepare.* I teach Graham-derived technique but (as did Graham) use technique as both physical discipline and creative exploration, encouraging personal variations on classroom exercises.

Improvise followed and proceeded along assigned themes. After ten minutes to half an hour all showed their improvs, then went into the third part, *Choreograph,* which yielded studies. After lunch, a two-hour break in China, we would spend the afternoon on *Keep,* putting the studies together as a group dance.

Improvs were selected in the hope that they would lead the dancers into new areas: Entrances (page 47), Character Study (page 62), Images (page 33), Step Study (page 22), Nature (page 33), Rites (page 51), Fabric (page 98), Roots (page 59), and Games (page 53). All were broadly interpreted; Games, for instance, generated studies based on children's games, sports, martial arts, and folk dancing.

I had brought an assortment of music: J. S. Bach, Frédéric Chopin, John Coltrane, Dead Can Dance, Depeche Mode, Morton Gould, Lionel Hampton, Scott Joplin, Joel Mandelbaum, Carmen Moore, Krzysztof Penderecki, Sergei Prokofiev, Nicolai Rimsky-Korsakov, and Igor Stravinsky, to name some. Dancers or groups worked in silence; when ready to show, I would select a tape by instinct, often gratified how dance and music came together.

The Guangdong dancers turned out brilliant studies but were reluctant to make final decisions, partly out of deference to me, partly because of a highly competitive spirit among themselves.

They listened to all the music but began to stick with John Coltrane and Morton Gould, eventually choosing Gould's Dance Variations. By the end of each day, moves that had started as individual improvs had been set on the entire group, anywhere from 1½ to 2½ minutes worth. After twelve meetings we had completed the 21-minute score. The remaining six meetings were used to trim, focus, and clarify. In every session the dancers made adjustments and improvements of their own. The final meeting was a showing to a group of teachers, dancers, and visitors, a three-ring circus of a dance, but thrilling to my eyes.

Judged purely as a dance, it needed drastic editing at the very least; but as a composition project, it revealed the dancers to be brilliantly creative and, I hope, it encouraged management to give the dancers more chances to choreograph. Extended P. I.C.K. is an experiment I want to try again.

ENDNOTES

1. Agnes DeMille, *Portrait Gallery* (Boston: Houghton Mifflin, 1990), p. 63.

2. Scheduled for release in 1998 by Sony Classical and Rhombus Media.

3. Graham reworked *Voyage* (also titled *Theater for a Voyage*) for two years, finally abandoned it, but not the set, which she used for *Circe*, a rip-roaring success in which the ship was placed in an ocean.

CHAPTER 8

DANCING OFF THE *MAP*

At the edges of very old maps of the world are pictures of mermaids and sea monsters. Ancient explorers needed daring to explore there. The *MAP OF MAKING DANCES* also has vast unknown regions where it takes courage to venture.

Before the 1960s, using text was virtually off the *MAP*, although explorers were at work: Martha Graham used poetry by Emily Dickinson in *Letter to the World*; Doris Humphrey used Federico Garcia Lorca's poetry in *Lament for Ignacio Sanchez Mejias*; Nina Fonaroff wrote a script for her duet, *Mr. Puppet,* eventually performed by ballet stars Alicia Markova and Anton Dolin; Valerie Bettis used text by William Faulkner for *As I Lay Dying.* At a time when dancers were not expected to utter sounds, all these forays were off the beaten track.

What lies unexplored today? That's not easy to say, for if we knew what we didn't know, we would have begun to know the answers. Nevertheless, some of the experimental areas suggested in the next section may tempt you into the unknown.

NEW MOVEMENT

Movement will forever be the alpha and omega of dance.

Circa 1967: Twyla Tharp is in the basement of the Judson Memorial Church on Washington Square. She, Sara Rudner, and Rosemary Wright move slowly, *passé-developé, ronde de jambe,* arabesque, and not much more for half an hour. The audience, five people, sit in silence. Afterward, Tharp, characteristically brisk, said, "New movement is finished. Modern dance has been doing that for fifty years. We're interested in other things."

If you've seen any of Tharp's dances, you know how striking her movement can be. Even a dance like *The One Hundreds,* an incandescent concept, glows from start to finish with the movement invention of its one hundred, all different, 11-second phrases.[1]

Where does new movement come from? Isn't there surely a limit that will kick in on the day that every possible move has been made? If the answer seems to be yes, know that the number of possible moves, like the number of possible curves is infinite. In no imaginable future will dancemakers run out of moves. Contemplating infinity, however, is not likely to find new moves. Here's how the pioneers went about it:

➤ Isadora Duncan observed nature. So did Erick Hawkins.

➤ Ruth St. Denis and Ted Shawn adapted from other cultures and also from their dance forms.

➤ Jack Cole, a Denishawn alumnus, mixed India's *Bharata Natya* moves with African-American rhythms, to create a powerful jazz vocabulary.[2]

➤ Katherine Dunham spent years in Haiti, where there were both Indian and African dances, to create a jazz vocabulary embraced by the world at large.

➤ Martha Graham, Doris Humphrey, Alwin Nikolais, Merce Cunningham, and Erick Hawkins each found a deep underlying principle, and built their movement on that.

Both Paul Taylor and Twyla Tharp began by absorbing all they could, Taylor first as an athlete, then as a student of Martha Graham and Merce

Cunningham. As a child, Tharp threw herself into a regimen that included ballet, tap, Spanish dance, and baton twirling. Eventually, both sought within themselves and wrote about it in their honest and absorbing biographies, two must-reads for dancemakers.[3] If their struggles and pain make you think again about making dances, well, no one said it was easy.

Every project on the *MAP* offers a chance to find new movement. You can use, say, an image study (page 33), to evoke a baseball game, utilizing the rich store of existing vocabulary, or you can go directly to baseball images in search of new dance moves. The second process is what we undertake here.

$\mathcal{P}$ROJECT 135   NEW MOVEMENT: A DIRECTED SEARCH.

Use any of the projects on the *MAP* with the specific purpose of developing new moves. ∎

PHYSICAL LIMITS   ### Violence and Stress

In 1961, when the group soon to be known as Judson Dance Theater was coming together, Carolee Schneemann, a painter and performance artist, began to work with dancers. In one of her experiments she had pairs of dancers run full tilt at one another, knees bent, arms flailing, until they smashed, a move that made people wince when they saw it in her dance *Lateral Splay.*[4]

Carolee Schneemann

Lateral Splay, by Carolee Schneeman, during which dancers run into one another full tilt.

In 1992, Memo Mehmet, a Turkish choreographer working in San Francisco, who may or may not have known about Schneemann, brought a brutal-looking form termed **hyperdance**, also **extreme dance**, to the American Dance Festival. His men and women slammed into each other, ran into walls, and fell flat on their faces and backs.

Elizabeth Streb, who, in the 1980s, danced while confined in boxes, is today the architect of a violent form that she calls **pop action.** Streb's dancers leap from scaffolds onto drum-like trampolines, producing fearful thuds, often the only accompaniment, to evoke the hustling clamor of training gyms full of pugs and kick boxers.

In 1980, Molissa Fenley startled the dance world with *Energizer.* It begins with a bang and goes on full out, nonstop, for forty-four minutes.[5] After a few minutes, watchers wonder how the dancers can keep it up. After twenty minutes, audiences just give themselves to it. *New York Times* critic Anna Kisselgoff exulted, "I have seen the future, and it works!"

One may be excited or repelled by the chaotic violence of a brawl or riot, but coldly choreographed violence is both unsettling and compelling. So is watching dancers make superhuman efforts that, unlike the competitive efforts of athletes, is done for the sake of effort itself.

Violence and stress have always been elements in our lives, yet dance mostly presents them in the muted tones of metaphor. With **hyper-dance**, **extreme dance**, and **pop action**, we get them straight. Watching such dances can be both exciting and disturbing.

$\mathcal{P}$ROJECT 136   VIOLENCE AND STRESS.

I do not suggest an expedition into this rugged territory; but to those determined to venture there, I say, proceed with caution and at your own risk. ■

Danger

Danger resonates in the human psyche. It draws people to auto racing and high-wire acts, and to sports like ice climbing, base jumping, hang gliding, and wild-river rafting, to name a few. Pseudodanger, too, has allure, as in roller-coastering and bungee jumping.

I danced in a structure of steel tubing made by Isamu Noguchi for Erick Hawkins's *Stephen Acrobat.* Twelve feet high and three feet wide, it felt like it would topple with the slightest unbalanced move. But after I was used to it, I could rock it across the studio floor. Audiences sensed the danger, which added to the dance.

Batya Zamir danced in a loft festooned with ropes that enabled her to swing, Tarzan-style, from one high perch to another.   Trisha Brown, a thoughtful, even meditative choreographer, made *Man Walking Down the Side of a Building,* performed by a dancer with a rigger's harness on the sheer face of a wall. Elizabeth Streb harnessed her whole company to a wall in *Lookup,* performed in the catacomblike interior of the Brooklyn Bridge Anchorage Building.

The primary goal when using danger—is safety. One recalls, with deep sorrow, the accident that befell the Butoh troupe when a rope failed and a dancer fell to his death.

A dancemaker who opts for danger must make painstaking preparations, take every precaution, and pay unflagging attention to details. If you essay a dance with danger, danger is your first concern; it must be prepared for as meticulously as a mission into outer space.

(No project here.)

Pain

Dance is often enlisted to convey painful emotions. Yet pure pain, existential pain, the pain of simply being human, is hard to capture in art. Attempts to do so risk shallowness, exploitiveness, mawkishness, bathos, and worse. Nevertheless, Paul Sanosardo managed to capture and abstract pain in his dance titled *Pain.* The dancers toiled beneath huge surreal bolders suspended inches above their heads, moving as if they bore intolerable burdens, to evoke unspeakable cruelties universally ignored. Sanosardo's *Pain* is a courageous dance.

$\mathcal{P}$ROJECT 137   INVOKING PAIN.

(Any project with pain is to be pondered before setting foot to floor.)   ■

TABOOS

Whether they are cultural, regional, local, or familial, taboos are societal, and a few, like murder, seem universal, although just what constitutes murder is defined differently in various cultures. Breaking a taboo may be an act of ignorance, defiance, or desperation. Taboos in art refract social taboos; if you break one, expect an outcry since it may seem to sanction or portend a change in a widely accepted value. Breaking an art taboo demands conviction and integrity. An empty urge to shock is soon recognized as a childish bid for attention.

Naked Bodies

The world is filled with little people
Who forbid us to bare our breasts to the sun
And walk among our tomatoes, simply naked as cats![6]
  MARGE PIERCY

Our Puritan fathers considered bodies a source of temptation and sin. All of Western civilization is still dominated by the Cartesian idea of separate spheres for the immortal soul, the realm of the Divine, and for the mortal body, the realm of temptation and evil. Today, after many court battles, performers are no longer routinely arrested for being scantily clad onstage, but the continuing power of nudity makes it clear that the taboo is still in force despite centuries of use by artists of many disciplines.

Sex

In the 1960s, when many taboos were breaking down, choreographer/ visual artist Laura Foreman predicted that there would one day be unsimulated onstage sex. But except for certain age-old exhibitions not deemed art, that prediction has not come to pass. Sexuality is the busiest place on the *MAP*, but sex is off it.

Obscene Gestures

Like profanity, obscene gestures derive power by being taboo. Some, like the upraised clenched fist or extended middle finger, have signal significance, and are thus widely understood. Others are only symbols, like the extended first and fourth fingers, which represent a cuckold's horns in Italianate cultures, where they are deeply insulting, but not elsewhere, since symbols are a kind of language and thus, not universally recognizable.

In the Broadway musical *Kismet,* choreographer Jack Cole inserted a sly sequence based upon the gesture language of Indian *mudras,* laced with subtly altered obscene gestures, which virtually no one in the audience recognized; however the dancers got a charge that likely added spice to their performance.

Martha Graham, whose Puritan roots influenced her art, used a shocking gesture to end *Phaedre,* about the Greek heroine whom Venus tormented with lust for her son-in-law. On the last musical note, triumphant Venus spread her legs in mocking derision.

Body Types

Lincoln Kirstein once described the New York City Ballet as having "one body," the long-limbed, long-necked, small-headed, small-breasted, slope-shouldered, short-waisted, reedy, medium tall, female Caucasian ecto-morph. Balanchine idealized that body type so powerfully that in classical ballet, all other types are virtually taboo. If you doubt it, count the number of ballet dancers with long waists, short legs, short necks, or other unfa-vored characteristics. On the other hand, in some Indian dance forms, the Western ideal is taboo.

To possess talent and a need to dance but have the "wrong" body type can be devastating. Modern dance was the first Western form to defy the taboo. In the 1940s, Martha Graham added shorter, taller, and sturdier dancers to her company, also Asians and African-Americans. Joanna Boyce, who could have been an Henri Rousseau model, populated her company with a wide variety of physical types. The broadest body range within a major troupe as of this writing is the Bill T. Jones/Arnie Zane Company. But body-type taboos still have enormous influence.

Age

How many 50-year-old dancers are dancing? What about 60-year-olds? Can it be they don't want to or that most dancemakers obey a taken-for-granted taboo against age? A piece in the Sunday *New York Times* about new works using older dancers was headed, "When Choreographers Bow to Older Dancers."[7] The article was not as condescending as the headline, which implied one used old dancers only with a reverential bow.

Condescension is better than a poke in the eye, but it's not as good as being needed. If old dancers are out, it's because they've lost the virtuosity and beauty of youth. But is virtuosity and beauty all that dance is about? If not, then the answer is simply that there is a social stigma—a taboo—against age. There are signs of change: a few experimental choreographers regularly use older dancers. In 1994, The Field, a dance organization based in New York City, produced *Staying Power*; in 1996, the American Dance Guild offered *Masters in Performance* and Dancers over 40, Inc. pre-sented *Prime Time*—each of the three featuring older dancers. This is all to the good, although as long as using older dancers is experimental and something special, the taboo is still in force.

Challenges

In the early 1970s at *ChoreoConcerts and Critiques*,[8] a young woman in a wheelchair said she wanted to make a dance for people in wheelchairs and

Eric Stephen Jacobs

After All, by Robert Koval. Left to right: Kitty Lunn, Robert Koval, and Chris Nelson.

asked what I thought. I considered it compelling, said so, and asked to be told when it would be performed. I never heard from her, but in the years since, the idea that physically challenged persons can dance has taken hold. A festival of wheelchair dances was recently advertised in the *New York Times.* A modern dance class I taught for Dancers over 40, Inc. included Kitty Lunn, director of Infinity Dance Theater, which presents dances for dancers with and without special challenges. Ms. Lunn took class in and out of a wheelchair and was inspiring to all. Ramps, kneeling buses, and other such accommodations evidence growing consciousness that all people should be full participants in whatever interests them, yet who would claim that the taboo is not still powerful? Certainly, in dance it is enough in force to provide exciting opportunities for imaginative choreographers.

Subtle Taboos

We are hardly aware of some taboos. Dance can convey a come-hither flirtatiousness, which is taboo to men. British comic Eddie Izzard points out that the taboo against cross-dressing applies only to men since women are free to wear men's clothing. Machismo, once taboo for women, has been replaced by fascination with the macho female. Yet that fascination comes from a lingering effect of the taboo, which betrays its presence because it is so often ostentatiously violated in comedy, satire, or parody.

Subtle taboos—putting on makeup in public, wearing unstylish clothes, audible eructation—lie just beneath the surface, like fossil bones on a desert floor. Prospect for your own by making lists of things you deem impermissible or improper. Allow yourself privacy and try for ruthless honesty. Whatever you learn is a plus. If it leads to a dance, it's a big plus.

Necessary Taboos

Taboos against murder, incest, and enslavement are virtually universal, and the fact that they are backed by powerful laws shows that they are needed to protect the vulnerable. Yet as some societies abandon taboos, for instance, against miscegenation, working on a designated Sabbath, even against dancing, others reinforce them.

This is social evolution, a complex process in which all participate. Politicians and policymakers eventually respond, but the prime movers are philosophers and artists. Philosophers function in a theoretical and coolly rational realm, artists in the hot flux where intuition rules—a realm that we are still unable to understand fully and that we only partially evoke through concepts like essence, soul, God, and the meaning of life.

*P*ROJECT 138   DANCE AND TABOOS.

Think about taboos. List all you can think of. Can any be engaged in a dance? ■

REFRESHING THE CLICHÉ

A **cliché** is a worn-out expression. It can consist of words, pictures, or moves.[9] Recycling is chic today, yet it is an ancient practice, says Walter J. Ong, who explains how Homer, an oral poet, created his epics:

> Virtually every distinctive feature of Homeric poetry is due to the economy enforced on it by oral methods of composition . . . [Homer] had some sort of phrase book in his head . . . he repeated formula after formula . . . stitched together prefabricated parts . . . Homeric poems, more and more appeared to be made of clichés, or elements very like clichés . . . Homeric poems valued and somehow made capital of what later readers had been trained to dis-value, namely, the set phrase, the formula, the expected qualifier—to put it more bluntly, the cliché.[10]

There are fascinating similarities between ancient oral cultures and dance today:

➢ In oral cultures, poems were passed from bard to bard, as today, one dancer learns roles from another, even if that other is on video or film.

➢ Ong notes that "in an oral culture, knowledge, once acquired, had to be constantly repeated or it would be lost." Today unperformed dances are soon lost.[11]

> ➤ The art of rhetoric developed from the need for spoken language to be lucid and powerful, allowing listeners to comprehend immediately. Many rules and forms of dance composition are adapted from rhetoric (pages 206, 232).

The invention of writing added a wholly new dimension to language, as notation did to music. Writing allows one to reread a difficult passage (termed "back-scanning"), encouraging complexity. In music, the fugue grew out of the simple canon only after notation made greater complexity possible; similarly, words written to be read can have more complex rhythms and vocabularies than those meant to be spoken aloud.

Dance, however, remains on what critic John Martin called a "verbomotor island,"[12] amid the literate seas of writing and music. Although dance now possesses good notational systems, few dancers know them. And even if general literacy does arrive, the audience's experience, as in music, will always be primarily sensate and unfolding, whereas the reader's is cerebral and subject to constant pause and review.

In the oral tradition, Ong noted, the familiar ready-made phrase is a structural element that the poet "was expected to use in original ways." This is congruent with the way the dancemaker is expected to use the ready-made moves and combinations from dance techniques.

The language-derived word, "vocabulary," applied to dance, means moves within a particular technique. These give dancemakers stores of ready-made components. Movement outside such a given vocabulary can be dismissed as unintelligible, as modern dance was often dismissed in its early years.

Highly codified vocabularies, like those of classical ballet, contemporary jazz, and *Bharata Natya*, as well as some modern dance techniques, can all be endlessly rearranged into new sequences—the familiar "combinations" of dance class. This recombining is akin to the way bards of oral cultures used language, and has the benefit of producing dances with built-in familiarity. That dances made this way can also be original and masterful is demonstrated by Homeric poetry and other masterpieces that have come down to us through the millennia.

The following project is somewhat related to use of a theme (page 194), in which a dance is unified by a movement statement. Here codified movement is the unifying component.

$\mathcal{P}$ROJECT 139   CLICHÉS: UNCOMMOMN USE OF THE COMMOMPLACE.

Use familiar movement in unfamiliar ways.

1. Pick out and put into a logical order some familiar moves from a dance technique, from a dance you know, or a study you've made. Because

the moves are familiar, they should be easy to remember. They should take one to three minutes to perform, and (unless you strike gold, in which case drop this project and start another), they should comprise a serviceable, if not compelling, study.

2. Now look for ways to heighten the moves. Familiarity makes them easy to remember but also, perhaps, bland. So inject something that jars, provokes, or even contradicts the moves. Shift the order, losing logic perhaps, but gaining excitement. Try to break the rhythm, repeat a move more than usual, expand the floor pattern or contract it. In these and other ways rework the study to make familiar moves memorable. ■

TECHNO-DANCE

The world is increasingly dominated by science and its offspring, technology. Painting and sculpture have new tools and materials; music is becoming increasingly electronic; most writers use word processors. Some arts, like photography, filmmaking, and video were born of technology. Dance, however, is largely exempt from technological dominance because its basic needs are still space, time, and bodies. Nevertheless, some fascinating experiments have happened.

In the 1960s, on TV's *Steve Allen Show,* choreographer Felissa Conde made a dance for the foreground of a TV screen. In the background, an orchestra and conductor could be seen. But the dancers were in New York City, the musicians in Los Angeles. In the live broadcast, the audience saw the production as it happened simultaneously on both coasts. Techno-gimmickry? Absolutely, but technology and dance continue to experiment.

𝒫ROJECT 140 A TECHNO-DANCE.

Consider transistor radios, tape and CD players, walkie-talkies, TVs, VCRs, video cameras, instant still cameras, computers, the Internet, in-line roller skates, scuba equipment, night-vision binoculars. Is there any way to use these and other technologies to make a dance? Can technology change an audience's perception of a dance? ■

REALITY

Circa 1953—in a seminar for dancers George Amberg, curator of dance archives at the Museum of Modern Art, asked dancers why they danced.

All the answers came down to: "Because I like to. Because I love to. Because I must." Performance, all agreed, was the goal.

"Performance is fantasy," said Amberg. "Do you perform to escape from reality?"

I jumped to my feet. "You have it backward! All the meaningless junk in our daily lives is fantasy! Dancing is real!" The dancers applauded.

Who hasn't wondered about the distinction between fantasy and reality? Luigi Pirandello's play *Six Characters in Search of an Author*, deals with it; so does Woody Allen's movie *Purple Rose of Cairo*. I once tried to make *Six Dancers in Search of a Dance*, but only got as far as a scenario.

In Thailand in 1956, I saw a martial arts exhibition followed by a fight between two men armed with clubs. As they whacked away, splinters of wood flew. Horrified, I was sure one would be maimed. When I discovered that every move had been staged, I realized I'd been fooled. It gave me an idea. Dancer Chad Block and I were to come onstage robed as boxers in a boxing ritual: take off our robes, shadowbox, insert mouth guards, listen to the ref, touch gloves, and at the bell, come out and really fight! Chad, a powerful guy, said he'd pull his punches, but I told him not to. When I was bloody and down for the count, Chad would just walk out of the theater. It would be last on the program, we'd tell no one, let people make of it what they could. But I never made that dance. It was 1957, and frankly, I think I didn't quite believe in it.

*P*ROJECT 141   FANTASY/REALITY.

The dividing line between fantasy and reality is not always clear. Are there ways to take creative advantage of the ambiguity?

- Find a "real" act or action that can become a dance.
- Seek other ways that dance can pass in and out of reality. ■

AUDIENCE PARTICIPATION

Dance began as a participatory rite; only after many ages did it evolve into an art form in which only a few dance while most watch. These days, to persuade people to take part is so difficult that audience participation is still pretty much off the *Map*. To succeed, the work must present the audience with a role and also get them emotionally involved.

Good examples of both occurred at the Kitchen Center in 1985 when Soviet expatriate artists Vitaly Komar and Alexander Melamid began by passing out bottles of vodka. Then they projected pictures against a large piece of framed canvas and led a discussion during which audience members came onstage to add pigment to the canvas. At the end, when the artists bowed to applause, a woman shouted, "There are still bare patches! That painting is not finished!" to which one of the artists replied, "Madam, if you were to consult any expert, he would tell you that this painting is finished."[13]

In the 1970s, cellist Charlotte Moorman gained notoriety by performing with lit light bulbs on her otherwise bare breasts. She also gave a performance in which she prepared to smash a violin in symbolic enactment of society's desecration of art.

A man in the audience yelled, "Stop! I protest destruction of that instrument! It should be donated to a poor music student." Moorman retorted, "This is not a participation piece!" When the protester attempted to wrest the violin from her hands, Moorman smashed it over his head. Now that's getting involved!

$\mathcal{P}$ROJECT 142   DRAW IN THE AUDIENCE.

Create a simple, but clear, role for audience members, something they can learn immediately, like speaking or singing a short phrase, moving props, switching something on or off, or joining an uncomplicated action. It becomes true participation when their action affects the dance, which acknowledges and accommodates their presence. Since you cannot know exactly how people will behave, there is a core of unpredictability in all audience-participation pieces. ■

DANCE IMMERSION/ INTERACTIVE DANCE

Putting the audience into the action has long been a popular feature of theme parks, whose guests can find themselves amidst *Bad Day at Black Rock*, a battle between American Revolutionists and British Redcoats, or on a ride in an antique choo-choo complete with a "Great Train Robbery."

Off-Broadway theater is enthusiastically storming the barricades between actors and audience. The audience enter the mise en scène at *Tony 'n' Tina's Wedding*, become invited guests, watch vows taken, attend a boisterous reception, eat Italian food, join a conga line and tipsy revels. *Grandma Sylvia's Funeral* takes somewhat the same approach but in a different vein, while elsewhere in town *Late Nite Catechism* subjects its audience to the stern teachings of an old-time parochial school. *Blue Man Group* gives people a choice; those who wish to participate in the improvisatory goings-on tie bandannas around their heads.

To my knowledge, works in this mode are rare in dance despite attempts at "knocking down the fourth wall" (page 71) and "audience participation" (page 147). An exception is Alice Teirstein's all-day event *Nexus,* in which the audience joins warmups, improvisations, and a dance made by combining the improvised and previously set material. She employed similar strategies in *Walking Shoes,* which moved along the promenade of Riverside Park from Soldiers and Sailors Monument to the 79th Street boat basin (page 150).

At the core of interactive dance is a cadre of well-prepared performers, who carry and foment the action, and who also assign meaningful roles to willing audience members. Perhaps by the time this is read, some dancemaker may have made it work in a spectacular new way. Until that happens, dance immersion, interactive dance, or whatever it may be called, is still off the *MAP.*

*P*ROJECT 143   AUDIENCE IMMERSION AND INTERACTIVE DANCE.

- *Dance paradigm.* Design a dance event of any kind that allows, encourages, and draws in its audience as participants.
- *Theater paradigm.* Find an event that brings people together for a purpose: an aerobics class, auction, beach party, clam bake, dance class, dance critique, faculty meeting, fashion show, funeral, garage sale, jury trial, parade, reunion, sales meeting, seance, stockholders' meeting, or wedding. Add to this list. Based on the purpose, create an interactive dance event that allows or inveigles audience members to join in. ■

MECHANICAL BODY PARTS

In 1970, an artist won an award from CAPS (Creative Artists Public Service) in the imaginative category of "art that fits no categories." He made what he termed *mechanical body parts.* A video showed him with scooplike sheaths on his arms and legs lunging bearlike up a grassy slope, accompanied by drawings and photos of the parts, which were wrought of leather and metal, some to be worn on the back and hips.

A few weeks later, I visited him in his loft to tell him that Martha Graham might be interested in the movement potential of his sculptures and that if used in a dance he'd earn a royalty and gain attention as an artist. He hadn't heard of Graham, didn't seem interested in money or fame, but invited me to join him in Central Park's Sheep Meadow, where he went on Sundays to "play" with his creations. I'm sorry I didn't go for I've never seen anything like his sculptures since, or the moves he made while wearing them. End of story. Yet, must it be?

Alice Teirstein

Ken Cooper

Alice Teirstein's *Walking Shoes* was danced annually from 1988 through 1992; it began at the Soldiers and Sailors Monument and continued along the Hudson River promenade to the 79th Street boat basin.

℘ROJECT 144   EXTEND MOVEMENT MECHANICALLY.

- Find a metal, plastic, wood, or leather-working genius. Collaborate to create bodily extensions. Use them to make a dance like no one has ever seen.
- Experiment with in-line skates; elbow, knee, thigh, and shoulder pads; hard hats; football or motorcycle helmets; stilts; pogo sticks; air mattresses; beanbag chairs; medicine balls—you name it. Seek new moves made possible by using any of these as adjuncts of your body. ■

KINETIC PUZZLES

This is how Carolyn Brown, Merce Cunningham's longtime partner, described her work with Cunningham: "The dances are treated more as puzzles than works of art; the pieces are space and time, shape and rhythm. The rest is up to us. We put the puzzle together, making of it what we can."[14]

What a liberating concept! No worrying whether this move goes with that one or with the music—or whether or not the dance says something. Find moves, fit them together, and make of them what you can!

Project 145 pretty much follows this scenario and will produce a sequence you can call a dance, although not necessarily a good dance. A good dance depends upon how well you solve the puzzle, which requires judgment. But if you like the process, you'll probably solve it well enough to like the results.

℘ROJECT 145   PUZZLE-PIECE STUDY.

1. Make from five to ten separate movement sequences. Don't try to relate them or imagine how they go together.
2. Decide on a process for putting them together: numerical order, coin toss, dancer's decision, or another device.
3. Find music or another aural environment; it doesn't have to go with the movements.
4. Dance the moves in the aural environment. ■

MICKEY MOUSING

In dance, **mickey mousing** is unimaginative one-move-per-beat proceedings, like you see in cartoons. A definite no-no! Yet in Charles Moulton's *Nine-Person Precision Ball Passing,* nine people in three rows of three pass tennis-size balls in clear precise patterns to music that underlines every move. But if that describes the dance, it doesn't even hint at what makes it such fun to watch or how it evokes games, sports, quilting bees, percolators, robots, production lines, city life. It boils down to:

Mickey mousing + Imagination = Brilliance!

*P*ROJECT 146   MICKEY MOUSE WITH FLAIR.

Find music that encourages you to move in-sync or that invites you to illustrate it with action; conversely, find music that is difficult to move in-sync with or to illustrate.

Make a dance in-sync with, or illustrating, the music. The specter—an unimaginative humdrum dance—is obvious, so you must work to avoid it. This premise is in some ways like Ruth St. Denis's *Music Visualization* but with a different thrust. St. Denis let music direct her, although not slavishly. Mickey mousing is slavish. How to be slavish and at the same time original is not easy. Charles Moulton did it, and danced off the *MAP!* ■

ACCENTUATE THE NEGATIVE

The fetish for fitness has everyone jogging, on a diet, or building abs. Yet it's not so much being fit as looking fit; so we also have shoulder pads, elevator shoes, hundred-dollar haircuts, and a multibillion-dollar makeup industry.

Dancers, justifiably concerned with their looks, have a habit of accentuating the positive. When choreographer Donna Uchizono asked me to be in an intergenerational dance in which everyone is briefly naked, I had to decline because dates conflicted.[15] Secretly I was relieved. I admire Uchizono and am relaxed about nudity, but no longer the demigodlike figure of forty years ago, I didn't like the idea of letting it all hang out today. This imperative to accentuate the positive creates an opportunity. If there's something about your physical self you dislike, confront it, confound it, offer it, flaunt it, transform it.

*P*ROJECT 147   "UGLINESS" INTO BEAUTY.

1. *Confronting:* Make a dance that confronts an aspect of your physical self that you wish were different: looks, mannerism, walk, laugh, turnout, arabesque, etc., or a "negative" feature: big ears, barrel chest, flat feet, big stomach, squinty eyes, long arms, birthmark, etc. Get

private; lock the door. Bring out that disliked physicality. Work it over. Wear it as a badge of honor! If it seems ugly, make it powerfully ugly! If it seems grotesque, make it proudly grotesque!

2. *Transforming:* We see many animals as possessed of pure natural beauty. But some, probably because they scare people, get tagged as ugly: tarantulas, centipedes, worms, snakes, bats, rats, hyenas, etc. Pick an animal you consider ugly. Capture its ugliness in movement. Celebrate that "big-bellied, flat-footed, ear-flapping crawl-hopper," or whatever magnificently ugly creature you can evoke. ■

I will eat evanescence slowly.
    EMILY DICKINSON

The personality of the performer always shapes the choreography. The reverse is also true, for choreography reaches deep into the dancer who performs it. In 1952, Bertram Ross made a dance titled *Solo*. Three dancers, Linda Hodes, Patricia Birch, and Chicki Cappel, danced sections named "Linda," "Patricia," and "Chicki." The title *Solo* referred to aspects of himself that Ross saw in each. In his *Nutcracker Suite*, Balanchine created "Coffee" for warm, sensuous Gloria Govrin. Martha Graham used quicksilver Helen McGehee for Yellow (Adolescent Love) in *Diversion of Angels*. All performers in Liz Lerman's *Short Stories* dance facets of their own lives which the choreography reveals and intensifies. Working directly with personality is a mother lode of ideas.

*P*ROJECT 148 CAPTURE A TRAIT IN MOVEMENT.

1. Solos:

- Make a dance out of someone's special traits or character. You can use a person you know well, or one you hardly know, working purely from impressions.
- Contemplate your own life. Is there something or someone you loved, feared, or otherwise remember that can seed a dance?

2. Duet/group:

- There's a tendency for groups to coalesce about charismatic personalities. Does someone around you have it? Can it be revealed in a dance?

- Groups have group personalities. Seek a dance that refracts the personality of you and your group.
- Is there a public personality who can spawn a dance? ■

PERSON-SPECIFIC DANCES

I first heard the term *person-specific* from Stephan Koplowitz, whose site-specific dance *Fenestrations* was made for the balcony windows overlooking Grand Central Station, a remarkable work that can be performed nowhere but there. His person-specific dances are just as explicit.

Every time *There Were Three Men* had cast changes, Koplowitz completely rechoreographed the role for the replacement, plus all movement for the other two where they interacted with the new dancer. The role and the dancer could not be separated.

Koplowitz began the creative process with conversations. He asked prepared questions, then ranged widely. When studio work began, he consulted his notes and asked for improvisations based on the conversations. In a later work, *Thicker Than Water,* about a family in which I played the father, Steve had me improvise before a video camera, calling out phrases like "Matthew's driving lesson!" and "Audrey's birthday!" From the tapes he selected moves upon which he developed the choreography.

Steve also had each dancer make up moves to be turned into individual themes. One day, after my theme moves were set, he had Alice Teirstein, as the mother, interfere, grab my arm, get in my way, jump on my back, to create a kind of kinetic argument between husband and wife.

Stuart Hodes and Michael Davis in Stephen Koplowitz's *Thicker Than Water.*

Steven Speliotis

As processes go, Steve's is untidy; he calls it "controlled chaos," and it tends to produce works that are complex. Yet controlled complexity describes the processes of life itself.

Working in so person-specific a way can seem to invade your very soul, which makes the process deeply collaborative, demanding mutual respect and trust. Because each personality is unique, every person-specific dance is automatically off the *MAP*.

*P*ROJECT 149   PERSON-SPECIFIC STUDY.

1. Find dancers you trust and who trust you.
2. Seek creative ways to draw upon that trusting relationship. ■

SURREALISM

The Latin root "sur" means over or above. **Surrealism** extends realism. It is said to have begun in Paris in the 1920s with the painter, André Breton. Well-known surrealist painters include Salvador Dali, Max Ernst, Gustav Klimt, René Magritte, and Egon Schiele. Surrealism is enjoying a renaissance and with good reason; its mix of reality and fantasy seems to reflect the increasingly surreal content of our lives.

Dreams are probably everyone's first experience of the surreal, and surrealist art has a dreamlike quality. In the surreal world, logic is twisted, yielding insights: Things exist in forms that they cannot—like Salvador Dali's liquid watches (yet time is highly liquid) and in contexts that they should not—like Egon Schiele's rain of umbrellas (but when it rains, out come umbrellas)!

Dance, whatever its stylistic means, is inherently surreal in the way it extends reality. In *The Gold Rush,* Charlie Chaplin cooked and ate his shoe—surrealism put to brilliant comic use. Talley Beatty's *Road of the Phoebe Snow* extends into the poignant humanity of people who live beside the railroad tracks, unnoticed by those in luxurious trains rushing by. Anna Sokolow's *Rooms* thrusts into the tormented inner worlds of individuals, who, despite proximity to one another, remain isolated within themselves. She offered a direct tribute to René Magritte in her dance *Magritte Magritte.* Martha Clarke's *Vienna: Lusthaus,* clearly surreal in its means, uses movement, images, sounds, and dancers suspended in space to explore the mysteries of a city which is itself surreal.

Surrealism in visual art has a firm place in history, yet remains a frontier. It is certainly off the *MAP OF MAKING DANCES.*

*P*ROJECT 150   SURREAL STUDY.

1. Spend time with surrealist painters: Pick a painting by one of them that you like; let it sink into your bones. Let your bones and everything else make the dance.

2. Generate movement from some recognizable activity, like entertaining friends, cooking a meal, painting a ceiling, crossing a street. Put it together out of order or skewed; set it against conflicting movement; employ startling props; establish an unusual context; add unexpected sound. ■

IMPLICATIONS

Implications can be read into virtually any text; some playwrights, Eugene Ionesco, Harold Pinter, and Sam Shepard, for example, deliberately imply multiple meanings. Directors and actors play these implications, which can become powerful subtexts (Project 99).

Dance, lacking the literalness of text, is always rich in implications, which can be clear, as in Paul Taylor's bouncy and mischievous *Company B,* yet sad with its wartime subtext, or ambiguous, like his *Three Epitaphs*, in which strange, silhouetted figures scamper on and off the stage, provoking laughter. It would be interesting to know what a dozen people, picked at random, say *Three Epitaphs* is about.

In the following project, implications are explored, then used as direction markers toward objectives not envisioned at the start.

*P*ROJECT 151   IMPLICIT BECOMES EXPLICIT.

You may use a dance or study already made, although it might be better to toss one together quickly and without much cogitation, especially for this project. Show it and then:

1. Discuss, brainstorm, and free associate, noting all implications.

2. Decide upon an interesting implication and make it the basis for revision; rework the dance to bring out that implication. Show it again.

3. Return to the studio to turn the implication into a declaration.

4. Show it again. Perhaps the revised dance has other implications. You may continue this process as long as you like. ■

In **performance art**, put the emphasis on *art* because this important movement began with painting, drawing, and sculpture created before an audience. A variant was termed **action art**, in which the images resulted from some action, as in the movie *Mondo Cane*, where naked women covered with blue paint, pressed their bodies against white paper.

Early performance artists were not good performers; they mumbled, stammered, guffawed; they had little focus, presence, projection, or energy—causing many to dismiss the movement. But eventually, performance art was recognized as something new. It took many forms:

> ➤ rambling lectures while the speakers painted or drew
> ➤ mumbling storytelling with haphazard "thing"-making
> ➤ collaborative constructions, sometimes with audience help
> ➤ enactments during which visual works were curiously formed, as by suspending leaking paint cans above panes of glass

Early performance artists considered themselves visual artists first—and since visual artists never paint the same picture twice, they *never repeated a performance*. But actors, writers, filmmakers, dancemakers, and others, attracted by the wide-open format, added a full range of performance skills, and they repeated performances. Today, performance art has its own paradigms and stars. Spaulding Gray's *Swimming to Cambodia* is a classic. Rachel Rosenthal, of San Francisco, a big woman with a shaved head, gives gripping performances that are part harangue, part *cri de coeur.* Eric Bogosian and Anne Magnusen have graduated to regular stardom.

Performance art is worldwide. The M. Raskin Shticting Ensemble, named for a triple spy who bamboozled Britain, the United States, and the Soviet Union, consists of German and Austrian artists who tease and bait their willing audiences. Florian Langenscheidt creates fiercely concentrated, meticulously crafted works out of almost unnoticeable trivia: slowly tearing or crumpling paper, shifting his eyes, clearing his throat.

Do these goings-on belong in *A MAP OF MAKING DANCES?* Meredith Monk once insisted her work be considered theater and has termed some of her works operas. She described her first recording as "dancing for the voice." Some deem her a performance artist. Stephanie Skura, a pianist, composer, and dancemaker, has made pieces so wide-ranging and original that she too is termed a performance artist. All broaden the definition of dance and demonstrate how unwise it is to define narrowly, that is, to pigeonhole artists. The dance world is wise to claim these artists as its own.

When we define something, we are attempting to understand it, to create conceptual order in a universe that can seem hopelessly chaotic. Artists seek order in response to the deep order they sense beneath this chaos. It is a way of cherishing and extending that life. The artist makes order by making art.

Performance art is a handy term for action, happenings, events, or assemblages that no other term quite includes. Yet some performance artists have clearly broadened the definition of *dance*. Along with critics, we must decide when something no longer fits our definition of dance, to become a sport, a put-on, gibberish. If performance art is not always on the *MAP*, it is a captivating place to explore.

*P*ROJECT 152 PERFORMANCE ART: AN OBJECT IS GENERATED.

Since performance art began with the public creation of a visual or plastic object, this project will take that direction.

Decide what you wish to make: you can draw; sculpt; or make a collage, soufflé, doll, mask, whiskey sour; or assemble a Tinkertoy; fix a bicycle; etc. The object is your nucleus—what you generate, your nuclear act. Now add, for instance:

1. Movement.
2. A lecture about what you are doing, or about something else.
3. Read or recite something: a poem, essay, letter from someone, plea for money, pledge of allegiance, precise description of a tonsillectomy, destruction of a rainforest.
4. Add any other action that underlines, undermines, or otherwise plays with or against the nuclear act.

Be ready for something to happen that is not remotely suggested by anything you read here. ■

CONCEPTUAL ART Art passes from mind to mind, sometimes gently, sometimes like lightning, mostly via an aesthetic object: a poem, painting, symphony, dance. **Conceptual art** does that, somehow, without the aesthetic object. In a real sense the consumer *creates* the work of art.

I saw a conceptual dance by Twyla Tharp, although I don't think Tharp intended it to be one. In her biography she tells of a dance that lasted all day and took place throughout Manhattan,[16] a bold concept right there. It began at dawn in lovely Fort Tryon Park. I arrived before dawn to join a waiting group, but we couldn't find Tharp. We climbed a low wall on a bluff facing east, overlooking Harlem rooftops. "Look!" said a voice, "The Sun's coming up!"

And there we were, city folk searching for a dance in a park at dawn, and it flashed upon me that *that* was what Tharp had intended! Smiling at her nervy ploy, I gazed with newly opened eyes upon the deserted dawn-bright streets far below. Leaving, we passed a field; and there were Tharp and her dancers, resting after their performance. They waved us over and danced for us. This time, it was vigorously physical, to contrast nicely with the conceptual dance I had seen minutes before.

John Cage's "silent" composition was premiered at Woodstock. About it Cage wrote:

> 4′33″, tacet, any instrument or combination of instruments: This is a piece in three movements during all three of which no sounds are intentionally produced. The lengths of time were determined by chance operations but could be any others.[17]

What was going through people's minds at that premiere? Bewilderment, irritation, outrage? Yet some might have noticed ambient sounds and wondered if Cage was asking them to listen to the music of nature.

In Merce Cunningham's *Winterbranch,* a stage light was aimed at the audience, who squinted and grumbled. Bertram Ross maintained that Cunningham was trying to make people seek out the dance through the light. Actually, the light cues were determined by chance. The chance cue to aim a light at the audience came up, whereas one that would have turned it off did not. Cunningham's concept came from traveling through a winter landscape at night when lights seem to appear and disappear at random. But Bertram Ross's concept holds up too!

When Robert Cohan was dancing with Martha Graham, well before he left to direct and make dances for the London Contemporary Dance Company, Leroy Leatherman, Graham's general manager, accused him of having created nothing as an artist. Cohan disagreed. "Well, what have you created?" challenged Leatherman. "My life!" Cohan replied.

The German conceptual artist Joseph Bueys designated some of his conversations as works of art, and found patrons willing to converse with him, and pay! A 1960s New York City artist gained brief notoriety by surreptitiously affixing stick-on labels bearing his signature to the clothes of passersby!

What Bertram Ross saw in *Winterbranch,* Cunningham may not have intended, yet who's to say it wasn't there? I sought in a park for a dance by Twyla Tharp, and found two. John Cage helped us hear music to which we had been oblivious.

*P*ROJECT 153 CONCEPTS OF ART.

A few of the statements I've encountered about art follow. If one strikes you, derive a dance from that statement. If you know and prefer any other or have your own definition, use that.

- Harold Bloom: "A gnostic aesthetic would say that the works of artists become objects of fear, even to those artists, because they are works of true knowledge."
- John Canaday: "The artist's first job, everything considered, is to grow up."
- G. K. Chesterton: "Art is limitation. The essence of every picture is the frame."
- Robert Dunn: "Art, in any acceptation of the term (including that of Marcel Duchamp), is precisely that which can be shared. This is in all reality a moment-by-moment and person-by-person negotiation, and the source of all the magic art still retains for us."
- William Earle: "A work of art is a kind of showing or recording or witnessing which gives palpable form to consciousness; its object is to make something singular explicit."
- Oscar W. Firkins: "The great art includes much that the smaller art excludes: humor, pain, and evil."
- Richard Foreman: "Art is really ninety-nine percent courage, the courage to follow your vision, and to remember what your particular vision is."
- Max Friedlander: "It is in the nature of a work of art to speak ambiguously, like an oracle."
- Glenn Gould: "All art is really variation upon some other art."
- Louis Horst, Carroll Russell: "Modern art is a free art and refuses to live within any boundaries."
- Suzanne K. Langer: "A dance, like any other work of art, is a perceptible form that expresses the nature of human feeling."
- Murray Louis: "Art is a stimulant for living and for life."
- Henri Matisse: "Truth and reality in art begin only at the point where the artist ceases to understand what he is doing and what he is capable of doing, and yet feels in himself a force that becomes stronger and more concentrated."
- Gustav Moreau: "Art is the relentless pursuit of the expression of inward feeling by means of simple plasticity."
- Friedrich Nietzsche: "Art is not an imitation of nature but its metaphysical supplement, raised up beside it in order to overcome it," and another, "Art is the army by which human sensibility advances implacably into the future."
- Isamu Noguchi: "All art is in some ways an accident, using accidents."

- Mary Overlie: "Art is partly working with the known and partly with the unknown, but pure creativity works with the unknown."
- Alain Robbe-Grillet: "If art is anything, it is everything; in which case it must be self-sufficient, and there can be nothing beyond it."
- David Ross: "If artists were sure what art is, they would stop making it."
- Susan Sontag: "Art is seduction, not rape."
- Leo Tolstoy: "Art is human activity having for its purpose the transmission to others of the highest and best feelings to which men have risen."
- Alexei von Jawlensky: "Art is nostalgia for God."
- Alfred North Whitehead: "Imaginative art suggests meaning beyond its mere statements. Art exists that we may know the deliverance of our senses as good. It heightens the sense world."
- My own statement: "A work of art is an intimate exchange between two minds that can exist in different and distant worlds."
- Your statement? ■

A DUNN DANCE

I had the notion in teaching of making a "clearing," a sort of "space of nothing," in which things could appear and grow in their own nature.

I . . . regard each dance I see as an animal of which there is only one of the species.

My refusal to provide a "recipe" toward which to work for approval or disapproval periodically got me in hot water emotionally with members of the class.[18]

Robert Ellis Dunn, along with Louis Horst, was an era-defining dance composition teacher. Both were musicians, neither a dancer (although Dunn had studied modern dance and could tap-dance), and both influenced many notable choreographers. Yet Dunn was in many ways Horst's antithesis. Horst made value judgements, Dunn rarely did. Horst gave clear and specific assignments, Dunn tried to create space for students to fill with dance. Horst was product-driven and expected assignments to be carefully worked out before showing, whereas Dunn was process-oriented and a master at evoking improvisations. Horst presented a famously crusty classroom demeanor, Dunn was notably beatific.

Dunn is credited with being the *éminence grise* of Judson Dance Theater. The Spring 1997 issue of *Movement Research Performance Journal*, #14, "The Legacy of Robert Ellis Dunn," is an absorbing testament to a teacher whose influence reaches virtually all who make dances today. Articles by Miranda Benedict, Paulus Berensohn, Al Carmines, Remy Charlip, Cate Deicher, Irene Dowd, Martha Eddy, Catherine Eliot, Ruth

Emerson, Anita Feldman, Simone Forti, David Gordon, Deborah Hay, Jill Johnston, Kenneth King, Paul Langland, Debra Loewen, Anastasia Lyra, Gretchen MacLane, Meredith Monk, Martha Myers, Mary Overlie, Steve Paxton, Wendy Perron, Yvonne Rainer, Leslie Satin, Jane Shapiro, Sally Silvers, Elaine Summers, Pauline Tisch, Nancy Topf, Nancy Zendora, and a poem by Mary Edsall and Oliver Cutshaw yield a portrait of a born teacher whose genius and originality stimulated, liberated, and exhilarated, yet never intimidated.

Dunn was avid for original concepts and ideas. Invited to write about his approach, he never really did, except for a few notebooks and articles. Perhaps his teaching could not be enough separated from himself to be captured in words, which he hinted at in a statement already cited, but worth repeating: "People don't come to study with you because of your technique, they want to be around your personality."[19]

Anita Feldman, who studied with Dunn during 1978–80, recounts one of his key stratagems after seeing a dance:

> First, we were to talk about what we saw as the strongest, most unusual flavor, action or feature of the work. Second, we were to freely associate, describing images, myths, and feelings brought out by the movement and structure. Finally, we were to give our ideas for further development of the dance.

Martha Eddy describes something similar in "a three-step version of a method he used for sharing opinions about someone else's work in a productive way," which she invites people to try as a way of honoring Dunn.

1. Describe a unique feature of the movement or dance or event.
2. Describe the system of contrasts that the performer(s) has (have) employed.
3. Share . . . "If this were my dream or fantasy I might have . . ." as a way to extend your views and ideas without taking authority away from the choreographer or performer."[20]

Nancy Zendora writes: "In a class of solo improvisation, he asked us to move across the floor. Then he asked us to sit and close our eyes and imagine ourselves moving across the floor. When we moved again, our choices were much richer."

Mary Overlie cites a way Dunn had of stimulating a dancer to find something new: "Drive your car around, get out, and look around." She writes: "This phrase is from Robert Dunn and I think that what it represents was one of the key reasons for a creative explosion in the dance world in the 1960s."

𝒫ROJECT 154   SEEK THE INFLUENCE OF ROBERT DUNN.

1. Experiment with one of Dunn's assignments.

   • Do something that's nothing special.
   • Make a five-minute dance in thirty minutes.
   • Make a thirty-minute dance in five minutes (credited by Dunn to James Waring).
   • Dare to do the "no-no."
   • Make a three-minute piece and don't work on it very much.
   • Don't worry about making a masterpiece.

2. Obtain a copy of *Movement Research Performance Journal #14*, read it, and respond.
3. Try to find other writings by and about Dunn.
4. Seek out and try to learn from someone who has directly or through association been influenced by Robert Dunn.   ∎

DECONSTRUCTION

Words choose the poet . . . The art of the writer consists in little by little making words interest themselves in his books. . . . Little by little the book will finish me.[21]
    JACQUES DERRIDA

Deconstruction is a way of extracting meaning from language. It first appeared in literary criticism, then proceeded into virtually all of the humanities. Its prophet is the French philosopher, Jacques Derrida, whose disciples remain committed and whose detractors rage. When deconstruction's American champion, Yale professor Paul De Man, was posthumously revealed to have been a Nazi apologist, business cheat, and wife deserter, it was a blow to deconstruction—which is not altogether fair.

"Words choose the poet" seems to evoke the magical process between ideas and the mind, as each affects the other. Can this concept be used for dance?

𝒫ROJECT 155   KINETIC DERRIDA.

Moves choose the dancer. The art of the choreographer consists in little by little making moves interest themselves in his dances. Little by little the dance will complete me.

1. Find moves that choose you.
2. Encourage their interest in your dances.
3. Make the dance that completes you!   ■

POSTMODERNISM

The first use of the term *postmodern* is said to have been by a Spanish writer, Federico de Onis, in the 1930s. What we understand by the term today took hold in the 1960s when architects began to insert old-fashioned, even kitschy, elements into their designs. Sly, irreverent, thought-provoking, it defied the canons of modern architecture, a defiance that spread into every area of intellectual endeavor: painting, theater, literature, criticism, economic and social theory, history, music, politics, feminism, and dance.

Definitions of **postmodernism** are now as numerous as its squabbling theorists, whose windy articles invoke the same nouns: deconstruction, problematization, poststructuralism, Derrida, Lacan, Foucault, and others; also, late modernism, high modernism; and distinctions between modern and modernist, postmodern and postmodernist, etc. Taken altogether, this is *Post Modern Syndrome*.

A grandiose, yet intriguiging, idea is offered by architectural critic Charles Jencks, who defines postmodernism as a permanent new category of thought that transcends the ancient conflict of old and new:

> Post-modernists look to the past and future equally and position themselves in the present . . . their typical style—radical eclecticism—hence their characteristic tone, a double-voiced discourse that accepts and criticizes at the same time.[22]

Yet if postmodernism is truly fundamental, it should be able to generate infinite tones and styles, like modernism, which began at the end of the nineteenth century with the rise of science and its ideology of progress. Modernism transformed the world, but it also amplified cruelty and destruction while generating little happiness, freedom, and justice, at least on a world scale. Political postmoderns, whose watchword is pluralism, hope their way can do better.

In literature, the postmodern premise indicates that meaning can never be certain or precise, which disturbs those to whom clear meanings are necessary. Others believe that de(con)struction of meaning leads to denial of universal standards for good and evil, which is moral relativism. In my opinion postmodernism does not deserve such an onus if only because it is so many-sided and is expressed so differently in different arts and fields of endeavor. Writer Don McDonagh said he first heard the term *postmodern* applied to dance by Yvonne Rainer when she broke with modern dance conventions in her ringing manifesto:

> No to spectacle no to virtuosity no to transformations and magic and make-believe no to the glamour and transcendency of the star image no to the heroic no to the anti-heroic no to trash imagery no to involvement of performer or spectator no to style no to camp no to seduction by the wiles of the performer no to eccentricity no to moving or being moved.[23]

Rainer's manifesto is a cry from the heart and in its passion for spiritual purity moves me deeply to this day. Rainer was working with dancers who came to be called the Judson Dance Theater and also, The Grand Union. They exchanged ideas and danced in each other's dances, but weren't really a group, didn't create an identifiable school, or even agree about much, except generational confrontation and a desire to reinvent dance. But that's just what they did, and they had a telling effect on dance.

Notable Judson alumni include Rainer, Trisha Brown, Lucinda Childs, Steve Paxton, David Gordon, James Waring, Deborah Hay, Barbara Lloyd, Douglas Dunn (page 161), and Judith Dunn. Twyla Tharp was there, and premiered *Re-Moves* in 1966, but rejected the manifesto: "All those noes would become my yesses."[24] Sally Banes's *Terpsichory in Sneakers* gives a good account of major Judson figures of that time.

James Klosty

Early days of The Grand Union. Left to right: Yvonne Rainer, Trisha Brown, Barbara Dilly, and David Gordon.

Here are some definitions of postmodernism:

➤ *Architectural:*

[T]he combination of Modern techniques with something else (usually traditional building) in order for an architecture to communicate with the public and a concerned minority, usually other architects . . . Post-modernism has the essential double meaning: the continuation of Modernism and its transcendence.[25]

➤ *Literary/political:*

In general terms [Post-modernism] takes the form of self-conscious, self-contradictory, self-undermining statement.[26]

➤ *Ideological:*

Post-modernism is . . . distinguished from modernism by the belief that artistic autonomy is neither possible nor desirable. . . . Mass or popular culture inevitably springs up to fill the vacuum created by elitist artists' divorce from a wide audience.[27]

➤ *Technological:*

The most significant post-modern movement of all is electronic democracy, information-age pluralism . . . Increasing information flow drives emergent democracies . . . just as higher energy flow drove modern nations in the nineteenth century.[28]

➤ *Dance:*

In the theory of post-modern dance, the choreographer does not apply visual standards to the work. The view is an interior one: movement is not preselected for its characteristics but results from certain decisions, goals, plans, schemes, rules, concepts, or problems. Whatever actual movement occurs during the performance is acceptable as long as the limiting and controlling principles are adhered to.[29]

➤ [T]here are . . . aspects of post-modern dance that do fit with post-modernist notions . . . of pastiche, irony, playfulness, historical reference, the use of vernacular materials, the continuity of cultures, an interest in process over product, breakdown of boundaries between artist and audience.[30]

*P*ROJECT 156   POSTMODERN SORTIES.

• Ask yourself: What is dance? Formulate your own answer and present it as a dance.
• Search through the definitions of postmodernism or any postmodern verbiage (there's lots) for an image. Explore it in movement.
• Give Rainer's manifesto a try. ■

Life evolved from the primal chaos that followed the big bang. Attempts of **DISPARITIES**
artists to create living works of art out of chaotic and disparate elements reflect that process. In *Predator's Ball*, Karole Armitage uses classical ballet,
hip-hop, rap music, video projections, and martial arts to illuminate a theme
from the life of Wall Street bond trader Michael Milken. Douglas Dunn's
Spell for Opening the Mouth of N uses high-tech music, text, dancers, singers,
and actors who respond to directions sent through wireless headsets.

As a project, Disparities is like Juxtapositions (page 102), except that it
drives toward unity from the start.

*P*ROJECT 157   DISPARITIES: A GROUP/TEAM CREATION.

1. Before starting, the group decides whether to limit the kinds of
   disparities, such as to movement styles, movement and text,
   movement with text and music, etc., or to set no limits whatsoever.

2. The group may choose a theme first, or else begin working on
   disparate elements, bring them together, and seek a theme in
   the result.

3. The group divides into three teams, which split up to work separately.
   The separate teams may choose to work together on one mutually
   agreed element or further split up into individuals, each responsible
   for a disparate strand. Disparate strands can be:

   • Movement: ballet, modern, jazz, folk, tap, ethnic, etc.—each member to
     make a phrase, all phrases to be woven together
   • Music, sounds, props
   • Text, poetry
   • Improvisations
   • Use of space, layering, or anything else

4. The teams put their own disparate strands together. If possible, work
   by consensus. If not, the team delegates final authority to one member.

5. The entire group comes together, teams present their assemblages,
   then all work together to unify as a single work. Again, work by
   consensus, if possible. If not, delegate an artistic director. If there is a
   wealth of strikingly disparate material, several artistic directors might
   each be allowed to complete different versions of the dance.

Note: The likely first results will be a disorganized, chaotic mishmash that
cries out for editing and shaping. This is consistent with the Darwinian

view of nature, which, after numberless experiments, allows only the best adapted to survive, as your dance will from its rich broth of life-giving disparities. ■

FOR THE FIRST TIME

Have you ever heard of "the principle of the dangerous precedent"? Its primary canon is: "Nothing should ever be done for the first time."[31] It forces one to reject a good idea simply because it is new. But its reverse is also bad: doing something *only* because it has not been done. Some things are not done for good reasons: a performance artist at the Kitchen Center ended his show by firing a shotgun at the ceiling. It blew a hole in the plaster, panicking the audience, who cleared out in seconds, and identified the artist as a nut case.

We can outwit this principle if we keep it from censoring a good idea, yet not allow it to substitute for no idea. Ideas are ultimately a mystery, but people who work for them, get them. Make a list of things that you've never heard done but that could be the kernel of a dance. I'll start:

➤ Have pizza delivered onstage during a dance.
➤ Use a cellular speaker phone to call Australia.
➤ Dance while tied in ropes or chains (likely has been done, but new to me).
➤ Have a dozen of the best audience seats occupied by St. Bernard dogs.

If some of your ideas seem far-out, don't reject them; one idea leads to another—and another.

$\mathcal{P}$ROJECT 158   DO SOMETHING FOR THE FIRST TIME.

1. List some things that, as far as you know, no one has ever done.
2. List things that you have never done.
3. Put an asterisk by those that are really stupid.
4. Pick the most interesting idea not asterisked and make it the core of a dance.
5. Pick the stupidest idea asterisked and use this to make a dance. ■

ORGANIZING PRINCIPLES

Movement

At the dawn of the twentieth century, virtually all the dance in the United States was imported. When American modern dance was born, its pioneers and first-generation artists sought to enlarge their palettes beyond European classical ballet technique. *New movement* became their organizing principle, and from the 1920s to 1960s there arose the seminal modern dance techniques of Martha Graham, Hanya Holm, Doris Humphrey/Charles Weidman/José Limon, Katherine Dunham, Alwin Nikolais/Murray Lewis, Jack Cole, Lester Horton, Merce Cunningham, and Erick Hawkins.

Form

Louis Horst began teaching dance composition in the 1930s and wrote *Pre-Classic Dance Forms* in 1937. In 1959, Doris Humphrey's *Art of Making Dances* presented clear explications of form and structure, and in 1961, Horst and Carroll Russell wrote *Modern Dance Forms*. These books, which made form an organizing principle, demonstrated that choreography had a rational basis at a time when it was often dismissed as instinctive, like a bird building a nest, and gave intellectual legitimacy to the growing presence of dance in American academe.

Process

In the 1960s, emphasis shifted to the underlying creative process, which became a new organizing principle. Movement and form were viewed as "products." Adherents of process did not "go for results" but instead concentrated on the process itself and accepted whatever results it generated. Process was seen as fundamental to all creative work, exemplified by Remy Charlip's "*Workshop in Making Things Up,*" which views making dances as basically no different from making poems, gardens, or hot rods. Process as an organizing principle minimized formal rules of composition and also broadened the definition of dance.[32]

Unity

Gravity, relativity, and quantum mechanics are three fundamental theories of physics; each led to a whole new understanding of the universe. Some scientists believe that no more fundamental principles remain to be discovered; others believe that all will one day be brought together in a grand unification theory, a "theory of everything."

Goodsell's book *The Machinery of Life,* presents the idea that in living creatures, movement, structure, and process *cannot be separated.* He could be speaking to dancemakers; for what is more compelling than the interrelatedness of elements in an art in which subject and object, process and product, dancer and instrument, are inherently one?

Everything in creation, from the universe to a dance, requires movement, form, and process. Conceiving of these three principles as one may be a fourth organizing principle. In dance each organizing principle yields a rich harvest of dances. What new dances will unity produce?

*P*ROJECT 159   UNIFYING STUDIES.

1. Make a new dance study or use one from another project, to be reworked here.
2. At each step of the creative act, or at the end, if you prefer, perform a second and a third creative act, each *in another art form*. The others may be musical, textual, verbal, or visual, may utilize video, other materials, or another discipline, like science or mechanics. Find an essence—an organizing principle—that belongs to all three.
3. Present as three individual works and as a single unified work. ■

*P*ROJECT 160   A PROBE OF ORGANIZING PRINCIPLES.

Fill a notebook or draft an essay with ideas and questions. Use it as the companion piece for another unified dance. Possible topics:

- an essay on how a dance might spring from the unifying process
- a discussion on the concept behind Remy Charlip's workshop
- arguments for or against the metaphor that links making dances with exploring landscapes
- a different paradigm for making dances ■

COMPUTER-ASSISTED CHOREOGRAPHY

Merce Cunningham makes up dances at a computer. Dissatisfied with the capabilities of his once-virtuoso physical instrument and not one to simply talk other dancers into enacting his ideas, Cunningham worked with Credo Interactive, Inc., to develop *Life Forms*, 3-D animation software that puts dance images on a screen. Cunningham designs sequences at his keyboard and presents the images to his dancers, who translate them into movement under his direction.

The process is somewhat akin to picture scores (page 42), except that the computer-generated images move and Cunningham himself directs the transformation from image to dance. It is a creative application of technology's cutting edge to the cutting edge of dance.

Will computer-assisted choreography spread? Art and technology constantly confound their prophets, and this is both. In the twenty-first century, making dances, like writing novels, might well be done on keyboards or with other input devices.

$\mathcal{P}$ROJECT 161   COMPUTER-ASSISTED CHOREOGRAPHY.

Research the possibilities. Merce Cunningham and the Dance Notation Bureau have programs,[33] but the field is rapidly evolving. Try the World Wide Web. The penultimate goal is to make a dance while sitting at a computer. The ultimate goal is to perform it. ■

CHAOS

Scholar/critic Harold Bloom argues that all art is in reaction to other art, and thus, what the artist does is primarily an act of criticism.[34] This startling idea is supported by the fact that seminal artists often react against other art forms and artists as, for example, Martha Graham reacted against ballet and as Merce Cunningham reacted against Graham.

But it doesn't quite cover Pilobolus, termed *sui generis* by critics, who began to make dances after very little formal study and thus had little to react against, drawing instead, upon an interior vision. An interior vision also inspired the Swiss troupe Mummenschanz, whose process was described by one of its originators, Bernie Schürch: "We needed to create chaos first by taking this and that and mixing it together and not knowing where it was going." Twenty-five years later, as Mummenschanz began to prepare a new program, Schürch said, "We're going to have to break loose and make a mess and start with chaos again."[35]

Since the universe itself appears to have condensed out of primordial chaos, why not chaos as a matrix for dance? One definition of *chaos* is complete disorder. Where there is complete disorder, any change at all is toward order; so chaos sets up a state of infinite potential!

Today, there is a new concept of chaos; one of its mathematical forms—fractal geometry—is held to be the mathematics of nature itself. Its graphical forms are compellingly beautiful and disturbingly mysterious. If they refract chaos, it is a chaos charged with energy, like the powerful provenance from which dances arise.[36] Much like the pioneers in the mathematical theory, the dancemaker begins to dance, courageously, without a plan, entering into apparent chaos with the faith that something unexpected and wonderful will be found.

The following project is for dancemakers who respect and trust one another, so that all feel free to offer ideas without being thought foolish. The hard part may be abandoning preconceived notions about what won't work. One more thing about using chaos: it's fun!

*P*ROJECT 162 FROM CHAOS TO DANCE.

Work with recorded music, live musicians, props, costumes, masks, texts, media—what have you.

1. Imagine that your consciousness has been transferred into another body that exists happily in an alien environment: another time, the ocean floor, another planet, outer space, a different dimension.
2. Every move and sensation is brand new, each prop—an alien artifact. When something interesting catches your attention, stop! Look it over. Try it out. Put it where you can retrieve it. Then plunge back into that alien environment for more treasures.
3. When you return to the here-and-now, put your discoveries together into a dance. ∎

BUTOH

In 1975, a young couple introduced themselves to me in these words: "We are Eiko and Koma, Japanese modern dancers not like Martha Graham." Thus, I encountered two brilliant artists who emerged from the influence of Butoh, a form I'd missed when in Tokyo with Martha Graham in 1955.

A Western commentator on Butoh said: "Butoh to exist has to remain dangerous. It cannot exist at center stage. To remain an exotic spectacle is to be dead. It can't be performed at Lincoln Center. If it is, it will cease to be Butoh." Butoh can seem like an exotic spectacle; but it is said to draw upon the essence of Japanese culture and is described as "a way of life." A Butoh master defines it as "total rejection of materialist values."

Butoh reaches extremes of agony, ecstasy, and affliction with images that are violent, orgasmic, entranced. Naked bodies are garish with paint, costumes sprout appendages, mouths pulled into grimaces, eyes rolled into skulls, tongues thrust out. Even in stillness, Butoh has the power of frozen violence. Butoh titles reveal overarching themes: *The Dead Sea, Civil Wars, Memories of Hiroshima*. What follows are quotes from a video, *Dance of Darkness:*

We let the body speak for itself. Reveal itself.

Butoh is a descent into the Earth. Butoh is a downward dance.

I wish to make the dead reenact their death, to make the dead die over and over again in me.

In severe weather, the body shrinks and cannot speak.

Dance is a way of life, not an organization of movement . . . I try to carry in my body all the weight and mystery of movement . . . to follow my memories until I reach my mother's womb.

Butoh is like a virus . . . spreading into the world.

We travel to other cultures . . . the influences mix and something new is created. Hidden memories awake . . . cultural exchanges begin with misunderstanding. We are not afraid of misunderstanding.

We shake hands with the dead.

American choreographers can learn from Butoh but not by aping its externals, as did a certain theater director who studied in Japan, returned, and gave a workshop in which he demonstrated techniques for flipping open a fan and the proper way to drink tea.

Beatriz Schiller

Eiko and Koma in *Tree*.

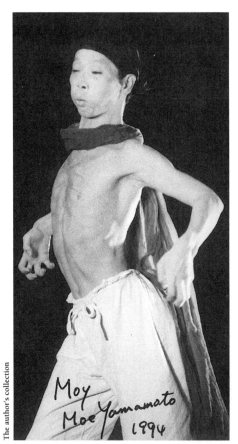

The author's collection

Moy Yamamoto, who performs in the Butoh tradition.

Some questions about Butoh:

➤ Since Butoh is not structured as we think of dances as structured, is it a kind of improvisation?

➤ What aspects of Butoh can be found in all human beings?

➤ Is the fervor of Butoh pancultural?

➤ How can we explore our culture as deeply as Butoh artists explore theirs?

➤ Does learning from Butoh mean we must produce something that looks like Butoh?

*P*ROJECT 163   BUTOH INSPIRATION: AMERICAN DANCE.

• Devise an improvisatory exercise with Butoh as a model. Set down rules for such an improv.

• Think about some aspect of life or society. Read works of Ralph Waldo Emerson, Jane Jacobs, or other thinkers and social critics. Respond with movement.

• Research a different culture. Read Margaret Meade, Erving Goffman, or other anthropologists. Compare your culture with another. Brew a dance from the differences.

• Banish your ego and your will; make no decisions; reject self-criticism; banish self-consciousness; turn attention inward. Leave your body free to dance. ■

Caution: A pernicious virus lurks in this project. It causes "tourist syndrome" (Value Judgments, page 237).

ENDNOTES

1. Tharp made one hundred eleven-second phrases, all one hundred done first by two dancers with four-second pauses, taking twenty-five minutes; then by five dancers, each doing twenty phrases without pauses, taking under five minutes; then by one hundred dancers, each taking eleven seconds.

2. You can see Jack Cole's choreography in the film, *Tonight and Every Night*. He also dances as Rita Hayworth's partner in the first big musical number. Notice that he never comes out of plié and does not smile.

3. Paul Taylor, *Private Domain,* (New York: Knopf, 1987). Twyla Tharp, *Push Comes to Shove,* (New York: Bantam, 1992).

4. Schneemann describes this and other works in *More Than Meat Joy,* (Kingston, NY: McPherson & Co, 1979.)

5. You can see *Energizer* on video, library catalog #MGZIA 4-98.

6. Marge Piercy, *Stone, Paper, Knife* (New York: Knopf, 1983) p. 61.

7. *New York Times,* 4 April, 1993, p. B8. The choreographers were Stephan Koplowitz, Donna Uchizono, and Phyllis Lamhut.

8. A series of experimental concerts produced by choreographer/visual artist/fiction writer Laura Foreman, head of dance at the New School for Social Research.

9. Its first meaning was a plate used in printing, which also became worn out.

10. Walter J. Ong, *Orality and Literacy* (New York: Routledge, 1988), pp. 20–24.

11. Ibid., p. 24. Recording dances on film or video is thought by some to make notation unnecessary. But recordings cannot serve for longterm preservation and are not comparable to notation, which is the only written, i.e., literate form of dance. Recordings deteriorate, use constantly changing technologies, cannot fully capture three-dimensional action in two-dimensions, and include performance errors and idiosyncrasies compounded by each succeeding recorded version. They are useful for preserving specific performances and in assisting those who already know a dance in restaging it. But once there are no more such people, a dance recorded only on video or film will inevitably be lost.

12. Ibid., p. 20. Ong cites Marcel Joust, who coined the term "verbomoteur," in 1925.

13. The event originated a decade earlier in Moscow in an amiable send-up of Soviet sloganeering titled *Art Belongs to the People,* which ended in the arrest of both artists and their entire audience. The discussions at the Kitchen about "John Hinkley's attempted assassination of President Ronald Reagan" were pointed toward a newspaper article. The work is described in Carter Ratcliff's *Komar and Melamid* (New York: Abbeville Press, 1989).

14. Susan Leigh Foster, *Reading Dancing* (Berkeley: University of California, 1986), p. 39.

15. Donna Uchizono's *A Sage Passage* played the same weekend in September 1993 as did Stephan Koplowitz's *Thicker Than Water.*

16. Twyla Tharp, *Push Comes to Shove,* (New York: Bantam, 1992) pp. 151–53.

17. Richard Kostelanetz, ed., *John Cage: Writer* (New York: Limelight, 1993), p. 52.

18. Robert Ellis Dunn, "Movement Research," *Contact Quarterly,* #14, Spring 1997. p. 1.

19. Paul Langland, *Contact Quarterly,* #14, p. 18.

20. Martha Eddy, "Another Way of Looking," *Movement Research Performance Journal,* #14, Spring 1997, p. 20.

21. Jacques Derrida, *Writing and Difference* (Chicago: University of Chicago Press, 1978), p. 65.

22. Charles Jencks, *The Post-modern Reader,* (New York: St. Martins, 1992), p. 6. Jencks, an architectural critic, presents his basic arguments in *What Is Post-Modernism?* (New York: St. Martins, 1989).

23. Used with permission.

24. Tharp, *Push Comes to Shove,* p. 89.

25. Jencks, *What Is Post-Modernism?,* p. 15.

26. Linda Hutcheon, *The Politics of Postmodernism* (New York: Routledge 1989), p. 1.

27. John McGowan, *Postmodernism and Its Critics,* (Ithaca: Cornell, 1991), p. 25.

28. Jencks, *The Post-Modern Reader,* p. 15.

29. Sally Banes, *Terpsichory in Sneakers,* (Hanover, NH: Weslyan University Press, 1979) p. xiv, citing Michael Kirby.

30. Ibid., p. xv.

31. Its originator is cited as the English academic, F. M. Cornforth, *New York Times,* 22 May 1993, A19.

32. The hold this principle had on the imagination is illustrated by a young video artist who wanted to shoot whatever traffic passed a groundfloor midtown Manhattan window between 12 noon and 1 PM. He set up his camera in my office, checked his watch, and at the stroke of twelve, started the camera. About two minutes later, a huge truck pulled up, its flat gray unlettered side filling the frame. I suggested he call a halt until the truck left, but this would have violated his process, which was to show whatever passed; so he shot the blank side of a truck for one full hour.

33. Dance Notation Bureau, 31 West 21st St, NY, NY 10010, 212-807-7899. Cunningham Dance Foundation, 463 West St, NY, NY 10014, 212-255-8240.

34. I trust that this does not misread Bloom's subtle and complex arguments. Among his words: "[T]he idea of poetry is always more founded upon the idea of criticism than criticism ever is founded upon poetry." Harold Bloom, *Agon* (New York: Oxford 1982), p. 45.

35. *New York Times,* 15 December 1996, p. H33.

36. The science of chaos is excitingly set forth in James Gleick, *Chaos: Making a New Science* (New York: Penguin, 1987).

CHAPTER 9

FORM

How do forms come to be? Are they imposed by external forces? Does form emerge from something deep and within? Is form a cause or a result? I can ask the same questions like this:

How
Do forms
Come to be?
Is form imposed
By external forces?
Does form emerge from
Something deep and within?
Is form a cause or a
Result?

Are the questions clearer in one form or the other? Are they more forceful in one form or the other? Does the treelike form, which is external to the content, affect the content?

Form empowers the dancemaker like a mountainside empowers the skier, who must respond to every nuance of the slope. The dancemaker too needs to be responsive and malleable, for dance is a chameleon of form; it can take traditional forms like the hora or tarantella, musical forms like the canon, rhetorical forms like theme and variations, and visual forms of pure shape and pattern. If the shimmer of form isn't there when you set out to make a dance, it is sure to emerge along the way.

You may choose to make a dance by following a plan, as an architect makes a building and as some believe the world was made, or by allowing the dance to grow from its needs, as the airplane evolved from the needs of flight and as some believe the world was made.

WHAT IS FORM?

Before God created the world, says the Bible, "the earth was without form, and void" (*Genesis* 1:2). Modern science describes the early universe as a chaos of radiation from which stars, galaxies, and life formed. Can we say that form emerges when order replaces disorder?[1]

The Bauhaus dictum, "form follows function," was an aesthetic statement; yet in nature it is often literally true. Fish have forms that function under water as birds' forms function in air.

Some cognitive scientists believe that forms we consider beautiful correspond to genetic imprints in the mind. Whether or not that is true, the mind responds to form:

➤ Form lets us extract meaning from perception. What we perceive as form is a reduction of infinitely complex reality into something we can comprehend.

➤ Form is at least partly a mental construct but an essential one. It lets the mind make sense of what the senses convey.

➤ Form allows us to conceive of what would otherwise be inconceivable.

A mystical definition of form appears as an unattributed poem on the last page of the first book ever published about Martha Graham.[2] It faces her photograph:

What is Form?
Form is the
Memory of Spiritual
Content. When
do Form and

Content Meet?
Form and Content
meet in Action.

Completely random patterns have no form. And yet the mind can extract form from virtually any pattern. The points of light in a starry sky are essentially random—yet looking up we see a Big Dipper, a Little Dipper, Hunter, Bear, and other earthly forms.

Form appears in all the modes of thought posited by Howard Gardner, the cognitive scientist who proposed the theory of multiple intelligences. These forms include linguistic, mathematical/logical, spatial/visual, musical, bodily/kinesthetic, interpersonal, and intrapersonal:

Linguistic forms include grammar, rhetoric, and the many forms of written language, which have long dominated Western concepts of intelligence and which some theorists believe hold keys to deciphering the deep structures of mind.

Mathematical/logical forms: Forms of nature can be captured by mathematics. Why this should be so is a stunning mystery. Yet, hidden aspects of nature—black holes, for example—are often discovered through mathematics. The simple act of counting extracts form. A heap of stones is a heap. Knowing that there are exactly three hundred ninety stones in no way changes the heap, yet conveys a sense of order. Contests that offer prizes for guessing the exact number of jelly beans in a jar play on our longing for order.

Spatial/visual forms are seen in cities, buildings, sculptures, sports, games, war, and dance, each of which also encompasses *bodily/kinesthetic* forms. Music merges bodily/kinesthetic and mathematical/logical forms, and may be the most direct experience we can have of pure form. How else can we understand the pleasure we get from rhythm, melody, and the ways they interact to create powerful, yet ineffable meaning?

Social forms arise from human nature and external conditions to generate behavior, mores, cultures, and traditions, surely the most complex of forms.

Form seems intrinsic to thought. It allows us to recognize not only material things but acts, attitudes, even moods. Human beings have an intrinsic feeling for form, and dancemakers would find it hard, perhaps impossible, to make a dance without form. Yet why not try?

*P*ROJECT 164   A DANCE WITHOUT FORM.

If you succeed in making a formless dance, show it, and ask if anyone can detect form in it. ∎

Microforms

The gross properties of objects depend upon the invisible form of the particles of which the objects are composed. Glass, rubber, and steel each gets its characteristic property—transparency, plasticity, strength, respectively—from the forms of its molecules. Might there be a dance correlate? Do the basic moves of a dance affect its overall form? Assume that the moves from the basic technique of a dance are its molecules. Would changing them change its form?

*P*ROJECT 165 MICROFORM INTO MACROFORM.

1. Select six generic moves:
   a. move through space
   b. move in the air
   c. legs/feet move
   d. body move
   e. move using arms
   f. change of direction
2. Select three styles or techniques—say, ballet, jazz, and modern.
3. Make a study using the six generic moves as found in one technique, then the same study using the same six moves in the second technique, then once more in the third.
4. Show and decide how each technique affected the dance. ■

Meaning and form are united. We don't confuse a frying pan with a shoe because the form reveals what each is meant to be. Yet form extends into context. In a museum, if we see a pair of shoes mounted in a frame on the wall, we see it as art. If a pair of shoes is lying on the museum floor, we might wonder: is it a work of art or did someone leave shoes in the museum?

*P*ROJECT 166 FORM AND CONTEXT.

Take any existing study and place it in a different context or frame of reference (page 104): change its music, surround it with an unlikely set, put other people onstage doing something unrelated—like eating lunch, or related—like staring at the dancers through binoculars. Seek other ways to change context and thus change the dance. ■

Once you have decided on moves, there is literally no end to how you can arrange them. The following sequencing exercise uses Body Shapes (page 11), but, of course, all moves can be sequenced.

SEQUENCING

*P*ROJECT 167   SEQUENCING: REARRANGING BODY SHAPES.

Select four body shapes—numbered 1, 2, 3, 4—and learn them by number.

1. Try patterns of sixteen counts, in groups of four. Some examples:
   1–2–3–4, 1–2–3–4, 1–2–3–4, 1–2–3–4
   4–3–2–1, 1–2–3–4, 4–3–2–1, 1–2–3–4
   1–2–1–3, 2–3–2–4, 3–4–3–2, 1–2–3–4

2. Still using four moves and sixteen counts, try other groupings:
   1–2, 1–3, 1–4, 2–1, 2–3, 2–4, 3–1, 4–4
   1–2–1, 2–3–2, 1–2–3–4, 2–3–4–1, 4–1
   Make up some others.

3. Try a random order. Write the numbers 1, 2, 3, 4 on slips of paper, then shuffle, deal, and replace—or otherwise randomize four groups of four. I got:
   4–1–3–2, 1–4–3–3, 4–1–4–1, 3–4–2–4 ■

There are more than 4 billion (4^{16}) possible orders of four shapes in four groups of four. Not that you can do anything with so many possible orders except use your intuition to find a good one.

You have a series of moves. If they constitute a coherent phrase, you can term it a theme (page 194). What now? You can make up another phrase or vary the one you have. A tree has dozens of branches, each a variation on the others. Variations involve specific actions:

VARIATION

➤ *Repetition.* Do one or more moves several times.
➤ *Inversion.* Reverse the order of moves.
➤ *Expansion.* Stretch moves out, elongate them, insert moves.
➤ *Compression.* Cut, compact, squeeze moves together.
➤ *Decoration.* Add frills and furbelows.
➤ *Change direction.* Left, right, front, back, up, down—and everything in between.

➤ *Change tempo.* Speed up, slow down.

➤ *Change levels.* Adapt a move to the air or the floor.

➤ *Change dynamics.* Hard/soft, calm/agitated, legato/staccato.

➤ *Other manipulations.* Reverse the entire sequence of movements (retrograde), change contexts (use different music, shift moves to a different place in a dance, different props, sets, frames), give moves to different dancers, etc.

All such manipulations are a kind of invention and demand the same sensibilities: intuition and instinct guided by reason. You may decide: "Now I'll repeat," or ask, "What if I try an inversion here?" as you manipulate the shape and flow of movement, its contrasts, its overall shape.

Inspiration is a gift but can be primed by simple decisions: to repeat, invert, change direction, etc. Sometimes what seems like an arbitrary decision can stimulate the imagination and pry loose a dance that seems to be stuck.

$\mathcal{P}$ROJECT 168 VARIATIONS ON A THEME.

Begin with a phrase you like. Vary it by using any or all of the preceding devices and any others you can think of. ◾

AUTHENTIC DANCE FORMS

I define as **authentic**, dance forms that began as dance, mainly folk, cultural, social, and ritual dances. Although they will often be closely associated with music and musical forms (pages 199, 202), they are dance forms first, and a rich resource for dancemakers. Here are a few:[3]

allemande	buck and wing	conga	farruca
bamboola	buffen	contredanse	fish
barn dance	bunny hop	cotillon	foxtrot
basse dance	bunny hug	courante	frug
beguine	cachucha	creep	funky chicken
belly dance	cakewalk	czardas	galliard
black bottom	cancan	dipsy doodle	galop
bocane	carmagnole	drehtanz	gavotte
bolero	cha-cha	electric slide	gigue
bossa nova	chaconne	emmeleia	gittana
bourrée	Charleston	estampida	grizzly bear
branle	circle dance	fandango	grossvater
break dance	clog	farandole	habanera

hambo
hip-hop
hoedown
hokey-pokey
hopak
hornpipe
hucklebuck
hula
hully gully
hustle
jerk
jig
jitterbug
jota
kordax
lambada
Lambeth walk
lancers
landler
lavolta
l'escargot

lindy (hop)
line dance
malaguena
mambo
mattachin
mazurka
merengue
minuet
morris dance
nautch
nizzarda
one-step
paso doble
passacaglia
passepied
pavane
Peabody
pecking
polka
polka-mazurka
polonaise

punk
quadrille
quaternaria
quickstep
rag
reel
rigadoon
ritmo svelto
rumba
saltarello
samba
sarabande
sardana
schottische
schuhplattltanz
seguidilla
Sevilliana
shag
shim sham
shorty George
Siciliana

sikinni
slide
slop
soft shoe
square dance
Suzy-Q
swing
tango
tarantella
tordion
turkey trot
twist
two-step
Varsoviana
villanelle
Virginia reel
voguing
volta
waltz
zambra
zapateado

A Virginia reel.

Schottisch, 1852.

The Newbury Library

Twyla Tharp's *Nine Sinatra Songs* draws on ballroom dance. George Balanchine drew on American folk dance for his ballet *Square Dance*. Laura Dean looked deep into her imagination to discover the earliest form of all for *Circle Dance*.

*P*ROJECT 169   FROM AN AUTHENTIC DANCE FORM.

1. Look over the preceding list. Choose a dance or move you like, or better, one you have never heard of. You may also choose a dance not on the list.

2. Obtain music of that form, or have a composer write an original piece for you.

3. Learn everything you can about where, when, and by whom it was first danced, what the times and culture were like, the art, fashions, politics, customs, etc.

4. Find something in your own life that you can relate to the dance you have chosen. Try to stretch the form; a square dance might work for a dance about gardening, the Internet, or a food fight in a cream-puff bakery. A Lindy hop might work to portray an argument with a significant other.

5. As for steps, moves, and patterns, the idea is to make up your own, although you are not obliged to avoid those belonging to your form.

6. Title the dance and show it. ■

DANCE AND MUSICAL FORMS

Dance forms and musical forms were probably one and the same when prehistoric peoples danced to rhythms pounded out on hollow logs. All cultures danced, and for eons, music and dance were closely interwoven. But once music notation was invented,[4] scores could be preserved, while dances, retained only in memory, changed, and the original forms were forgotten. The minuet, for example, began as a rustic folk dance of Poitou, France, to become the rage of kingly courts. Composers wrote music for the minuet, and eventually, it was favored for the third movement of four-part sonatas. We still have authentic musical minuets, but experts disagree on precisely how they had been danced. What we call pre-Classic dance forms are really the musical forms to which those dances were danced.

A sixteenth-century French canon and dance lover, Jehan Tabourot, realized that old dances were being lost; under the anagramatic nom de plume Thoinot Arbeau, he wrote *Orchesography,* hoping to preserve dances of his time:

> As regards ancient dances all I can tell you is that the passage of time, the indolence of man or the difficulty of describing them has robbed us of any knowledge thereof.[5]

The invention of music notation did more than preserve music; it gave composers the power to organize their compositions in ways far more complex than the simple forms that could be kept in memory. Simple rounds evolved into complex fugues, suites became sonatas. With so powerful a tool, music produced the magnificent fugues of Johann Sebastian Bach, upon which dancemakers can piggyback their own compositions; although lacking a practical dance notation, they must still work on their feet and from memory.[6]

In all the arts, traditional forms are essentially descriptions of what artists have done in the past. They are a rich treasure but cannot help us predict what some seminal genius will do next. What follows calls attention to a number of landmark forms. If any interest you, take them into the studio and put them to work in a dance.

LOUIS HORST'S PRE-CLASSIC DANCE FORMS

In 1937, Louis Horst, Martha Graham's composer, conductor, and mentor, published *Pre-Classic Dance Forms*, a compendium of material from his course in dance composition.[7] Students gained factual knowledge of the musical forms of European court and folk dances, and under Horst, a loving curmudgeon, were urged to use the forms in new ways. Forms included were *allemande, bourrée, chaconne, courante, galliard, gavotte, gigue, minuet, passacagalia, passapied, pavane, rigadoon, and sarabande.* Students learned musical time signatures and tempos, and for each form, something about the time, and people who danced it. If the course has a weakness, it may be that it seems to bind dance to music.

From my old notes on the *allemande:*

> . . . four-quarter time, slow and dignified, yet flowing with much use of decorative 16th notes . . . only courtly dance of German origin . . . "knights in armour treading a warlike almain" . . . somewhat melancholy, slower, not so dexterous and agile as a Galliard . . . sentimental . . . image of a contented or happy mind delighting in order and repose . . . not popular among modern composers who prefer the less sentimental pavanne or sarabande.

Horst played several short allemandes by different composers, describing the structure of each: A, AB, ABA, etc., with the exact measure count for each. In the following list, again taken from my notes, the numbers given after each allemande indicate the number of measures of four in each section:

Johann Froberger, AB, 6/6
Handel Suite XI, AB, 6/8

Rio Grande Allemande, A, 14

John Blow, AB, 6/9

Chambonnier, AB, 10/13

Couperin "Le Tenebreuse," AB, 9/9

J. S. Bach, French Suite #4, AB, 10/10

Horst would say, "Work between the bed and the bureau," students would choose an allemande, and come to the next lesson with a titled dance made to its exact counts. After each showing, Horst would offer a critique. Legend has it that he was devastating, but in my experience he was calm and matter-of-fact, with glints of humor; if he said your dance was chaotic or trite, he explained exactly why, and there was always the implication that you could do better. Legend also has it that Louie was a great teacher and there legend is right!

*P*ROJECT 170   *PERUSE PRE-CLASSIC DANCE FORMS.*

In its umpteenth printing, Horst's book is likely to be found in any dance library. If you want to make a dance based on a preclassic form, you can either dig up the music or have a new piece written in the form. In any case use the form as a springboard for your own ideas. ■

**DANCE AND
MOVEMENT
CORRELATES**

Sound, Tones, and Notes

The basic matter of dance is movement; the basic matter of music correlates sound. So we can think of movement as the dance correlate of sound. Musicologist Edith Borroff wrote an interesting definition of *music*: "Sound given impetus through time, or conversely, time given shape by the energy of sound."[8] The *dance* correlate could be: movement given coherence through time, or time given shape by the measure of movement.

Each of the following statements about sound or music is followed by one or more questions on dance correlates.

➤ *Statement:* Sound is vibration in a fluid medium, usually air or water, detectable by our ears, caused by other vibrations: reeds in clarinets, vocal chords of animals and people in air, wind in trees, whale songs in water.

   Questions: Is there a kinetic correlate of vibration? Can space be considered dance's fluid medium, or is it the light that reaches one's eyes?

➤ *Statement:* A tone is sound of a specific pitch. It can have quality or timbre, like a violin or human voice. Thus, an explosion cannot produce a tone, nor can the many-tone "white" sound of a waterfall. A tone lasts long enough to be perceived but not a measured amount of time.

Question: Is a dance movement, like a glissade, or a nondance move, like a karate chop, a kinetic correlate of a tone?

➤ *Statement:* A musical note represents a specific tone (pitch) as well as its duration. Notes are arranged according to pitch, forming scales. Before scales were invented, notes were grouped, three to a trichord, four to a tetrachord.

Questions: Is a single move on a count, a kinetic correlate of a note? Can one make a kinetic **trichord** (a chord with three notes) or **tetrachord** (a chord with four notes)?

SCALES

Pitches are notes with an assigned rate of vibration. Middle C has 440 vibrations per second. A scale is a succession of pitches, ascending or descending.

The diatonic scale most of us know, *do-re-mi-fa-sol-la-ti-do,* has seven tones—eight if you count both top and bottom *do.* The chromatic scale, all half steps, brings the total to twelve—or thirteen, counting top and bottom. This is the "well-tempered scale" of Western music. Non-Western music has other scales.

The modern piano, tuned to the well-tempered scale, can play eighty-eight notes, or pitches. From the lowest stop on any organ, made by a 64-foot pipe that utters a note five octaves below middle C, a note you feel more than hear, to its highest, made by a 3/8-inch pipe that produces a pitch six octaves above middle C and close to the upper limit of the human ear, there are eleven octaves of twelve pitches each—in all, one hundred thirty-two notes. All of Western music is made out of these, greatly fortified by the overtones that give each instrument and voice its distinctive character.

Adding in the quarter tones of Eastern music greatly expands the number of available notes; yet if it seems like a lot of basic material, dance has far more. You can use your index finger in at least twenty-two different ways:

1. pointed
2. curved slightly
3. curved a lot
4. almost crooked
5. completely crooked
6. wagging side-to-side and pointed

7. wagging side-to-side and slightly curved
8. wagging side-to-side and curved a lot
9. wagging up and down and pointed
10. wagging up and down and slightly curved
11. wagging up and down and curved a lot
12. wagging up and down and crooked
13. circling and pointed
14. circling and curved
15. folded at the knuckle and pointed
16. folded at the knuckle and curved
17. folded at the knuckle and crooked
18. folded at the second joint
19. folded at the knuckle and second joint together
20. in stabbing motions
21. in figure eights
22. in circles

This seems trivial, yet indicates the seemingly infinite possibilities of an entire body. The projects that follow develop correlates between musical and dance figures.

*P*ROJECT 171   A MOVEMENT SCALE.

1. Moves can be made to stand for pitches. Decide which move constitutes a note or tone—for instance, a step, a torso bend, an arm thrust, a plié, a turn, a weight shift, a shake.
2. Devise a kinetic scale. Learn to play it back in any order, like musical notes. ■

Movement Melody

A music melody is an agreeable succession of tones or notes for a single voice. One dance correlate is the classroom combination. Some teachers are known for challenging classroom combinations, just as some choreographers are known for extended passages of exciting movement.

*P*ROJECT 172   A MOVEMENT MELODY.

Using the kinetic scale you have devised, make a movement melody. ■

Kinetic Chords: Movement in Contrast

A chord consists of different tones played simultaneously; they can sound harmonious or they can clash.

℘ROJECT 173 CHORDAL MOVEMENT STUDY.

1. Select kinetic tones from your kinetic scale.
2. Using three dancers, create the movement correlate of a trichord; with four dancers, make a tetrachord.
3. Build a chordal study. ■

Kinetic Tranposing: Notes into Moves

In music, transposing moves the pitch or key of music up or down. Here we change notes into moves.

℘ROJECT 174 KINETIC TRANSPOSING: MOVEMENT FROM MUSICAL NOTES.

Substitute kinetic notes for the musical notes of a simple melody, like "Yankee Doodle." Dance the movement melody to the musical one before setting it to different music. ■

Canon

The canon is one of the most widely used musical and choreographic devices; it is a phrase begun by one musician or dancer, repeated exactly by a second, who starts after the first. A round is a simple canon. Canons are immediately perceived as such; the eye sees a movement phrase, and a few moves later, recognizes that phrase when it is begun by another. This is comforting; it assures us that we and another intelligence are communicating.

℘ROJECT 175 KINETIC CANON.

Make a canon for two, three, or more. ■

MUSICAL FIGURES

What follows are various musical figures, most of which suggest projects. Some figures not discussed here will be found later.

Cadence

From the Latin, *cadere,* to fall. A **cadence** is a melodic conclusion that sounds natural. It is achieved in music with a *tonic* or *key* note, which, in the context of the musical piece, feels like "home."

$\mathcal{P}$ROJECT 176   KINETIC HOME OR TONIC MOVEMENT.

Establish a movement or phrase as home, the musical equivalent of a tonic note, a move that the dance flows into at the end. Make a study that comes home to that move. ■

Dissonance

Dissonance is the sounding together of tones not in harmonic resolution so as to produce beats. The kinetic equivalent of dissonance might be moves that clash or feel awkward or clumsy. Modern dance was once derided for flexed feet, which seemed "dissonant" to people used to pointed feet.

$\mathcal{P}$ROJECT 177   KINETIC DISSONANCE.

Find moves that seem dissonant to you now. Make a dissonant dance. ■

Drone

A **drone** is a continuous underlying pitch or several pitches. Drones solidify the background. In Indian music the tambura's only function is to provide a background drone for the melodic sitar and rhythmic tabla.

$\mathcal{P}$ROJECT 178   KINETIC DRONE.

Find background action that supports the foreground action without drawing attention from it. ■

Continuo

Continuo, or **figured bass,** performs like a drone but with alternating notes and added rhythm. Doris Humphrey used the kinetic equivalent of continuo in a rondo made by her students at the American Dance Festival, 1948 (page 200). It was a simple yet powerful repeating phrase done by the group, from which individuals emerged to perform brief solos. The same structure is seen in dances that place soloists in front of a group and in musicals where a singer performs before dancers who move in the background in ways that point up the foreground.

$\mathcal{P}$ROJECT 179   KINETIC CONTINUO.

Devise a repeating move that can be performed continuously. Explore ways to use it behind a solo you create for the occasion. ■

Harmony

Harmonious notes generate a pleasing concordance when played together. But what pleases one ear may grate on another. The same is true of movement.

$\mathcal{P}$ROJECT 180   KINETIC HARMONY.

Experiment with kinetic harmony. Decide for yourself what is pleasing. ■

Hocket

Hocket (from "hiccup") means breaking a melodic line with short notes and rests. Two "hocketing" singers can carry on a musical dialog.

$\mathcal{P}$ROJECT 181   KINETIC HOCKETS.

1. Make or remake a short study. Learn to dance it and teach it to someone else. Break it into short movements with frequent stops. Dance as a movement dialogue.
2. Do the same using two different studies. ■

Melody

Melody arises when one voice utters a succession of notes. The dance correlate is one dancer doing a succession of moves. Incidentally, just what makes a melody memorable or pleasing is truly mysterious.

$\mathcal{P}$ROJECT 182   KINETIC MELODY: A SUBJECTIVE EXPERIMENT.

Begin by recalling a sequence of moves you have choreographed or danced and can dance from memory. Dance it through; then consider whether the moves are consonant, that is, fit comfortably together, or dissonant, that is, clash; whether the sequence is lilting or spritely or sighing or grave or something else; whether the sequence is simple or complex, forthright or subtle. Try other sequences. ■

Rubato

Rubato (from "**robbed**") indicates stealing time from one place to add in another; slows down here, speeds up there. Composers indicate rubato by writing the word on the score, but it also comes from interpretation. Exaggerated rubato can be overly romantic, even corny. A conductor prone to rubato can spell trouble for dancers because bodies are less easily slowed down and speeded up than fingers. Nevertheless, rubato offers interesting choreographic challenges.

*P*ROJECT 183   RUBATO STUDY.

Use a study previously made and greatly vary its tempos. Work without music; then see what happens when you set the tempo-changed movement to music.   ■

Schmaltz

Schmaltz means "grease." It is a mix of rubato, vibrato, tremolo, trilling, attacca, glissando, and other extravagant carryings-on. It was concocted in the Romantic period and many still lap it up.

*P*ROJECT 184   SCHMALTZ STUDY.

Select a dance or study. Schmaltz it up!   ■

CELL, FIGURE, MOTIF

Cell, **figure**, and **motif** in music denote small identifiable sections. They may be rhythmic, melodic, or both. The three terms are often used interchangeably in music, but "figure," is perhaps most easily related to dance.

In Martha Graham's *Every Soul Is a Circus,* the central character dreamt of being a star; at moments of triumph, Graham gave her a saucy wiggle. She sometimes used the same figure *offstage* when she felt mischievous, saying, "I'm switching my tail!"

Musicologist Paul Cooper defines **motif** as "the smallest unit of musical measurement," whose length "varies from two to nine notes . . . related to an easily recognizable rhythmic pattern."[9] A motif recurs and can be heard or sensed throughout the movement or work. The famous first four notes of Beethoven's Fifth Symphony constitute a motif rather than a theme.

I saw a solo dance in the 1950s in which the dancer thrust out her leg and slapped her bare foot briskly on the floor. Lyrical moves followed, to be constantly interrupted by the thrust-slap, a motif powerful enough to make me remember the dance, although I can't recall its title or the dancer.

PROJECT 185   MOVEMENT CELL, FIGURE, AND MOTIF.

1. Think about any dance or study you've made. Does it have a small part that stands out? If so, does the dance develop it? If you were to develop it further, would the dance be strengthened or weakened?
2. Make one of the following: a movement cell or figure, a motor fragment, a space pattern or rhythmic pattern, a short phrase, a body shape. Treat it as a motif, and build a study around it. ■

THEME

Theme is placed here among musical forms because dance and musical themes are so closely conjoined; but it is important to know that theme originated in rhetoric (page 206) as a unifying concept in the form of a statement. Today the thematic statement in music and dance is just as important as in language. In dance it can consist of: identifiable moves, a movement sequence, a pattern, a contrast, a dynamic, or any other movement device to:

➤ engage   (mind, attention, thought)
➤ orient   (consciousness, attention, thinking)
➤ concentrate   (a thought, an image, an impression)
➤ focus   (an idea, a concept, a perception)
➤ conceptualize (an inkling, a feeling, an intuition)

Themes underlie all the diverse ways of making dances. Although most dancemakers gain by studying and sharpening thematic awareness, the underlying drive for order and coherence is so strong that most dancemakers tend to create themes instinctively.

Each of the projects suggested uses a somewhat different definition of the theme.

PROJECT 186   A THEME OF PURE MOVEMENT.

Use body shapes, steps, space, patterns, time, tempo, tempo changes, dynamics, physical sensibilities and prowess, attack, dynamics, change of dynamics. ■

$\mathcal{P}$ROJECT 187   MOVEMENT FROM A MUSICAL THEME.

Music is the dancemaker's primary resource; even though one may properly resist becoming dependent on it, music and dance will always be wedded. The musical definition of the theme as a musical statement comes straight from rhetoric, although music can be considered pure form without content or a merging of form and content. Towering musical themes are heard in the music of Johann Sebastian Bach. Listen. Dance! ■

$\mathcal{P}$ROJECT 188   A MOVEMENT THEME FROM A VISUAL THEME.

A painting's theme can be a plate of fruit or a human figure. It can also be a line, shape, or color. Dance also uses image, line, and shape; does it have a kinetic corollary of color? Martha Graham put a dancer in a red dress (page 39)—but can color be evoked by movement alone? ■

$\mathcal{P}$ROJECT 189   LOGICAL/ILLOGICAL MANIPULATION OF A THEME.

1. Make a logical movement sequence Exactly what constitutes logic is left to you.
2. Reorder the same moves, making it as illogical as you can. What makes one logical, the other not? Which do you prefer? ■

Theme from a Literary Image

The image is to be objectified by a signature movement plus some other element upon which it can be focused. For instance:

➢ "Tomorrow and tomorrow and tomorrow . . ."—a hesitation or broken rhythm, plus a rope or mask or bone.

➢ "It was the best of times. It was the worst of times . . ."—a spiral or a leap and fall, plus an utterance.

➢ "Now is the winter of our discontent . . ."—a contraction, plus a mirror or empty picture frame.

➢ "A rose is a rose is a rose . . ."— a repetition, plus a partner or a rose.

$\mathcal{P}$ROJECT 190   A LITERARY/POETIC THEME.

Find a movement statement in literature for which you can find a signature movement, plus a focusing element. Develop both interactively. ■

*P*ROJECT 191 A CONCEPTUAL THEME: MOVEMENT FROM AN EMOTION OR IDEAL.

Find movement in an emotion or idea: anger, anticipation, body building, body odor, boredom, celebration, cowardice, dissent, electricity, flirting, flying, fury, ghostliness, heroics, impatience, libido, mourning, nervousness, oafishness, pickles, pleasure, regret, rejection, slyness, sneezing, soreness, surprise, sympathy, teasing, watchfulness, yearning, etc.

Open a dictionary at random and pick a word that expresses an emotion or idea from the two pages before you. Extract moves from this word. ■

*P*ROJECT 192 MOVEMENT FROM AN UNDERLYING CONCEPT.

"Equal opportunity" and "pursuit of happiness" are social concepts. The multiplication table and $E = mc^2$ are mathematical concepts. What can be deemed dance concepts? Is it Martha Graham's concept that the center of the universe strikes from the center of each human being? Is it Erick Hawkins's concept that the universe comes to a center in each human being? Is it Merce Cunningham's concept that everything in the universe is equally centered? Ponder a concept that can become the theme of a dance, a lifetime of dances, a way of life. ■

Thematic Transformations

Martha Graham, inspired by a Kandinsky painting that had a shaft of red running through it (see p.39), transformed it into dance when she had Pearl Lang, costumed in red, dash across the diagonal in *Diversion of Angels*.

*P*ROJECT 193 A THEME TRANSLATED FROM ANOTHER ART WORK.

Find a theme in music, visual art, or literature. Transform it into dance. ■

Thematic Concepts

*P*ROJECT 194 THEMATIC EXPRESSIONS.

Dance your understanding, pro or con, for the following:

- A first or early phrase is not necessarily the theme.
- A theme is different from a motif.
- A theme must be stated at some point in a dance.

Left to right: Miriam Cole, Robert Cohan, Pearl Lang, Linda Hodes, and Matt Turney in *Diversion of Angels,* by Martha Graham.

- A theme can be inferred, if not specifically stated.
- A dance must have a theme.
- It is possible to make a dance without a theme.
- Themes can be weak or strong.
- A strong theme is better than a weak one.   ■

Life proceeds through an organic cycle: birth, growth, climax, decline, death. Marcel Marceau displayed it brilliantly in a solo that lasts less than three minutes: *Childhood, Youth, Old Age, and Death.* Big bang cosmologists ascribe such a cycle to the universe, although other cosmologists prefer the steady state theory.

Most choreographers trace an organic cycle—beginning, middle, climax, end—in their dances, and you even find it in classroom exercises. Dances by Merce Cunningham, however, seem to open up upon something eternal, to end when he calmly turns away. If Graham and

CLIMAX

André Maier

The climactic moment of Lynn Shapiro's *Silent Night*. Romina Pedrole and Matthew Brookoff.

Cunningham had been cosmologists, Graham would have been a big banger, Cunningham a steady stater.

What constitutes the climax of a human life? Is it the physical peak, which comes early; mental acuity, reached later; or wisdom and understanding, later still, or never? Is climax, like beauty, in the eye of the beholder?

Where should one put the climax of a dance? Sometimes the dance decides. When discussing *Cloven Kingdom*, Paul Taylor observed that the explosive male quartet is its climax. "It comes early in the dance," he said. "The women's quartet was supposed to top it later on, but it didn't."[10]

$\mathcal{P}$ROJECT 195   THE CLIMAX OF A PHRASE.

Make a phrase or select one in a prior study. Dance it a few times. Then consider the following:

- Does the phrase have continuity?
- Does it begin, build, end?

- Does it have a clear high point?
- Is its high point kinetic, dramatic, something different?
- Is it possible to dance the phrase so as to change the climactic point? ■

PROJECT 196   AN ARBITRARY CLIMAX.

In the phrase used for Project 195, move the climax, putting it first, last, or elsewhere. Show at least two versions of this phrase with the climax in different places. ■

PROJECT 197   CHART A CLIMAX.

Use any completed dance or extended study and identify its emotional highs and lows. Some choreographers trace the dance with graphs, even to the extent of allotting separate lines for kinetics, dynamics, drama, tempo, decibels—even audience response. It sounds very scientific, but the call— how to act on the numbers—is one of pure judgment. ■

MUSICAL FORMS INTO DANCE FORMS

ABA

The ABA is a musical form that began as a poetic form set to music. It requires two themes, "A" and "B," with the B-theme relating, through contrast or comparison, to the A. When A is repeated, usually with changes, it becomes ABA. You hear it in popular songs that begin with a *lyric,* A, followed by a *bridge* B, then a return to the lyric, A.

> A: Twinkle, twinkle, little star. How I wonder what you are.
> B: Up above the world so high. Like a diamond in the sky.
> A: Twinkle, twinkle, little star. How I wonder what you are.

Variants are almost endless, ABBA, ABaB, or a complex ABaAabAB, where A is the first theme, B—the second theme, a—the subsidiary first theme, and b—the subsidiary second theme. Everyone should make an ABA somewhere along the way. It keeps cropping up in bigger forms and is fun. The hazard of ABA is the highly formal or symmetrical demand it seems to make. You'll get more out of ABA if you are not too strict.

PROJECT 198   ABA STUDIES.

1. Make up two movement themes. *Arbitrarily* make one A, the other B. Try as ABA. Reverse A and B designations and try again.

2. Create a theme specifically to be an A theme. Now make a related or contrasting B theme. Dance as ABA. Can these themes be successfully reversed?

3. Follow-up. Construct subsidiary a and b themes. Try as extended sequences, such as "AaBabA." Try other arrangements.   ∎

Canon

A **canon** is a restatement; moves are introduced by one figure, then taken up by succeeding ones. Thus, it takes two or more to make a canon. A "canon for one" would be like the sound of one hand clapping.

Music notation made the **crab canon** (*canon cancrizans*) possible. It is a canon that can be played forward or backward, and even when the page is turned upside down. Haydn's *Ten Commandments* is a crab canon, also Luigi Dallapiccola's *Notebook of Anna Libra*. Paul Hindemeth's *Ludus Tonalis* (the title means play with tones) is a highly complex one. An enthusiastic user of something like the crab canon is Twyla Tharp, who sometimes requires dancers to do complex phrases of movement *retrograde,* or backward.

𝓟ROJECT 199   CANON STUDY.

You need another dancer, or several.

1. All learn a sequence at least eight counts long, to be repeated. To make it a four-count, three-count, two-count, or one-count canon, a dancer starts four, three, two, or one count(s) after the preceding one.

2. If it works, try running it backwards.   ∎

Rondo

The word "rondo" derives from *rondel,* which is old French for circle. In music, a **rondo** is a recurring theme interspersed by related themes. A rondo goes around.

Doris Humphrey directed an exciting student dance at the American Dance Festival in 1948. She had students create a strong, simple theme to open and to be continually repeated in the background, while individuals emerged to dance their own solo and duet variations. Variations came in rising order of excitement to bring the dance to a high pitch before the final closing group restatement of the theme.

I copied that idea with Linda Hodes, Miriam Cole, and Jack Moore, using Françoise Couperin's *Musette,* to which we all made variations. *Musette for Four* opened our concert.

*P*ROJECT 200   A RONDO (FOR THREE OR MORE DANCERS).

1. Make a group theme; select or collaboratively make a 32-count phrase to be used as the theme. Dancer's counts = four eights. Musician's counts = eight measures of four. All learn it cold.
2. Each dancer makes up a 16-count variation.
3. Perform as follows:
   a. Open with all dancing the group theme.
   b. 1st-variation dancer comes front as others in the group theme go to the rear, to the sides, or divide up.
   c. After the 1st variation, the first dancer blends back into the group and all repeat the group theme strongly.
   d. 2nd-variation dancer emerges for similar solo turn, then rejoins the group, which repeats the group theme with new wrinkles, if desired.
   e. Repeats for variations 3, 4, 5, and so on.
   f. Dance ends with finale which expands on the group theme.

Take liberties with this scheme, varying individual and group themes in any ways that appeal. ■

Counterpoint

Counterpoint, from the Latin *punctus* contra *punctus*, "point against point," pits two different melodies against one another, is thus different from a canon, which uses the same or very similar melodies. The adversarial implication is no accident; by pitting two individual melodies against one another, a counterpoint creates a new and exciting whole. A counterpoint can be thought of as a marriage of two competing, yet complementary, melodies. Counterpoint is implied elsewhere on the *MAP*, as Juxtapositions (page 102) and Layering (page 108). Here we regard it as a thing-in-itself.

Classical counterpoint has highly codified rules derived from harmony, most of which do not apply to dance. Yet there is a difference between dancing harmoniously together or merely in the same space without regard to how moves play. One can try to formalize prescriptions, yet it is largely up to dancemakers to decide what goes with what.

As you undertake counterpoint, you need to decide what you want it to do. People can dance on the stage at the same time doing different moves, dancing alongside, but not with the others—which is all right if it's what you want. But the aims of counterpoint are complementarity and complexity—toward a higher unity.

$\mathcal{P}$ROJECT 201   DOUBLE AND TRIPLE COUNTERPOINT.

1. Double counterpoint:
   a. Make two separate and different lines of movement, using the same tempo or using the same music.
   b. Perform both together.
   c. Make changes to improve this marriage.
2. Triple counterpoint: Add a third line and perform with three dancers. ■

OTHER MUSICAL FORMS

Below is a list of musical forms (not complete by any means) that are intriguing on their own and that may suggest dances. Delve into any that interest you.

> ➤ *aria* (from the Latin *aër*, air). A musical idea for a single voice. Arias are distinguished from airs by being more elaborate.
> ➤ *aria da capo*. A vocal form usually in three parts: theme, second theme, return to first with embellishments. In other words, ABA.
> ➤ *ballade* (from the Italian *ballare*, to dance). A dancing song, or song that can be danced. It is light, melodic, and of two or more repeated stanzas.
> ➤ *cantata* (from the Latin *cantare*, to sing). A vocal form in four movements: recitative, aria, recitative, aria.
> ➤ *canzona* (Italian for a short, graceful song). Also an instrumental form based on the *chanson*, French for canzona.
> ➤ *chorale* (from the Greek *choros*, a band of dancers and singers). A chorale is a sacred song sung by many voices in unison.
> ➤ *concerto* (from the Latin *consertus*, joined together). A composition in sonata form premised upon rivalry and the passing of phrases and figures back and forth. The solo concerto pits an instrument against the orchestra. The *concerto grosso* contrasts instrumental orchestra sonorities.
> ➤ *descant* (from the French *descanter*, to sing). The accompanying part of a theme. An early form of counterpoint. Descant also has other meanings.
> ➤ *divertimento*. Music written to amuse. This form peaked in the late sixteenth century, in works of Haydn and von Dittersdorf.
> ➤ *fancy* (from a Greek root for imagination). A free improvisation.
> ➤ *fantasia* (from a Greek root for imagination). A free form related to sixteenth-century improvisations, often used to show skills and virtuosity.

➤ *fugue* (from the Latin *fugere,* to flee). A harmonic combination of independent melodies, consisting of a single subject worked out polyphonically for two or more voices. The first fugue was published in 1607. The fugue is a product of music notation.

➤ *glee* (Greek for jest). An unaccompanied song, not necessarily gleeful, by a vocal group—a glee club.

➤ *madrigal* (possibly from the Latin *mandra,* a herd of cattle—consequently, something pastoral). A secular musical form of three to six parts.

➤ *motet* (French. Diminutive of *mot,* meaning word). Unaccompanied polytonal composition based on a sacred text.

➤ *paraphrase* (*para:* beyond and *phrasis:* to speak). Repetitions of sections of songs varied and enhanced with different meters or proportions.

➤ *prelude* (from the Latin *prae:* before and *ludus:* play. Then from the French *préluder,* to improvise). An instrumental opening of a larger work.

➤ *recitative* (from the Latin *re:* again, and *citare:* to name). A declamatory song in a speaking tempo with free rhythm.

➤ *rhapsody* (from a Greek root, meaning stitched together). Its oldest meaning is literary, a recited portion of an epic poem. The musical rhapsody has no strict form and has an improvisational feel.

➤ *ricercar* (the root means to search). One musical idea which is explored by alternating a familiar passage with new ones. The title of Glen Tetley's ballet, *Ricercari,* uses the plural.

➤ *ritornello* (from the Italian *ritornare,* to return). A repeat or return to a theme.

➤ *sonata* (from the Italian *suonare,* to sound). Musicologist Paul Cooper terms the sonata "an energizing organizational premise" based on exposition, development, and recapitulation, which descends from a rhetorical triad: statement, argument, summation (page 206).[11]

➤ *suite* (from the French *suivre,* to follow). Groups of pieces that come one after another, united by an idea, often melodic. The earliest suites were dance suites.

➤ *symphony* (from the Greek *phonein:* sound, and *sym:* together; also, *symphonos,* agreeing in sound). An orchestral composition, usually with three or four movements.

➤ *toccata* (from the Italian *toccare,* to touch). A free form, like a *fantasia.*

➤ *tone painting, tone poem.* The tone painting tries to evoke colors with sounds, for which there is an impressive German word, *Klangfarbenmelodie,* which means "tone-color melody." The tone poem attempts musical description. Both are examples of artistic *transubstantiation,* one art trying to become or do the work of another. These forms are not favored by classicists, yet interesting music has been written in them.

SACRED SONG

Edith Borroff writes: "Chant [a sung prayer] must be conceived not only as a musical construction, but as an entire aesthetic experience."[12] Making any dance is assuredly an aesthetic experience, but sacred dancing or making a sacred dance—a danced prayer—adds yet a deeper layer.

Dance had been a rite of Europe's pre-Christian religion, to be suppressed when the medieval Church sought to replace that religion. Thus, although music gained an important place, the early Christian Church had no dance. Prayers could be made as *plainsong*, also called *chant* and *plainchant*, giving *Introit*, *Kyrie*, *Gloria*, *Alleluia*, *Credo*, *Offertory*, *Sanctus Benedictus*, *Agnus Dei*, and *Communion*.

Sacred songs include: *psalm*, a song of praise from the Book of Psalms; *canticle*, another song of praise; *antiphon*, sung before or after a canticle or psalm; *hymn*, a poem, usually of adoration, sung to music; *lesson*, a sung reading from scripture; *responsorium*, an answering refrain; *nocturne*, a series of psalms, antiphons, and responses.

Today sacred dance is beginning to return. The Cathedral of St. John the Divine has a resident company, Forces of Nature. Sacred dance deserves to return, for dance generates profound awe at the miracle of existence.

$\mathcal{P}$ROJECT 202   SACRED DANCE.

Create a dance to celebrate something you hold sacred. Perform it in conjunction with a liturgy, as part of a ceremony, at any assemblage, or as a private act of devotion. ◼

MODERN MUSICAL FORMS

➤ *antiromanticism*. Erik Satie is its epitome, a romantic who opposed romantic extravagances. Satie's younger colleagues became *Les Six*: Arthur Honegger, François Poulenc, Darius Milhaud, Georges Auric, Germaine Tailleferre, and Louis Durey.

➤ *atonality*. Begun in the early twentieth century with Jan Sibelius, Richard Strauss, Gustav Mahler, and Aleksandr Scriabin (Scriabin is great for dance), embraced by Arnold Schoenberg, Anton Webern, Alban Berg, and others, who broke with the major-minor tonal system of keys and harmonic rules.

➤ *computer music*. In the late 1950s, Iannis Xenakis and Lejaren Hiller started experimenting with computers, developing sophisticated sets of rules, termed *algorithms*. Experimentation continues.

➤ *electronic music*. It began in the 1960s with tape as a recording medium. Now there is a wildly expanding technology of digital sound, MIDI (Musical Instrument Digital Interface), sound processing, sampling, and more.

➤ *futurism.* A form prominent in the early twentieth century, as composers attempted to capture the machine world in music. *Examples:* George Antheil's *Ballet Mécanique,* Arthur Honegger's *Pacific 231,* Sergei Prokofiev's *Le Pas d'Acier,* Alexander Mossolov's *Steel,* and much by Edgard Varèse.

➤ *indeterminacy/aleatory music.* Aleatory (from the Latin for chance) music is associated with John Cage, yet has roots in the philosophical view that absolute control is impossible, and thus one should relax control in favor of indeterminacy. Another composer with this orientation is Morton Feldman, whose delicate, attenuated scores were used by dancers in the 1950s. Since his death, Feldman's reputation has grown and his music is ripe for rediscovery.

➤ *machine-generated music.* Compared with today's electronic keyboards, sound generators, and samplers, early machine music is archaic. The pioneer was a Canadian, Thaddeus Cahill, who made his telharmonium in 1906. Twenty years later, came the theremin, whose eerie wail was heard in horror movies, the trautonium, for which Hindemeth wrote a concerto, and the Ondes Martenot, which had to be fingered like both a piano and a violin, cost a fortune, broke down often, and could be repaired by only two people in the whole United States.

➤ *musique concrète.* Begun in Paris, it is a form of electronic music that re-arranges and alters natural sounds. Two leading figures, Pierre Schaeffer and Pierre Henry, collaborated on *Symphony for a Man Alone.*

➤ *nativism.* In the United States, Charles Ives and Aaron Copland put American folk songs and melodies into their compositions. In Europe, Béla Bartók's music is notable for folk melodies of his native Hungary. Works by Leoš Janáček, Bedřich Smetana, Antonin Dvořák, Manuel de Falla, and Igor Stravinsky, among others, use such materials.

➤ *neoclassicism.* In 1935, Igor Stravinsky produced a kind of neoclassicist manifesto: "I consider that music is by its very nature essentially powerless to express anything at all. . . . The phenomenon of music is given to us with the sole purpose of establishing an order in things . . . particularly, the coordination between man and time."[13] Can this be the same Stravinsky who wrote *Le Sacre du Printemps* in 1913?

➤ *new music.* The name came from a publishing project, New Music Editions, of composer Henry Cowell, who wanted to publish experimental composers of the 1930s, including John Cage, Harry Partch, Charles Ives, Carl Ruggles, Edgar Varèse, Arnold Schoenberg, and Henry Cowell.

➤ *non-European forms.* European and American composers, including John Cage, Olivier Messiaen, Henry Cowell, Alan Hovhaness, Colin McPhee, Erik Satie, Pierre Boulez, and Karlheinz Stockhausen, were influenced by music of India, Bali, Arab countries, Japan, and Africa. So too, were Igor Stravinsky and Nicolai Rimsky-Korsakov, among others. Works by Terry Riley, Steve Reich, and Philip Glass don't sound particularly Eastern, yet they give an Eastern centrality to melody and rhythm.

> *popular music.* Mass-audience music is going international as composers from the United States, Africa, Australia, Northern and Eastern Europe embrace technology and mix genres, tonalities, rhythms, and other influences. When in China in 1992, from a window I heard the melody of Johann Strauss's waltz, *The Beautiful Blue Danube,* but with a cha-cha rhythm and Chinese lyrics!

> *serialism.* Atonality had already taken hold when Arnold Schoenberg devised the system of rules called serialism. Serial composers have written some fine music and lots that sounds pretty dry. Schoenberg's *Pierrot Lunaire* was an inspired choice for a stunning dance by Glen Tetley. Even Stravinsky, in old age, tried serialism. It is alive today.

> *symphonic poem.* This is musical translation of narrative, credited first to Franz Liszt and taken to extravagant heights by Richard Strauss. The symphonic poem pours out emotion. The symphonies of Gustav Mahler are not unlike tone poems in their emotional expression.

> *synthesized music.* This began in 1963 with a composition by Milton Babbitt for a special instrument built by RCA. Robert Moog's synthesizer, although costly, put electronic music into many hands. Today, synthesizers are low-cost substitutes for acoustic instruments. Used with "sampling," they can produce astonishing sound admixtures, a low-flying jet, say, its wave-form adjusted to play *"Flyin' Home."*

DANCE AND RHETORICAL FORMS

In 1992, I was astonished to learn that familiar compositional devices, like theme and variation, repetition, parallel construction, and many others, originated in rhetoric. The early Greeks had no written language, and so, like all people in oral cultures, their spoken language preserved all their knowledge—the very culture itself. And since spoken language must be held in living memories, rhetoric was a mnemonic stratagem, eventually to become an element in the *trivium*—rhetoric, logic, and grammar—which became the core of Western education in the Middle Ages.[14]

Formalisms from language spread into music and dance. The basic rhetorical triad: "statement, arguments, summation," in music became "theme, variations, recapitulation," to be taken up by dance.

But despite the many congruencies among language and dance, they differ importantly. Dances can tell stories, but not the way language does (this is a good subject for explication). Language, on the other hand, tells stories very well, but describes movement poorly. (Some dance critics keep trying, but few other writers do; so you rarely encounter movement description in literature.) Despite or because of their differences, dance and language have an exciting resonance. Dancemakers constantly make dances out of ideas found in language, although the opposite is rare. (This is another subject needing explication.)

In what follows, think of rhetoric as an anthropological site where one can find fascinating and useful artifacts that can be put to use. Those that seem most adaptable are listed first, but the rest may also be useful to the bold and ingenious.

*P*ROJECT 203   A STUDY FOR EXPERIMENTS WITH RHETORIC.

Most of the projects in this section will be best accomplished using a short prepared study. Make five to ten measures of movement, with each measure four counts long. The whole study should take from fifteen to forty seconds to perform. After you've made it, learn it in silence. Know it cold.   ■

Alliteration and Rhyme

Who said, *"Nattering nabobs of negativism"?*

Where is it written, *"From fishes to knishes: One call, you got it all."?*[15]

The first is **alliterative**; each word begins with the same sound. The second is internally **rhymed**. Alliteration and rhyme are used by politicians and ad writers because they are memonic; they stick in the memory.

Neither alliteration nor rhyme appears in the two texts I have on rhetoric, but both have always played a powerful role in oratory. You're not likely to hear rhymed couplets in political speeches, but you do find internal rhyme; they are also found in sermons, sales pitches, and sound bites. Internal rhyme catches at memory without calling quite as much attention to itself as end rhyme.

*P*ROJECT 204   KINETIC FORMS FOR ALLITERATION AND RHYME.

1. *Alliteration:* the same sound at the beginning of each word. Something like kinetic alliteration would be successive phrases or motor fragments that start in the same way, with a move, a shape, a sequence, or other recognizable motion, or a distinctive floor pattern or rhythm.

2. *Rhyme.* Rhyme has other meanings, but here it is the same sound in the middle or at the end of a sentence or phrase. The movement equivalent of rhyme, like alliteration, is recognizable similarity. Use the prepared study, altering it so that a rhymed move happens two or more times. You can use a rhyme scheme, such as ABAB, ABBA, or another.

3. *Manipulation of alliteration and rhyme.* As raw material use the rhymed or alliterative study made in items 1 or 2. See what happens when you move it about. *Suggestion:*

   a. Take the first move of the first phrase and put it early in the second phrase.

   b. Take the first move of the second phrase and put it anywhere in the third phrase.

   c. Take the first move of the third phrase and utilize it to end the first phrase.

   d. Take the three moves you've just manipulated and put them all into the fourth phrase.

This or any manipulation may be made more interesting by what happens when the rhymed or alliterative moves fall into new places. ∎

Allusion

Allusion in language is indirect or symbolic reference, a hint, even word play. "The light fantastic" alludes to dance, "coffin nails," to cigarettes. To his political opponents, President Franklin D. Roosevelt was "that man in the White House." Reference is more direct than allusion, although the word is considered a synonym.

Gestures, moves which have immediate significance, can act in a similar way. Like words, gestures can refer or allude. Doris Humphrey developed these possibilities in her "ritualization of gesture," using familiar gestures in new ways or transferring them to other parts of the body. Her own book *The Art of Making Dances* describes it best.[16]

Gesture in dances alludes to real-life actions. In Martha Graham's *Appalachian Spring,* the bride makes cradling gestures as she imagines her future child, and all the dancers fall to their knees in prayer.

The art of mime uses a foundation of familiar moves: jaunty gaits; postures of fear, yearning, or resignation; gestures of pleading, greeting, or farewell—which allude to recognizable states of mind. Marcel Marceau's *Walking against the Wind* does more; it turns a series of recognizable moves into a metaphor for life (page 223).

*P*ROJECT 205 MOVEMENT ALLUSION.

- Use moves from a familiar chore.
- Use recognizable moves from a social or folk dance.

Stuart Hodes and Martha Graham in *Appalachian Spring,* circa 1954.

- Use recognizable gestures.
- Use a tableau that alludes to a statue (*The Thinker*), a painting (*Nude Descending a Staircase,* page 210) a photograph (*Flag-raising on Iwo Jima*), a poster, a sport, a quote from another dance or dance form.
- Is it possible to make an entire study into an allusion? ■

Marcel Duchamp, *Nude Descending a Staircase, No. 2.*

Anaphora

Anaphora is repetition at the start of a statement. It builds momentum. Preachers and politicians love it. Winston Churchill's stirring World War II speech to the British House of Commons is a classic example:

> We shall fight in France, we shall fight on the seas and oceans, we shall fight with growing confidence and growing strength in the air, we shall defend our island, whatever the cost may be, we shall fight on the beaches, we shall fight on the ground, we shall fight in the fields and in the streets, we shall fight in the hills; we shall never surrender.

*P*ROJECT 206   KINETIC ANAPHORA–REPETITION OF SELECTED MOVES.

1. Pick one of the moves in your prepared study and add it to every one of the others, so that it begins with the double move. For example, if your study consists of moves A–B–C–D–E–F–G, anaphora might make it: AB–AC–AD–AE–AF–AG or ABC–ACD–ADE–AEF–AFG.

2. Invent a new move, X, to be added to the moves in your study. Then do: XA–XB–XC–XD, etc.

3. Instead of arbitrarily adding X to all moves, scatter it at random or where you want to emphasize something. For instance: XA–B–C–XD–XE–XF–XXG. Notice the doubled X at the end: XXG. It was impulsive. Go ahead—engage your impulses! The goal is to generate force and momentum. You can think of this device as something like smacking a fist into the cupped hand for emphasis, although if done too often, it diminishes the effect. ■

Antiphrasis

Antiphrasis is the use of words to mean their opposite: an insane asylum termed a "funny farm"; a dangerous mission termed a "piece of cake"; a tyrant termed "Big Brother" in George Orwell's *Animal Farm*. Kinetic antiphrasis would be use of movement to gain an impact opposite to its usual effect. This isn't something often seen, but a stunning example sticks in my memory.

In Martha Graham's *Embattled Garden,* the Stranger (Satan), in a fierce interpretation by Glen Tetley, pounded his thighs so furiously he raised welts. When Paul Taylor took over, he leaned his arms and shoulders into the beating, yet his hands barely brushed his thighs, to create an eerie, scary Satan. Another example can be found in Chinese theater, where an actor, no matter how short in stature, can indicate tallness with a lowered gaze, indicating the ability to look down upon others.

*P*ROJECT 207   KINETIC ANTIPHRASIS.

Use jumps to evoke earthbound creatures, space to evince confinement; create a sense of vastness with one foot or both rooted; evoke old age with spritely movement; evoke wisdom with clownish moves; evoke foolishness with dignified moves. Dream up more kinetic antiphrasis. ■

Asyndeton

Narrowly defined, **asyndeton** means omission of conjunctions; more broadly defined, it is use of fragments.

> No low blows, no butting, shake hands, come out fighting.
> Attention! Left face! Forward march!
> Wall Street. The money chase, directionless juggernaut, mad free-for-all, losers litter the landscape, winners lose their souls.

Asyndeton is rare in written language because to the eye it looks sputtering and jerky. But spoken, it can have breathless urgency and is used in election speeches, sales pitches, sermons, and other exhortations.

Dance lacks the formal connecters of language, such as articles and conjunctions. But bodies, which prefer to move connectedly, insert their own connectors, and codified movement disciplines—techniques—are designed with built-in connectors. It is not difficult for dancemakers to identify these connecting moves, although removing them may not be so easy.

If asyndeton breaks word flow, adding potency and crispness, something similar can be achieved in dance, as Helen Tamiris did in the "Wild Horse" dance of the Broadway production of *Annie Get Your Gun.* Modeled on the bucking, battering moves of an untamed horse, it was slammed out in an erupting succession of powerful moves with virtually no connectors.

*P*ROJECT 208   KINETIC ASYNDETON.

1. Take an existing study and remove its connecting moves.
2. Make a dozen percussive moves, string them together, then thrust them out as abruptly as possible.
3. Is there something harsh, sharp, strident, cruel, or brutish which

you can utter in dance? Seek moves to project its furies. Hurl them at your audience. ▪

Balance of Opposites

In rhetoric, *opposing elements* yield *balance* and a sense of completion: question and answer, assertion and proof, assertion and refutation, threat and its consequence:

- Stop, or I'll shoot!
- Live free, or die.
- The best things in life are free, but I prefer second best.
- You love French fries? How about high blood pressure?

Balance of opposites is related to Contrast (page 216), except that here the opposing elements are more directly related or tied together.

PROJECT 209   A BALANCE OF OPPOSITES.

1. Make a study in which directly contrasting elements play against each other: lyrical/percussive, zigzag/curving, vertical/horizontal, peaceful/agitated, jumping/falling—or any other.
2. Look at any study you've made. Consider its balance. ▪

PROJECT 210   AN EXERCISE IN OVERBALANCE.

Relentless symmetry becomes predictable and boring. Can the same happen with relentless balance? To find out, balance every phrase or move in your study. Conversely, unbalance them. Consider what role balance and unbalance play in your dances. ▪

Catachresis

Modern dictionaries define **catachresis** as abuse of terms or incorrect usage, like a strained or mixed metaphor. Critic Northrop Frye defines it as "the unexpected or violent metaphor."[17] An older definition is "the practice of using the nearest term to describe something for which no actual term exists."[18] This last definition implies an attempt to *express something for which there is no expression.* Dance does that better than any other art form. The following are examples of kinetic catachresis.

➤ *Forbidden desire.* In *Phaedre,* Martha Graham had the heroine peek at her son-in-law through panels that opened to reveal body parts: a thigh, a pectoral, an ab, an arm. It so shocked a congresswoman that she said it should be banned.

➤ *Fallen Idols.* In Paul Taylor's *From Sea to Shining Sea,* Dan Wagoner, costumed as Superman, gave a mighty punch to his girlfriend, Lois Lane. The Statue of Liberty, played by Betty De Jong, sank into New York Bay!

➤ *Artist versus society.* Ishmael Houston Jones danced f/i/s/s/i/o/n/i/n/g in heavy boots, head swathed in black fabric, body naked. Blind, vulnerable, he moved inexorably toward the audience, as if urged by an unstoppable force.

*P*ROJECT 211   CATACHRESIS: EVOKING THE INEFFABLE.

Pick a strong emotion: shame, regret, fear, awe, ecstasy, or another. Seek to convey it kinetically and with surprise. *Suggestions:*

- *Shame:* Dance with a toilet seat.
- *Regret:* Dance moving backward, never forward.
- *Awe:* Dance on one leg.
- *Fear:* Dance with mouth wide open (ugh!).
- *Ecstasy:* Half the dances ever made go for ecstasy, usually with lifts. What else can you do? ■

*P*ROJECT 212   CATACHRESIS: OBJECTIFYING THE INEFFABLE.

1. Find an issue on which you feel strongly, in politics, education, law, customs, attitudes, roles, medicine, or something else.
2. Seek a kinetic catachresis, an outrageous movement metaphor, that paints your issue in stark colors. ■

Chiasmus

From the Greek, *chiasmós,* a crosspiece, **chiasmus,** in rhetoric, is the inversion of order of elements in the second of two parallel phrases. A simple example: *He's a superman in body but in intellect, a wimp.* Ordinarily it would be: *He's a superman in body but a wimp in intellect.* Changing the order adds punch: "*. . . in intellect (pause), a wimp!*"

The kinetic equivalent of chiasmus is common. Here's a ballet class example of this:

Glissade, assemblé, glissade, jeté,
glissade, jeté, glissadé, assemblé

Instead of exactly repeating the order, in the second line, jeté and assemblé are reversed. Kinetic chiasmus is often intuitive and comes out of a feel for pattern, rhythm, and flow. But when intuition needs a rest and you wish to work intellectually, it's good to know about chiasmus.

PROJECT 213   KINETIC CHIASMUS.

Select three *motor fragments*, A, B, and C from your prepared studies. A **motor fragment** is more than a single move but shorter than a phrase. In any case, it should be easily learned.

Now make an order: AB, AC. Get the feel of it by dancing it half a dozen times or so.

Finally, make a chiasmic reversal: AC, AB, and then dance both phrases: AB, AC, AC, AB. Chiasmus can be much more complex and is handy to have around when you need it.   ■

Clarity

Clarity is important in speechmaking. If you are reading text you can reread it; but if listeners miss a passage, they have missed it, period. Lacking text, the spoken word is as ephemeral as dance! Of course, you can rerun (the attenuated image) of a dance if it is on film or video; but we are dealing with live performance, where dances must be clear. However, what is clear to one person, another can find ambiguous or impenetrable. Even a fable, soap opera, or cartoon can be viewed in different lights. What is clarity in a dance?

> ➤ Is it simplicity, organization, harmonious elements?
> ➤ Is it attention to detail?
> ➤ Is it lack of ambiguity, or deft use of ambiguity?
> ➤ Can a dance be clearly ambiguous (an oxymoron)?
> ➤ Can clarity be carried too far?
> ➤ Can clarity, like beauty, reside in the eye of the beholder?

PROJECT 214   AN EXPERIMENT IN CLARITY.

1. Write down four action verbs. *Example:* walk, shake, turn, stop.
   a. Make a strong move for each word.
   b. Make a speech pattern of your four words; recite it on a slow $\frac{3}{4}$ beat as one stanza. *Example:* walk–walk–turn, shake–walk–shake, stop–shake– shake, turn–turn–turn.
   c. Now do appropriate moves as you speak the words.
   d. Extend the speech-with-movement pattern to four stanzas, repeating or varying the order.

2. Do the same exercise, but use adjectives. *Example:* hot, slippery, yellow, intelligent.

3. Do it using nouns. *Example:* bicycle, president, omelet, alligator.

4. Compare the three studies for clarity. *Questions:*

- For which study was clarity easiest: verbs, adjectives, or nouns?
- Is *clear* in this context the same as *understandable?*
- Can some words be hard to translate clearly into movement?
- Can a movement be clear, yet not expressible in words?

There are many ways to experiment with clarity. Seek others. ■

Contrast

In rhetoric, **contrast** is used to present an opposing argument and then expose it as faulty. In art it has less devious uses: to engage, surprise, delight, shock. Dance uses change of tempo, rhythm, line, direction, dynamics, and others. My first dance, *Lyric Percussive,* a solo, was a simple study in contrast—smooth lyrical moves pitted against sudden broken ones. Auditioned for Doris Humphrey, it got me my first concert at the 92nd Street YM-YWHA in 1952.

*P*ROJECT 215 EXPLORE CONTRASTS.

1. Create a contrast study.

a. Make a "pretty" movement—4 counts.

b. Make an "ugly" movement—4 counts.

c. Combine these contrasting moves to make a 16-to 32- count study.

d. If pretty/ugly doesn't attract you, try calm/excited, delicate/crude, gentle/fierce, cool/hot, silly/serious, or another contrast.

2. Add contrasts to a study. Start with your prepared study. What is its dynamic quality? Does it cover space, stay put, stay on one level, have many steps, have torso moves? If it already has contrasting elements, intensify them. If not, create them—place them strategically or seed them at random into your study. ■

Economy

Economy was important in the ancient art of rhetoric, when spoken language was the primary means of communicating—long before rhetoric became "mere rhetoric," meaning empty words. Perfect **economy** demands there be not an iota more than necessary, like Mozart's music, about which it has been said that removing a single note can throw a whole piece out of kilter. Doris Humphrey's classic admonition comes to mind: "All dances are too long."19

Ideas of what constitutes economy differ. Those weaned on television and action movies might be put off by the deliberate pace of Japan's *Noh* theater, India's *Kathakali* dance drama, and closer to home, the intense duets of Eiko and Koma, Philip Glass's and Robert Wilson's five-hour opera, *Einstein on the Beach,* or a long novel like *War and Peace,* although in their own terms these use their materials with economy. It is left to each dancemaker to decide just what constitutes economy.

*P*ROJECT 216   AN EXPERIMENT IN ECONOMY AND EXCESS.

On the theory that you can learn about economy by experiencing its opposite, this project asks you to extend your prepared study.

1. Repeat individual moves. Repeat groups of moves. Repeat entire sequences of moves. Decide when you've reached terminal boredom.
2. Vary moves as you repeat. See if variation makes it possible to go longer before the onset of ennui.
3. See what can be trimmed from your prepared study without significant loss of coherence. ■

Ellipsis

Ellipsis picks up the pace by leaving out words whose meaning is clearly implied—for example, the end of Lincoln's Gettysburg Address:

> . . . this nation of the people, by the people, for the people, shall not perish from the earth.

Lincoln left out the "and" before "for the people," but we don't miss it. A less lofty example: "I've been to Rome but my wife hasn't." Although not uttered, the second "been to Rome" is understood.

Kinetic ellipsis often occurs in a dance with a theme and variations. When a theme is repeated, as is the A theme in ABA, the final A is often changed by tightening or shortening, that is, leaving out a move or moves from the original statement. Can kinetic ellipsis sharpen your study?

$\mathcal{P}$ROJECT 217 ELLIPSIS: LEAVING OUT SUPERFLUOUS MOVES.

1. Look at connections between moves in your prepared study to see if any, particularly near the conclusion of a phrase, can be cut to advantage.

2. If your study is too short for kinetic ellipsis to work (as is likely), try it on any longer dance you've made.

3. Cast a critical eye on all the dances you see in class or in concert to see if they might be enhanced by judicious trimming. ■

Emphasis

Louis Horst, reviewing one of my early dance concerts, wrote, "Mr. Hodes works on only one level, full out." It was a telling criticism. Dancemakers, like speechmakers, must carefully choose what to emphasize. Dance **emphasis** is achieved in different ways:

1. *Range:* nearness has more impact than distance; big moves prevail over small; moves covering space are noticed more than confined moves.

2. *Change of tempo:* emphasis can be changed either by slowing down or speeding up.

3. *Dynamics or intensity:* loud or soft, calm or agitated, bound flow or free flow.[20]

4. *Attack:* gentle or forceful, gradual or sudden.

5. *Contrast:* changes of any attribute.

6. *External emphases:* music, sounds, lighting, props, costumes, etc.

7. *Repetition:* emphasis placed on repeated moves.

Other means include use of colors, as in costumes, hiding or partially revealing, as in the striptease, and the whispered conversation that makes one strain to hear.

$\mathcal{P}$ROJECT 218 AN EXERCISE IN EMPHASIS.

Use any of the preceding devices to rework your prepared study giving it at least one clear emphasis. If that makes it longer, fine. ■

Euphemism

A **euphemism** says something gently or inoffensively that would otherwise be harsh or shocking. "Gosh!" is a euphemism for "God!," "Darn!," for "Damn!," "He passed on," for "He died." Dance can evoke powerful feelings with acceptably constrained movement, as in almost any love duet and also in somber drama, such as *Swan Lake,* with its romantic portrayal of suicide.

Euphemism is narrower and more specific than Metaphor (page 223), which casts a large action wholly in terms of another. Martha Graham's depiction of Medea's jealousy and vengeance, a violent dance, is nevertheless a euphemism for Medea's still more violent murder of her own children.

Euphemism projects a point of view. One euphemistic expression for death, "the big sleep," implies resignation or defiance, whereas its personification as "the Grim Reaper" evokes fear or horror. Dances whose subject is disease and death are unavoidably euphemistic, even while projecting sympathy, sorrow, despair, or rage.

One can make a kinetic euphemism for anything from breaking a light bulb to an exploding sun. Similar projects are suggested in Metaphor, which is broader. But euphemism has its own special flavor.

$\mathcal{P}$ROJECT 219   DANCE FORCEFULLY, YET GENTLY.

Find a harsh reality or minor nuisance, like: advertising, bad drivers, bad manners, bereavement, blisters, confinement, illness, junk mail, machismo, madness, poison ivy, politics, pollsters, talk shows, traffic jams, TV news, or any other. Euphemize it with movement. ◼

Focus

Because speech is serial in nature and spoken words can address only one subject at a time, speakers must keep focused upon the main argument. Too much wandering distracts and confuses. But dance is only partly serial since we happily watch two or more dancers at once, which allows separate simultaneous actions. Canon, counterpoint, and harmony all require separate simultaneous voices and actions.

A dance-composition dictum warns against splitting the audience's focus, and although we don't want a chaotic, tangled dance, it often makes sense to have two or more things happening at once. **Focus**, in dance, is a matter of directing the eye, or misdirecting it: In *Fact and Fancy,* Paul Taylor purposely crossed a slow moving line of figures downstage, forcing the audience to look through them to the more central action going on upstage, like at a dinner party, where one tunes out a nearby conversation to hear one further away.

*P*ROJECT 220 EXERCISES IN FOCUS.

1. *Focus in space.* Two or three dancers perform their prepared studies onstage together. It's likely to be confusing. Seek ways to change the focus.

   a. Begin close together, then move apart, separating the focus, or else one go downstage, the other(s) upstage.

   b. Dance at different tempos. Speed may draw the focus. So might slow motion.

   c. One of the dancers freezes. This will likely draw attention to the one who freezes, although if continued, focus will return to the movers.

   d. Vary the attack and other dynamics.

   e. Expand one study into the space as the other contracts.

   f. Someone break into song, or do some other focus-drawing action.

2. *Focus in time.* A dance unfolds in time and thus has a sequential aspect in which rules of rhetoric can be applied. Sequence affects coherence as well as continuity. Consider whether your prepared study would be better focused if its sequences are changed. ■

Grouping and Separating

Good rhetoric sticks to the subject, keeps related ideas together, and side issues apart. In dance, this is generally observed, but it should not be a rule since movement flows differently than prose. Sometimes an illogical or irrational move works very well. Expecting dance to act like language is an occupational hazard of dance critics, who are writers, after all.

Critic George Steiner could have been writing about dance, which, like poetry, is a lyrical art, when he wrote:

> Poetry leads toward music . . . it passes into music when it attains the maximal intensity of its being. . . . By a gradual loosening or transcendence of its own forms, the poem strives to escape from the linear, denotative, logically determined bonds of linguistic syntax into what the poet takes to be the simultaneities, immediacies, and free play of musical form.[21]

Student dances are sometimes much in need of *grouping* and *separating,* especially when made by someone with a gift for invention and a tendency to keep everything that pours out.

*P*ROJECT 221   EXPERIMENT WITH GROUPING AND SEPARATING.

A prepared study may be too short for this project, but if three to five are willing to pool their studies, making a suite, grouping and separating may make it a better one.

1. *Whole studies.* To become a suite (page 203):
   a. Run the (three to five) prepared studies in any order.
   b. Each participant group and separate elements for a better order.
   c. Run the studies in different orders.
   d. Mutually decide on a best order and run that.
2. *Movement elements.* For those with an analytical bent, a wholly new dance can be fabricated from the prepared studies using their moves, which are handled like Lego or Tinkertoys.
   a. Decide on one of the following ways to regroup all the moves.
      • by speed
      • by levels
      • by any other characteristic
   b. Rework each individual study so that the same kind of movement is grouped. The study will vanish.
   c. Perform the grouped moves together. For instance, if you decided on speed, each dancer first do, say, fast moves, then slow moves, and so on.
   d. Explore other of the endless ways to regroup. ■

Hyperbole

Hyperbole is exaggeration for effect. Some common hyperboles: "ruby lips," "sharp as a tack," "old as the hills," "nervous as a long-tailed cat in a room full of rocking chairs." Here's one I heard in an army tent: "Rain's comin' down like an old cow pissin' on a flat rock."

The art of caricature uses a kind of visual hyperbole, exaggerating features so shrewdly that we can recognize faces. Charles Weidman, a master of kinetic caricature, could capture a character or even another dancer's movement style with a single gesture or kind of walk.

To achieve caricature or any other kind of hyperbole, you must sharpen your ability to sense and reproduce kinetic attributes. Seek individual characteristics—what makes the person unique. Hyperbole can reveal, flatter, and also ridicule. Use with care.

$\mathcal{P}$ROJECT 222 OVERSTATEMENT AND CARICATURE.

1. *Kinetic caricature.* Choose a dancer, actor, or anyone you know with distinctive moves. Get into that person's skin. Then:

   a. Walk, run, sit, rise, carry something heavy.

   b. Improvise or do a simple combination in ballet, jazz, modern, or tap.

   c. Make a bed, wash dishes, thread a needle, hammer a nail.

   d. Do other moves while inside that person's skin.

   e. Repeat the moves, first to identify, then to emphasize, then to exaggerate that person's characteristics.

   f. Extract the most characteristic moves and put them together as a kinetic caricature.

2. *Kinetic charades.* Each time I tried this, I doubted that it would work—yet it always did. There are two versions—easy and hard.

   a. The easy way:

      i. Divide into two teams.

      ii. Each team selects five or more people that everyone is likely to know.

      iii. Write their names on slips of paper and fold the paper.

      iv. The teams exchange sets of folded slips.

      v. The first team up selects one of the folded slips, reads it, then in movement alone tries to convey the identity of the person whose name is on the slip to the other team.

   b. The hard way: same as the easy way, but omit step iv. ■

Litotes

Litotes (lye-toe-tees) increases an effect by appearing to diminish it, or expresses an affirmative by negating its opposite. *Examples:* "hardly unusual," for ordinary; "no mean feat," for an impressive feat; "not unexpected," for expected; "not a dull party," for a barroom brawl; "an offer you can't refuse," for a threat. If the following does not qualify, it is close.

> Driver stopped by police car: "Was I speeding, officer?"
> Policeman: "No. You were flying too low."

Might the following be kinetic litotes? When Charles Weidman gazed out upon the unicorn in *The Unicorn in the Garden,* he sighed, leaned against a post, and tilted his head—gentle moves of one dazzled by magical beauty.

*P*ROJECT 223   LITOTES: EXAGGERATION BY UNDERSTATEMENT.

Use your prepared study: Set it to a powerful beat. Begin full out, then make the movement smaller, smaller, still smaller, without losing the beat. Turn off the music. Now evoke it with the merest echo of the original movement.

What other ways can you create kinetic litotes? ■

Metaphor

In rhetoric, **metaphor** is a term placed where its meaning cannot be literal, yet where it performs better than a literal term. For example, a copious flow of tears becomes "a flood of tears." Some common language metaphors: dance of life; valley of death; shades of the past; wave of the future; currents of thought; torrent of abuse; Lamb of God.

Daniel Nagrin wrote: "Every action, in or out of art, can be seen as a metaphor for something else. Metaphors are what we do for a living."[22] One can find metaphoric meaning in any dance, even those deemed abstract. Of Alwin Nikolais, critic Jack Anderson wrote: "Audiences began to realize that by showing dancers interacting with mobile props and constantly changing lighting effects, he had created kinetic metaphors for the interrelationship of man and the universe."[23] And as noted earlier, George Balanchine said that every time a man and woman dance together, it is a metaphor for love.

Martha Graham's *Errand into the Maze* is a metaphor for a woman's sexual rite of passage; the monster of the labyrinth, a metaphor for exigent impersonal male desire. Rachel Harms's *Toxic* is a metaphoric portrayal of two people who poison one another. In *Side Ring,* Jack Moore portrayed a clown out of the limelight, a metaphor for all the dutiful decent toilers trying to bring a bit of happiness into the world. When performance artist Karen Finley smeared her bare upper body with chocolate syrup, she outraged many with a powerful metaphor of woman as a defiled sexual object.

*P*ROJECT 224   MOVEMENT METAPHOR.

Use your prepared study. Even if all you had in mind was pure movement, look for its metaphoric possibilities.

1. Show your study, asking all to jot down images or ideas evoked.
2. Read all evocations aloud.
3. Select one or more that you like and rework the study to bring out this metaphoric potential.
4. Show the new study. ■

Order of Climax

Order of climax holds that arguments go from the least to the most important point, each building upon the preceding, until all come together in the persuasive moment, the climax.

This eminently logical progression is uncommon in music, with notable exceptions: Ravel's *Bolero,* Dukas's *The Sorcerer's Apprentice,* and many songs by Jacques Brel. Music has the freedom to put climax almost anywhere, and so does dance.

Merce Cunningham rejected climax altogether to give all events equal importance. (Importance is a value attached by people. The universe may regard the fall of a leaf as no less important than the explosion of a sun.) This is one of the ways Cunningham defied rules that long dominated dance composition; many other dancemakers followed.

May we ignore climax? Certainly. But climax is less a rule than a perception. It arises like a wave from within. It you want your dances to surf on that wave, order of climax is worth pondering. The rhetorical order— least to most important—is only one possibility.

*P*ROJECT 225   AN EXERCISE IN CLIMAX.

1. *Dynamic climax.* If you have taken dance technique, you have done grand battements—high brushes to some modern dancers. Try making one of a series of battements the climax, or one of almost any repeated move.
   a. Stand in first position. After warming up, do sixteen grand battements. Place the climax on the sixteenth. What did you do to put it there?
   b. Place the climax on the thirteenth. Did you succeed? If so, how?
   c. Place the climax on any other battement.
2. *Movement climax.* Dance your prepared study through. Most likely, it already has a perceived climax. How might you build it? Rework the study for maximum climactic effect. Ask for group responses. ∎

Order of Complexity

The good speaker begins simply and builds toward *complexity,* giving time at the end to explain and recapitulate the arguments. This is not unlike theme and variations, which starts with a statement, the theme, and develops increasingly complex variations upon it. I have nowhere read that theme and variations descended from order of complexity, yet, imagine there is a link.

$\mathcal{P}$ROJECT 226 SIMPLICITY TO COMPLEXITY.

Use your prepared study.

1. Extract the simplest moves and do them first.
2. Add the other moves in increasing order of complexity.
3. Combine moves, original plus whatever add-on moves you need. Let them grow as complex as they will, but don't force the issue.
4. Dance the study.

Consider whether this study, which will start simply and end less simply, points toward theme and variations. ■

Ornamentation

Something is deemed **decorative** or **ornamental** if its function is purely aesthetic. Yet the line between ornamental and functional is not always clear. Nineteenth-century speeches sound ornate to our ears; but is spare modern language more functional than older flowery language? Critic and essayist George Steiner says no:

> The style of Hemingway and his myriad imitators is a brilliant response to the diminution of linguistic possibility. Sparse, laconic, highly artificial in its conventions of brevity and understatement, that style sought to reduce the ideal of Flaubert—*le mot juste*—to a scale of basic language.[24]

Modern architecture threw out Victorian ornamentation (which, however, returned with postmodernism). Modern dance came along just after the austere Bauhaus "form follows function" era. Not surprisingly, modern dance too is somewhat austere.

Two photographs of Martha Graham tell that tale: in the first she is a Denishawn exotic, gaze averted, holding a parasol, in a clinging costume, all swirls and curves spiraling to a hem that flowers out from her ankles. In the second she is an all-out modern dancer, gaze front, arms stuck up like poles from which hangs a sack that ends a foot above her bare feet. The pictures were taken a year apart.

$\mathcal{P}$ROJECT 227 PLAIN AND FANCY.

1. Walk across the studio, first in a plain walk, then a "decorated" walk. What did you add?
2. Walk across the studio with the following ideas or images:

- for exercise
- to attract attention
- to model clothes
- to the beat of music in your head
- on your way to see the most exciting person you've ever met
- past hostile-looking strangers
- aware that someone you want to impress is watching
- on your way to the dentist for root canal

How do the walks differ? Are all the differences embedded in the walk or do some constitute decoration?

3. Do each of the following moves as plainly as possible, and then do them highly ornamented:

- *Gesture:* That way! Stand back! Come here!
- *Military drill:* Forward march! About face!
- Any aerobic exercise.
- Solo waltz in a circle.
- *Pantomime:* Don a scuba suit. Open a gift.

4. Add ornamentation to your prepared study. Perform it with and without. ■

Paralleling

Parallel construction is a basic choreographic device assumed to have originated in music. But parallels in language certainly go back to the origins of speech itself. *Examples:*

➤ "Me Tarzan. You Jane."
➤ "*Veni. Vidi. Vinci.*" (I came. I saw. I conquered.)
➤ "What a surprise, what a pleasure to meet you at the party."
➤ "My life is studying dance, dancing dance, making dances."
➤ "Don't call us, we'll call you."
➤ "Scared to audition, scared not to audition, I auditioned. I got the job."

Repetition plus small changes creates parallels. In speech it reinforces and advances the argument to build an insistent, rhythmic, even hypnotic urgency. In language, parallels can consist of words, clauses, phrases, whole sentences. It's much the same in music and dance. But there are pitfalls: a well-known choreographer began a dramatic dance giving the ballerina a slow soulful reaching gesture toward the audience—then the same

Repetition and parallels. July 4th dance at American Dance Festival, Connecticut College, circa 1970.

(Philip A. Biscuti. Print: Courtesy of American Dance Festival Archives)

gesture facing stage left—then stage right—then again toward the audience—again left—again right. The dance had barely begun and I was bored out of my mind.[25]

$\mathcal{P}$ROJECT 228   PARALLEL CONSTRUCTION: REPETITION PLUS CHANGE.

Even a loose parallel can reinforce a dance if watchers recognize or sense the original move. Use your prepared study.

1. Add a parallel, slightly changed, move to each individual measure, like a distorted echo. It will double the length of the study.
2. Shift the parallel moves to other places in the study.
3. Add a parallel phrase to the first or second half of your study. ■

Proportion

An old saying: "You don't use a sledgehammer to swat flies."

Proportion is the relation of one part to another or to the whole in matters of dynamics or scale. In rhetoric, proportion is concerned with seeing that each argument gets the right amount of attention. For instance, a speech to consumers on protecting the ozone layer would give more weight to gases escaping from aerosol cans and air conditioners, less to the intricate chemical processes. A speech to scientists would reverse the preceding proportions.

ℙROJECT 229   A STUDY IN PROPORTION.

Proportion operates in any comparison: more to less, quick to slow, calm to agitated, near to far, etc.

Use your prepared or any other existing study. After each of the following suggested exercises, judge the effect of the change in proportion.

- *Repetition proportion:* Repeat the first three moves as a sequence—4, 6, or as many times as reasonable—then continue to the end of the study. Try it with other moves. Decide if any of these changes strengthen the study.
- *Tempo proportion:* Start at a slow tempo, end with a fast one, and vice versa. Pit one or more tempo changes against another.
- *Dynamic proportion:* Dance part of the study serenely, another part intensely. In other ways vary the proportion of internal dynamics.
- *Space proportion:* Expand some of the study into all of the space, collapse the rest, and vice versa. Dance some of the study as far from the audience as you can get, then move as close as you can get.
- *Other proportions:* Air work to floor work, footwork to torso, articulation to gesture, bound flow to free flow, etc. ■

Quotation

Quotation is used in public speaking and in expository writing. Few term papers are complete without them. Quotation also has interesting applications in dance. In the 1970s, Laura Foreman was producing *ChoreoConcerts and Critiques,* a series at the New School to which she usually contributed a dance. One year, she offered *Laura's Dance,* largely quotes from the dozens of works she had presented over the years, an expression of her commitment to these dances and of the pressure that had kept her from her own work. In Martha Graham's last dance, titled *Maple Leaf Rag,* a dancer in a dark drape stormed through the light-hearted frolicking with histrionic quotes from Graham's dramatic works, to hilarious effect.

ℙROJECT 230   MOVEMENT QUOTES.

1. All show a dance. Each dancer then selects a move or two from someone else's dance and quotes it in her own.
2. Pair off; each dancer show his study to the partner, then quote a few moves from the partner's dance in his own.

3. All decide on a few moves to be quoted by everyone. They can come from any study or from a well-known dance. Each quotes this in her own study. ■

Repetition

Repetition turns atoms into molecules, molecules into cells, cells into organisms, organisms into societies. When our prehistoric ancestors began to stamp their feet and pound drums in repeating patterns, they were reenacting the pattern of the universe.

Repetition is language's oldest mnemonic device, used by poets, storytellers, and minstrels, in ceremonies, chants, and rites. Repetition in the works of Homer, once thought to have been for rhythmic and musical reasons, was understood to have been for mnemonic purposes when it was realized that he had been an oral poet.[26]

Minimalist music is based upon extravagant repetition. The term *minimalist* denotes limited melodic and rhythmic material, although bounteous repetition can produce music with a sense of abundance. Interestingly, modern speechmakers seem shamefaced about repetition. "Artful" repetition is accorded a place in giving rhythm to speech. "Necessary" repetition is tolerated for emphasis. If shunned by literati, repetition is nevertheless used in sermons, in political and sales pitches, and it remains fundamental to music and dance.

ᛔROJECT 231   A STUDY IN REPETITION.

Expand your prepared study through repetition.

1. Extract a move that you like. Repeat it three to a dozen times in different places in the study.
2. Do the same with two or three moves.
3. Triple or quadruple your study by repeating every move. Repetition need not be exact; it probably shouldn't be—but don't worry about that now. If you wish to, rearrange the order. ■

Scope

In language, *scope* refers to coverage and breadth of subject matter. In dance, **scope** can cover movement, space, dynamics, tempo, relationships, subject matter, or anything else. In a sense, scope is the opposite of focus, or perhaps focus from the other end of the tele*scope*. In general, broad scope gives weak focus, narrow scope gives strong focus. Narrow scope demands ingenuity—yet if successful, it can make a dance memorable. In

Esplanade, Paul Taylor limits his moves to walks, runs, falls, baseball slides, and other "nondance" moves. In Lynn Shapiro's *Silent Night,* a blindfolded woman pitches her weight so completely into the arms of a man that all he can do is support her and follow.

Broad scope demands a unifying element. Works like Michel Fokine's *Petroushka* and Martha Graham's *Clytemnestra* contain dance after dance, but all are united by a powerful dramatic focus.

$\mathcal{P}$ROJECT 232   AN EXERCISE IN SCOPE.

Try both limiting and expanding the scope of your prepared study.

1. Examine your study for its range of movement.
2. Narrow its scope by removing moves but adding repetition, so that the dance stays at its original length.
3. Broaden movement scope by adding one or more new moves—not variants of any existing moves. The study will be longer.
4. Show:
   a. the original study
   b. the narrowed variant
   c. the broadened variant ■

Simplicity

> *The language of truth is unadorned and always simple.*
> MARCELLUS AMMIANUS

Art is deemed a form of truth, but it is not always *simple.* Yet even if complex, when it coheres, it can appear to be simple, like a Japanese garden. Simplicity can be powerful. About the fifth time I saw Helen Tamiris's *Spirituals,* I noticed that the first section had only four moves, a sidling rush, a strutlike walk, a run, a leap. Those moves, repeated, reversed, accumulated, directed hither and yon, and made into canons, created a wildly energetic stage that was never chaotic because of the underlying simplicity of its materials.

$\mathcal{P}$ROJECT 233   SEEK SIMPLICITY.

1. From your prepared study remove one element, such as turns, a particular move or change of level, direction, or dynamics. Extend the remaining elements—with variations.

2. Emphasize a prominent attribute—a walk or jump, for instance, to make it dominate the study. If a space pattern, develop that pattern and diminish other patterns. ■

The Time-honored Rule of Three

There are three wishes, three Fates, a Holy Trinity. Statements involving threes abound.

- ➤ New York City is noisy, dirty, and crowded.
- ➤ The trouble with Yanks is that they're overpaid, oversexed, and over here. (London, circa 1944)
- ➤ Dancing is a tonic for body, mind, and soul.

Threes appear so often that some ancient rhetorician decided there was a **rule of three**. Is it a rule in dance?

*P*ROJECT 234   THE RULE OF THREE: A TEST.

1. Search for a pattern of threes—first in your own studies, then in other dances.
2. Add a pattern of three to your study:
   a. Repeat a study three slightly different ways.
   b. Arrange three moves in three orders of three—for instance, ABC, ACB, BAC.
3. Decide if the rule of three makes sense in dance. ■

Understatement

In speech, *understatement* can be used to mislead, to make a "measured response," to give an appearance of objectivity, as well as for humor. Bob Bowyer and Jo Ann Bruggeman used both understatement and overstatement in *Minuet* to create a hilarious portrait of a weak, pompous man wooing a powerful, lusty woman.

Kinetic understatement is tricky. A woman can be noticeable by her absence; and something similar can be achieved by leading an audience to expect a move, which, not done, calls attention to the omission.

Understatement is a peculiar challenge to dancemakers, for audiences expect performances to transcend ordinary existence; the dancemaker, imbued with the passion that underlies all dancing, is usually glad to oblige. Yet the understated moment has unique uses.

PROJECT 235   EMPHASIZE THE UNDERSTATED MOVE.

1. Set up a move, then do something else.
   a. Make a small swift passage that ends with a flourish. Repeat it several times, each time broadening the flourish. On the final repeat, omit, drastically reduce, or merely wave away the flourish.
   b. There's an old kinetic joke; a ballet dancer elaborately prepares for an outside pirouette, then does an inside one. Look for other ways to make people anticipate a particular move, then do something else.
2. Rework a section of your prepared study as an understatement.
3. What happens to your prepared study if you "mark" a move, or a few moves, or the whole study? ■

Variety

Variety in rhetoric simply means the inclusion of all arguments, appeals to reason, and use of varying tones for emotional breadth. In dance, it is a far bigger subject, leading inevitably to variations. Yet even a simple dance requires variety in movement, pattern, direction, tempo, dynamics, and in other basics. If a dance is soundly made, yet a bit dull, variety may be what it needs.

PROJECT 236   USES OF VARIETY.

1. Vary moves by repeating, parallelling, building upon, limiting.
2. Vary the old standbys: direction, level, space, order, dynamics. Such changes can add variety without adding or subtracting moves.
3. Vary tempo, intensity, movement quality, range, attack, and all other variables. ■

OTHER RHETORICAL AND LOGICAL FORMS

There are many other rhetorical and logical forms in spoken and written language, some of which are strongly applicable to dance. However, I am often astonished at the ways dancemakers spin language into dance, so I include rhetorical figures both likely and unlikely of dance applications. **Allegory**, for instance, is a prolonged metaphor that tells one story in terms of another, as in *The Sleeping Beauty* and other story dances. A **lemma** is a premise or proposition that supports another proposition, and thus may be likened to a dance figure that initiates and builds into a theme.

But other rhetorical forms seem so closely tied to the unique characteristics of spoken language that it is hard to imagine related music or dance forms. **Metonym** and **synecdoche**, for example, are figures of speech in which the name of one object is used to indicate another to which it is related; thus, "sets a good table" for serves good food, and "he's reading James Joyce," that is, Joyce's writing; or a part is used for the whole: "fifty rifles" for fifty soldiers or "wheels" for an automobile.

Pattern is a major dance concern, particularly in folk dance forms, where it is ordinarily a pattern in space (pages 16, 92), whereas in rhetoric it refers to chronology, description, importance, complexity, logic, and cause-and-effect. Dancemakers with a rhetorical bent might wish to consider how any of these might be reflected in dance patterns.

> ➤ *Time patterns:* A speaker can assign more or less importance to time. Although dance can compress or expand time, as action, it occurs in "real time," where what happens first is first.

> ➤ *Space patterns:* Speakers can only describe space, and poorly. The dancer experiences and projects it. Space is dance's turf.

> ➤ *Patterns of importance:* Rhetoric demands that an argument proceed from least to most important. In dance, patterns of importance shift, as they do in life, where memorable moments are interspersed with the forgettable. Similarly, dance can change the pattern of importance.

> ➤ *Patterns of complexity:* In rhetoric, patterns of complexity are linear, and go from least to most. Dance is less constrained since the goal is not to convince but to absorb people in an experience.

> ➤ *Patterns of logic:* Rhetorical logic is deductive, from general to particular: where there is dancing, there must be dancers. It is also inductive, from particular to general: where there are dancers, there must be dancing. Critic Sandra Kemp has asked, "Is it possible to present a conceptual framework for the analysis and interpretation of movement?" No one has yet offered such a framework or formulated a convincing logic of movement. Patterns of logic in dance have many variables, including those that lie within the watcher; these patterns remain as mysterious as the innermost workings of the atom.[27]

> ➤ *Patterns of cause and effect:* Rhetoric organizes arguments using immediate detail and also the sweep of history. In dance, causes and effects are a function of the action. To put it another way, the cause of dance is also its effect.

Other rhetorical forms worth mentioning include **rhythm**, which, while of importance in oratory, is fundamental in dance. Similarly, **space order** in rhetoric only asks that speakers keep things clear: front, behind, above, below, etc. Dancemakers do this almost without conscious effort, for dance inherently makes order of space.

The **syllogism** is a complex form consisting of a major premise, a minor premise, and a conclusion—for example: dancing is exercise, and exercise is healthful, thus dancing is healthful. In dance it can be seen as a special case of statement, argument, conclusion, which leads us, once again, to theme and variations.

Time order is limited in rhetoric: "[T]hings are arranged according to their occurrence in time—what happened first is mentioned first, what happened second, is mentioned second, and so on."[28] Words can be about action, whereas dance is action; whatever you dance first, is first. Dance also condenses and expands time: Martha Graham's *Night Journey* opens as Jocasta begins a slow back fall. The Furies enter, then Oedipus, and the story unfolds. About forty minutes later, Jocasta completes her dying fall.

Tone, the last rhetorical device to be mentioned, brings up a question. Rhetoric has the speaker deliberately manipulate tone in order to project the underlying point of view: arrogant, pleading, beseeching, bombastic, disdainful, pious, etc. Does something like that manipulation exist in dance?

Certainly, a dancer can portray any emotional state or attitude. But does this mean that movement, like speech, can be used to dissemble, or is there truth to the dictum favored by Martha Graham, "Movement does not lie"?

When I first saw Maria Benitez dance, I felt like a leaf in a whirlwind; when introduced to her, I met a modest person who spoke barely above a whisper. Was her mighty power onstage dissembling, or artistry? I vote for artistry, believing that truly arrogant dancers come off as strident, pompous, or just boring. Dancers can portray any attitude or emotion, but by engaging their convictions and skills—not via calculated manipulation of tone, as speakers are capable of doing. Thus, I doubt that tone as a rhetorical device has a kinetic correlate of the sly, calculated uses to which it is put by speakers. And yet, I can't be certain.

*P*ROJECT 237 TONE.

Changing no moves, dance your prepared study arrogantly, fearfully, humbly, proudly, or in some other way so as to project an underlying attitude or emotional state. ■

OTHER FORMS

Dances can take the forms of liturgy, ceremony, soliloquy, or a story. They can be rhapsodic, episodic, like poetic stanzas, possess the continuity of narrative, or be in short takes like blackouts. Martha Graham's *Letter to the World*, with poetry of Emily Dickinson, is a series of episodes, yet not a suite: "*Dear*

March, Come in!" is a frolic between Graham and the spirit of Spring, "*The Little Tippler,*" a solo celebrating nature, "*After Great Pain,*" a rite of bereavement. Barbara Roan conceived a dance for the main street of Blue Mountain, Colorado, *The Blue Mountain Paper Parade,* later performed in theaters.

PROJECT 238 FORM FROM CONTENT.

Base a study on:

- an episode, occurrence, or incident
- a vignette, description, or portrait
- a dream or a slice of life
- a gift or an offering
- a soliloquy, monologue, speech, presentation, or argument ■

PROJECT 239 POETIC FORM.

Make a study from a formal element of poetry:

- Use poetic rhythms; make a study in, say, iambic pentameter.
- Make a dance sonnet, jingle, couplet, haiku, or following another poetic form. ■

ENDNOTES

1. I owe the question, "What is form?" to Dawn Lieber, who asked it at the American Dance Festival, setting off a fusion of cogitation in an attempt to find answers.

2. Merle Armitage, *Martha Graham* (Los Angeles: Lynton R. Kistler, 1937).

3. Perhaps some on this list, the cha-cha, say, began as musical forms to which people responded, making up the dance. However, cha-cha is listed because it is generally thought of as a dance form. There is more on dance and musical forms in the next section.

4. An eleventh-century monk, Guido d'Arezzo, developed a notated scale; a thirteenth-century theorist, Franco of Cologne, developed rhythmic notation, with advances by others. The most powerful force for music notation was Pope John XXII, who, in 1324, decreed that liturgical music be played from scores in order to retain its religious character.

5. Thoinot Arbeau, *Orchesography* (New York: Dover, 1967), p. 15.

6. Dance notation systems now enable dancemakers to compose on paper, and two, Labanotation and Benesh, can be written with computerized notation processors. Unfortunately, few dancers know dance notation.

7. Louis Horst, *Pre-Classic Dance Forms*, (Princeton: Princeton Books, 1937).

8. Edith Borroff, *Music in Europe and the United States*, 2d ed. (New York: Ardsley House, 1990), p. 11.

9. Paul Cooper, *Perspectives in Musical Theory* (New York: Dodd, Mead, 1974), p. 47.

10. Taylor said this to a small group, including the writer, at the American Dance Festival, 1992.

11. Cooper, *Perspectives in Music Theory*, p. 197.

12. Borroff, *Music In Europe and the United States*, p. 11.

13. *Igor Stravinsky, Chroniques de ma vie (Paris: Denoel et Steele, 1935).*

14. Ideas expressed here were gained from Walter J. Ong's *Orality and Literacy (New York: Routledge, 1988).*

15. "Nattering. . .," said by Spiro Agnew, campaigning with Richard Nixon. The knish motto was seen painted on a delivery truck in New York City.

16. Doris Humphrey, *The Art of Making Dances*, (New York: Grove, 1959).

17. Northrop Frye, *Anatomy of Criticism*, (Princeton: Princeton University, 1957), p. 281.

18. Patricia Parker, "Metaphor and Catachresis," *The Ends of Rhetoric*, eds. Bender and Wellbery, (Stanford, CA, Stanford, 1990), p. 60.

19. Humphrey, *The Art of Making Dances*, p. 162.

20. Bound flow and free flow are terms used to denote movement qualities. They were coined by the Hungarian dancer and teacher, Rudolf von Laban, whose work continues today at the the Laban-Bartenieff Institute of Movement Studies, the Center for Laban Movement Analysis, and the Dance Notation Bureau, the center of Labanotation, one of the leading dance notation systems.

21. George Steiner, *Language and Silence* (New York: Atheneum, 1967), pp. 42–43.

22. Daniel Nagrin, *Choreography and the Specific Image: Improvisation* (Pittsburgh: University of Pittsburgh Press), 1997.

23. *New York Times*, 2 May 1993, p. A17.

24. George Steiner, *Language and Silence*, p. 30.

25. The choreographer shall remain anonymous; as far as I know, the dance is no longer in repertory.

26. Ong, *Orality and Literacy*, pp. 16–27.

27. Andrew Benjamin and Peter Osborne, eds., *Thinking Art: Beyond Traditional Aesthetics* (London: ICA, 1991) Sandra Kemp, "But What If the Object Begins to Speak?"

28. Vincent Ryan Ruggiero, *The Elements of Rhetoric* (Englewood Cliffs, NJ: Prentice Hall, 1971), p. 97.

CHAPTER 10

VALUE JUDGMENTS

All dance is universal, and there are only two kinds of dance, good and bad.[1]
MARTHA GRAHAM

Three young professional choreographers once asked me to critique a study on which they had collaborated. It was short and bland, with simple patterns and no clear character; so I asked to see it a second time. They began laughing. "But it's so terrible!" said one.

They had conspired to make a deliberately bad dance in order to test whether I, their teacher, would condemn it. Their premise seemed to be that a teacher's role is to teach judgment: how to tell excellence from adequacy, brilliance from competence, art from craft. I failed their test.

Young choreographers, remembering perhaps, the feared and adored tyrants who trained them in technique, may long for a wise, all-knowing authority to do the same for their judgment. But the two processes are different. The only way to develop taste is to exercise it. Diligent notes from one hundred lectures achieve less than half as many dance performances closely watched. And far fewer dances, honestly made, can achieve even more.

Composition workshops kindle the imagination, loosen constraints, release potential, and hone a discerning eye—but achieve less by laying down rules or offering superior judgments than by challenging dancemakers to test their own ideas. Nevertheless, those memorable young dancemakers taught me not to ignore the issue of *good* and *bad*.[2]

ON GOOD DANCES

Excellence

Often we know a good dance when we see it—but how to explain why it is good? We avoid the issue by enumerating virtues: inventive movement, striking dynamics, clear designs, powerful drama, etc. What makes some moves inventive, others merely busy? What makes for striking dynamics, compelling design? Why is one pattern clear, another bland? Why are the contrasts in one dance exciting, in another clashing? Why does skill come across as virtuosity here, as shallow display there? Excellence is an enduring mystery.

Originality

We admire but also disapprove of originals, people who separate themselves from the herd. Isadora Duncan, very much an original, achieved fame, yet to many was a pariah. Originality brings risk.

In the 1960s, originality became chic. A dance was made to the sound of urinating and flushing, another used a prop of raw beef entrails. Performers smeared themselves with ketchup, Instant Whip, and nastier things. A man danced with an intact 19-inch TV tube, endangering himself and everyone in the tiny loft. The problem was how to be original when originality was what everybody was trying to be. Jules Feiffer nailed it in a cartoon character who cried, "I want to be different like all those others!" It took nerve to refrain from making gestures against conformity.

Paul Taylor's early dances may have seemed like that, but were soon revealed to be his alone. And at a time when most dancers were having scores written for them, Taylor used Vivaldi, Bach, and folk music. Asked why he used "old" music, he answered, "It's new to me."

There's an unclear line between originality and pretention, originality and self-advertisement, originality and self-indulgence. The only place to seek originality is deep within one's self.

Complexity

The seeming chaos of subatomic particles is unified in the atom. Atoms coalesce into molecules, and molecules join to create the miraculous complexity of life. Each step adds complexity. Remove complexity and you destroy upward potential. A drop of sterile water has unity but no life.

The human brain is the most complex structure known. Yet it supports the greater complexity termed mind, and many minds, given time and proper conditions, create culture. Might the present chaos of competing cultures one day become a many-cultured totality within which each can strive toward individuality while contributing to a higher unity?

A dance emerges from an infinite store of moves; but the moves have no significance until mind extracts meaning. Then the dance appears—and vanishes. Yet it leaves a trace as enduring as those left by tradition, culture, friendship, and love, precious ephemera without which life would be less than human.

A dance opens with a woman standing in a pool of light. Her gaze is lowered, her arms folded across her stomach.

We sense tension.

A clatter of drum beats, a shriek of woodwinds; she shudders, moves an arm, makes a hobbled quarter turn, then another . . .

Is she embattled, exalted, doomed?

A dark figure appears, arms laced over a huge bone propped across its shoulders.

There is ominous intent as movement and drama unify. Martha Graham's *Errand into the Maze* proceeds to its mighty climax.

Errand into the Maze (1946): Choreography, Martha Graham. Music, Gian Carlo Mienotti. Set, Isamu Noguchi. Martha Graham used the myth of the Minotaur as a metaphor for the sexual drama between woman and man, told from a woman's point of view. She enters his labyrinthian lair by following the track of a curving tape on the floor, to encounter the Creature of Fear, a male figure bearing a giant bone across his shoulders. The first costume included a literal bull's head, later just horns, still later a grotesque makeup. His first approach is leaden—the embodiment of impersonal male desire. She shrinks away and fends him off, and when he returns, fends him off again, until, in a fury of resolve, she obliterates the curving tape on the floor—her escape route—to face the Minotaur's third pounding approach, mount its thighs, and press it backwards into the ground, where it stays as she dances above in triumph.

The dance is a plum for those who like symbolism. The curving tape is clearly an umbilical cord, the huge Noguchi-sculpted bone, a phallus to which he is linked. When I was learning this role, Graham told me that after being conquered, the bone should slip from the Minotaur's grasp, its body to relax as in satisfied sleep—a detail lost in later performances in which the Minotaur ends up in a position of tormented defeat, still clutching his erect bone! Another tidbit—in conquering the man, the woman mounts *him*.

Authority

Authority, expressed as a clear-seeing inner eye, is essential to making dances. No one is born with it, but dancers can cultivate it, just as shy people can learn to assert themselves. It generally comes sooner to those who make many dances in a relatively short time, later to those who agonize a long time over a few. Yet nothing is settled about authority. Dancers seek it in technique and intensive rehearsals, dancemakers in mastery of craft and an ever-expanding vision of dance.

There is serene authority in the commanding essays of George Balanchine, the imaginative probes of Merce Cunningham, the thrusting flights of Paul Taylor. There is a searching authority in the dances of Martha Graham, which spring from interior storms, as Antony Tudor's do from vulnerable sensibility, Trisha Brown's from a questing spirit, Twyla Tharp's from gladiatorial ferocity.

Craft

A work of art needs both concept and craft. Concept alone has a sort of quasi-reality and is hard to capture, like conceptual art. Craft without concept produces artifacts.

In the 1970s, there were choreography conferences intended to help dance teachers make better dances for student recitals. When the organizers applied to the National Endowment of the Arts for funding, the panel was chaired by Robert Joffrey, who had adjudicated some of these conferences and confirmed the claim that participants had produced over five hundred ballets. Panelists were impressed. One asked: "Do you plan to take any of them into the Joffrey Ballet?"

Joffrey seemed taken aback. "Oh, no," he said. "They're not *that* kind of ballet."

I had attended one such conference and regret to say that the dances consisted largely of stitched-together classroom combinations. They reminded me of those jigsaw puzzles in which all the pieces are white; after putting it together, you have a blank square. Joffrey's answer shot down the application. Grants were intended for choreographers with concept as well as craft.

New Movement

Have you ever seen a movement, only to realize suddenly that you had never seen it before? Louis Horst loved new movement and urged dancers to seek it in every study. Horst believed that there was an endless supply of new movement and passed that faith to many.

In 1970, more than twenty years after I took Horst's courses, a brashly confident young choreographer said to me, "For forty years modern dance has been looking for new movement. That's over now. We're interested in other things." It was Twyla Tharp, whose success owes much to her sheer genius for movement. Soon after that, Pilobolus burst upon the scene with what seemed like a whole new vocabulary.

The brief period between speaking with Tharp and seeing Pilobolus was the only time I questioned the faith in new movement I gained from Louis Horst. New movement is not the only way to make original dances; yet it will forever be a boundless wellspring.

Coherence

One definition of **coherence** is logical consistency. Something coheres—holds together—if it is logically consistent. Can we use logic to analyze the coherence of dances?

To try is an absorbing exercise, although logic is a discipline that employs abstractions—words and symbols—whereas dance uses associations, signs, symbols, and more. A military salute is without inherent meaning; thus, it is symbolic. But thrusting out the arm and extending the index finger indicates direction to speakers of many languages—thus, it has "signal" significance. Dance is rich in signal significance and also in something we can term inherent or corporeal significance. When people run, jump, fall, etc., they evoke bodily associations and sympathetic sensations. Even a person unable to run can comprehend a running dance from knowledge possessed deep within.

A smile can be given in mirth, pleasure, happiness; also, to entice, beguile, and deceive; and seemingly, in the rictus of pain or death. Yet whatever its cause, the smile is never confused with a frown; it is shared by peoples of all languages, cultures, ages, and races. So are tears, leaps, and articulated torsos. Culture gives special meaning to some moves, yet all moves possess corporeal significance. With good reason dance is deemed a universal language.

How then judge coherence, especially in your own dances? At the root of judgment is *intuition.* You develop it best by learning to dance—by dancing, by seeing and making dances. Familiarity breeds confidence!

A Dialogue on Coherence

Q. *What do you mean by coherence?*

A. A dance that grows from its premise and hangs together.

Q. *What premise?*

A. The premise of the movement itself. Before you move, literally, anything can happen. But the instant you move, you create expectations. For example, if the first move is slow, it establishes a tempo. If the next is fast, it establishes a change of tempo. If tempo changes randomly, it establishes an unpredictability of tempo.

Q. *Aren't those just audience expectations?*

A. Certainly. But that's where the dance exists.

Q. *No. It exists first in my own mind.*

A. True. But would you deny that you are your own first audience?

Q. *I have to think about that.*

A. Fair enough. A dance leaves no trace except in the mind, where every move leaves a trace. In a coherent dance those traces capture the mind and lead it through the dance.

Q. *Doesn't that make a dance predictable?*

A. Exactly the opposite. Coherence allows continual surprise by providing a way to place the most unexpected actions into the dance as a whole.

Q. *Do I have to worry about coherence if I make a dance by chance?*

A. Of course. Chance alone can't keep an audience interested because it eliminates the human element; anyway, an audience soon tumbles to it. It's boring.

Q. *You were bored by Cunningham's* Suite by Chance?

A. Heavens no! Cunningham had prepared compelling moves, his dancers were brilliant, the chance element operated before your eyes, and it dazzled you to think you were seeing a unique dance, because the combinations wouldn't come up again for millennia. *Suite by Chance* developed its premise brilliantly.

Q. *I have a problem with the idea that dance exists only in the mind. Doesn't it mean that I am making something that can exist only in another's mind?*

A. Can you think of a better place?

Q. *Still, coherence and unpredictability seem contradictory. How can you achieve both together?*

A. A premise offers enormous latitude, far more than, say, a theme. A premise begins with the first move and extends deep into the dance. In one sense it isn't completely stated until the end.

Q. *Isn't that saying that the premise is the whole dance?*

A. I'd prefer to say that the whole dance embodies its premise.

Q. *Sounds like the premise and dance are one and the same.*

A. I'll admit they are closer than theme and variations.

Q. *Then how can you violate a premise?*

A. I spoke of not fulfilling it.

Q. *Explain that.*

A. The curtain goes up on a dramatically lit stage. Half a dozen dark figures are slowly swaying to a growly hum that gets louder. The figures sway faster. Do you have the picture?

Q. *Yes.*

A. It's ominous and dramatic and goes on for maybe a minute. Then, pow! A heavy beat, the lights bump up, the dancers peel off plastic raincoats to reveal brightly colored beach clothes, and it's hip-hop for ten minutes.

Q. *I've seen dances like that on MTV.*

A. Sure. It sets up, then gaily abandons a premise. The ominous opening is to get your attention, after which everyone relaxes and has fun. I can enjoy such dances.

Q. *You don't mind that it doesn't fulfill its premise and is probably incoherent to boot?*

A. Not if it's high-spirited and done with energy.

Q. *Is premise all there is to coherence?*

A. Premise and coherence are like a tree and its roots. They shape the moves, relationships, dynamics, story, whatever. But a dance needs more. Inventiveness is important, and so is craft. A dance can be coherent and boring. Because the audience is not you, and everyone in it has a somewhat different sense of what coheres is another reason you can't just apply rules of logic. You must trust your intuition and your own judgments.

Q. *In the final analysis, isn't it all about talent?*

A. Yes, there must be talent. But a Biblical parable teaches that talent must be put to use. If you wait until you're sure it's there, it will probably wither. Make your dances now.

Ideas

Dance *ideas* can begin with a body in motion or an abstract idea. A dance by Manuel Alum opened with all the dancers standing on their heads, their legs waving in the air—a good and also an original idea. I'd never seen a stage that looked like that.

Monkshood's Farewell, by Pilobolus, is full of fine delineations of character, all springing from its vaguely medieval mise en scène, in which four befogged oafs are yanked into a dance and left dazed in its aftermath. Even more poignant is the feeble bent figure who brings them to life, strong and joyous in the dance, to be led painfully away when it ends. Ideas are not dances, but a strong idea offers powerful support. Ponder the ideas underlying dances you like.

Drama

Drama is life writ large: the death of a bullfighter in Doris Humphrey's *Lament for Ignacio Sanchez Mejias,* the death of children in Antony Tudor's *Dark Elegies,* all of Martha Graham's beleaguered heroines. Dance thrusts so powerfully into drama that it is hard to make an undramatic dance. Merce Cunningham seems to purge emotion from his dances and sets them in eternity; yet what is more dramatic than human consciousness afloat in such vastness? Steve Paxton's Contact Improvisation© draws directly on the drama of trust between people. Many choreographers draw drama out of pure movement, some in the sheer stress it can inflict, others in dramatic intellectual games.

Can good dances be undramatic? My personal opinion: no. In the 1960s, the Judson Group strove to eliminate drama. It was important research and they made real discoveries—among them, that to eliminate drama, they had to eliminate much that makes dance an art. If you want to get off the *MAP,* try to make a sound, interesting, yet nondramatic dance!

Focus

The usual assignment of *focus* is to direct audience gaze by organizing the performing space. Focus crops up in many places on the *MAP.* Yet it is also an interior attribute, which is why virtually any part of the stage can be the focus, if one is drawn by that attribute.

Authenticity: The Voice of the Artist

If a ritual, traditional, folk, or social dance is done by its possessors in their own setting and for its own sake, it is assuredly authentic. Is authenticity lost when the exact same dance is done for audiences? Assuming that *Swan Lake* in its Moscow premiere, February 20, 1877, was authentic, if that production were somehow transported to Kennedy Center today, perfect in every detail, would it be authentic? Is any modern *Swan Lake* authentic?

My personal definition of *authenticity* is simply the voice of the artist. To dancemakers, finding that voice is the highest challenge; for only in one's own voice can one make a truly authentic dance. I am elated every time I perceive that voice, for through it the world is seen afresh.

I glimpsed it in Martha Graham's *Primitive Mysteries,* Merce Cunningham's *How to Pass, Kick, Fall and Run,* Paul Taylor's *Rehearsal,* Antony Tudor's *Dark Elegies,* Jerome Robbins's *Cage,* Alvin Ailey's *Cry,* Doris Humphrey's *Day on Earth,* Alwin Nikolais's *Kaleidoscope,* Sophie Maslow's *Village I Knew* (page 246), Pearl Primus's *Strange Fruit,* Daniel Nagrin's *Indeterminate Figure,* Sybil Shearer's *In a Vacuum,* Valerie Bettis's *Desperate Heart,* Eiko and Koma's *Night Tide,* Rachel Harms's *Toxic,* Lynn Shapiro's *Silent Night* and *Charades* (page 247), and in a recent work by Ellis Wood, *After Darkness,* which struck me as different from any dance I

Merce Cunningham in *How to Pass, Kick, Fall, and Run.*

James Klosty

Philippe Halsman

Donald McKayle, Irving Burton, and William Bales in *The Village I Knew*, by Sophie Maslow.

had ever seen. Louis Horst liked to say, "There's one great dance in everyone," which means that every dancemaker can make at least one authentic dance. Those who succeed heed the question, "Is this a dance I must make?" and answer, "Yes!"

Surprise

Virtuosity always surprises because it violates our sense of the possible. One is never entirely ready for that suspended leap, perfectly centered turn, or extended balance; each thrusts the dancer into an unearthly

André Maier

Charades, by Lynn Shapiro, danced by men, evokes the thoughts and voices of women. Top to bottom: Niles Ford and Marlon Barrios.

sphere. Virtuosity reveals the demigod or demon within.

But there are other ways to surprise. A tap riff in a classical pas de deux is a calculated surprise and can be joyous. But have you ever encountered, early in the morning, a perfect spider's web, and been taken by surprise at the delicate tenacious pattern, a dance of life and death suspended in space and time? Can any choreographer produce a surprise equal to a spider's web?

Seek surprise in what delights you. A dance unfolds, tries to stay ahead of its watchers with unanticipated contrasts, patterns, movements, and dynamics. But surprise that is too calculated loses force. To infuse your dances with surprise, try to surprise yourself. If you do, the audience will be a pushover.

Good Bad Dances

ON BAD DANCES

Critic Clive Barnes distinguishes between "bad dances," and "good bad dances." He said to me in a telephone conversation, "Where a good dance is brilliantly discrete, the good bad dance is flamboyantly successful." He noted that the same thing applies to theater, and I'm sure we can add movies, novels, paintings, architecture, fashions, decor, food—anything that requires taste to create and enjoy.

Taste is influenced by social trends, including the debate about elitism, and distinctions between "popular art," "high art," "folk art," and "fine art." These matters deserve debate, yet heaven help us if we ever abandon the concept of excellence. A dance made to garner public favor may be of the "good bad" kind, which is not bad! If flamboyant, let it be unselfconscious;

if kitschy, then energetic; if sentimental, then unashamed. If it is vigorous, joyous, desirous of approval, yet not pompous—and the mass market loves it—may it be enjoyed by millions!

Right and Wrong

Bad is no easier to define than good, nor does listing bad attributes—chaotic, confusing, empty, disorganized, glib, pompous, pretentious, self-indulgent, slick, superficial, unfocused, etc.—explain what makes one dance chaotic, another complex; one glib, another flowing; one slick, another seamless.

There is also the problem of audiences so unused to dance that they don't trust their own taste. Martha Graham's *Every Soul Is a Circus* is flat-out comedy. The first comic move—a meaningful look—comes about twenty seconds after the start. Every audience has laughed except one, circa 1948. The look came, followed by laughter, followed by a loud "Shhhhh!" from those who deemed Martha Graham *high art,* thus categorically unfunny. So everyone sat in stony silence through one of the funniest dances ever made.

Even today there is widespread ignorance about how dances are made, although not as profound as in 1949, when following a performance, a woman who said she had loved the dances, asked, "Do you make them up as you go along, or do you practice them first?"

That began to change after Doris Humphrey's *Art of Making Dances,* the first text to reveal that choreography had an intellectual foundation, was published in 1959. Dance was struggling for acceptance, and Humphrey showed, in terms academicians could accept, that making dances was as rigorous as writing dissertations. Humphrey's book reached academe in time to support the 1960s dance explosion, in which colleges played a significant role.

The author's collection

Martha Graham about to tap Erick Hawkins with a rose in *Every Soul Is a Circus.*

The Art of Making Dances spawned a host of clones and some outright plagiaries. It has line drawings of dancers in arabesque at different angles relative to the front, some labeled "Right," some "Wrong." I have one such clone with photographs of the exact same poses and captions.

Humphrey well knew that in a theater not everyone sees stage figures from the same angle, and also that dance is in motion, not still. Her illustrations are schematic, meant to generate awareness. When I audited her class at the American Dance Festival in 1948, I met a warm-hearted, open-minded welcomer of student ideas, who never expected dancemakers to work from lists of rights, wrongs, do's, and dont's.

At that same American Dance Festival composer Norman Lloyd took issue with Doris Humphrey's statement that center stage is strongest, saying that lighting can make any area strongest.[3] Martha Graham had her own rule: "The strongest spot on the stage is the spot were I happen to be."

Certainly, stage lighting and star power shifts the focus. Yet Humphrey is perfectly right in stating that the center is the strongest part of the stage. This was only one of many insights and discoveries that put solid theoretical ground beneath dance composition. As a pioneer record of creative discovery, *The Art of Making Dances* is an important book today.

Clutter

Who would want to make a cluttered dance? Before you answer, let me tell you about a studio I visited in the late 1950s, a Victorian rummage of carvings, bearskin rugs, wrought-iron lamps with tooled leather shades, damask-covered love seats, bentwood chairs, shelves of bric-a-brac, papered and tapestry-hung walls with elaborately framed pictures. It belonged to Denishawn photographer John Lindquist and was another world. One person's clutter is another's collectible.

Murray Louis made clutter the mise en scène of *Junk Dances*, strewing the stage with all manner of objects, among which people capered, squabbled, and behaved as if completely at home, a whimsically thought-provoking comment on modern life.

Martha Graham's youth and seniority presented a contrast; in 1950, her apartment was spare. Thirty years later, it was crowded, yet not cluttered. In both there was an organizing force. Only when things are dumped or shoved thoughtlessly from place to place is there clutter, and its message is ominous; chaos is gaining. Yet lovingly arranged, even a plethora of objects assure us that we are in human space, where life is thriving.

The pejorative "busy," denotes kinetic clutter—which can be too much movement, unclear focus, too little order, sloppy dancing, or all of these. If you find clutter in your dance, you may try to strengthen the focus, arrange the moves better, remove moves, or rehearse the performers. If none of that helps, well, maybe the dance is just cluttered.

*P*ROJECT 240 GAUGE CLUTTER.

1. Make up many small moves and motor fragments. Set aside.
2. Put half of them together into a single short study.
3. Now into every other measure add a move. Don't take more time—just compress the moves. Your study will become a lot busier.
4. Repeat step 3, making the study as dense as you can, still trying to keep it orderly.
5. Show the study. Then decide if it went too far and if it's truly cluttered. ■

PRINCIPLES OF DANCE COMPOSITION

In science, a principle is a fundamental law that reveals one of nature's laws, such as the law of gravity. In the social sciences, if there are immutable laws governing human behavior, they involve so many variables that they are quite unlike scientific principles. Many variables are also at work in what are termed *dance composition principles,* which come down to judgments about what makes dances good. Here are a few gleaned from various sources.

Some Dos

Keep group designs simple. State your theme clearly. Develop one theme before introducing another. Use movement material appropriate to the dance idea. Make images clear. Look for contrasts. Be logically consistent. Make a strong, clear theme and build upon it. Keep movement within its established style. Build a dance phrase with the same precision that you construct a sentence.

Some Don'ts

Don't mix movement styles. Don't mix metaphors. Don't introduce movement material out of context. Don't go for effects. Don't blur a theme with extraneous material. Don't split audience focus. Don't ignore or mutilate the music.

Some Bewares

Beware the three Ps: Predictable, Pretentious, Precious. Beware extraneous or decorative movement. Beware dry intellectualism. Avoid self-indulgent emotionalism. Beware distracting or extraneous patterns. Beware continuous symmetry. If you must mix movement styles, know that mixing styles can be jarring. Too much repetition produces monotony. Too little invention yields a dull dance. Too much invention yields a busy or confusing dance. Unless you do something about it, the center is the most powerful part of the stage. Be wary of mixing techniques. In group design simplicity sometimes produces clarity, sometimes, boredom.

There is much more, but even if all are true principles, they are hard to put to work, not to speak of the burden of trying to keep so many do's and don'ts in mind. Finally, if you follow every dictum and avoid every pitfall, it doesn't guarantee a good dance.

PURSUIT OF EXCELLENCE

With all its hazards, it is exhilarating to ponder how and why dances work, why some are wretched, some good, some masterpieces. Although excellence is difficult to comprehend (Robert Persig, in *Zen and the Art of Motorcycle Maintenance,* almost went mad trying), that should not discourage us from striving. Making a dance engages intuition and intellect, a sense of spatial and temporal engagement, a feeling for social relationships, an awareness of aesthetics. It enlists all forms of human intelligence. It is an ever-challenging frontier. And it's fun!

ART, SCIENCE, AND THEORY

Albert Einstein proceeded, *a priori,* from the general to the particular, from theory to fact; he predicted that gravity would bend light, and when it was measured in a solar eclipse, he was proved right.

Isaac Newton went the other way, *a posteriori,* from particular to general, from fact to theory, when, as the story goes, he divined the laws of gravity from the fall of an apple. Newton's success emboldened other theorists. Some ponder art by seeking a theory to explain it. But do art and science work in quite the same way?

A choreographer makes a movement, ponders—I like it, I don't—and decides what to do next. Pondering can be deeply complex, yet happen in a flash, after which the choreographer goes back to step one, making more movement.

When watching dances, we take this process in a slightly different direction. We see a dance, ponder, make a value judgment, and sometimes justify it in terms of a theory. Might this be where art and science part company?

TWO DANCES: AN ANALYSIS

Despite reservations about principles, I'll try to analyze two dances with principles in mind; for knowledge of principles can alert one to pitfalls or superficiality, help through sticky places, or simply bolster confidence in a choice. The first is a study by Jill Caradonna.[4]

A Study

> A white sheet spread on floor, Jill lying on it face down. She raises her body in an inverted "V," rolls onto her back, draws up into a "V," subsides, sits up, reaches for edge of sheet at her feet, does back rollover, winding into the sheet.

Opening piques interest—there is an excellent integration of fabric and movement.

> Jill rolls off sheet, stands, makes movement gestures, leaves fabric, returns, does hopscotch on fabric.

The dream/sleep/night image is interrupted by waking and rising. I'm not sure why she moved downstage right then back to the sheet. Again at the sheet, she evoked an image of a childhood game.

> Jill picks up sheet, drapes it, and does a sinuous dance.

A new element. Whatever was downstage right is dismissed in this serpentine dance that suggests a temptress, a jump from childhood to adulthood, a change of place or time, or a new game.

> Jill holds fabric near her face, her fingers seeming to be knitting its edge. She continues to manipulate sheet, then lets it fall to the floor.

I'm not sure of the intent.

> Jill steps around fabric, then onto its edge, does a slow paddle pivot on one foot, winding up the sheet. Turn continues until the foot is wrapped in a spiral of cloth.

The study ended in another transformation of the sheet into a snare that caught her foot. She had begun by evoking a constricted space, perhaps a bed, perhaps a dream. She emerged from the dream (or did she?) to play a child's game. The sheet became a costume, her dance was seductive.

Then the sheet become a snare, a montage of images, although none of them predominated.

The first strong image—a person in a ritual space or dreaming in bed— was not followed up, but the study, at only about two minutes, leaves plenty of scope. The sheet was also used to evoke different aspects, or ages of the person, or the dreamer's dream. Then again, the study could be developed into a dance about a woman and a sheet.

To summarize: Jill's study has lots of thematic material, may even be a bit burdened by the *tyranny of the theme,* which holds that once a theme is presented, it must be developed. I consider it a promising study, showing lively imagination, abundant imagery, good ideas, and an audaciousness that is lost in my description. Even the extra thematic material, which her short study could not develop, might work well in a longer dance.

An Open Showing

A man dressed in a black martial arts costume stands upstage right. Japanese flute music is heard. His moves are small with an inner focus. Suddenly, he lunges into whirling, kicking jumps suggestive of martial arts. Then back to the meditative moves. For about ten minutes he repeats this succession, progressing from up-right to down-left, quiet contemplative moves followed by martial arts action.

The intensity caught one's attention. The slow moves looked like tai chi, likely were, and hinted at interior depths. The sudden furious karate- like strikes that followed provoked questions. Was a drama unfolding? The sequence was precisely repeated, slow moves followed by strikes, and when it happened again, and again, and again, and again, the dance faded away. With its portentous music, a swinging lantern, and moves along a stark diagonal, it wasn't a clean display of martial arts either. The dancer began to look out of context in his regalia, a tourist pretending to be a native. The furious arm moves, first evocative of katas, became pointless, desperate—a man swatting at bees.

The problem is superficiality and undigested cultural content. Despite sincerity and physical competence, the dance came off as specious, a toy- ing with attitudes. Good moves in themselves, the martial arts material was neither presented nor developed as moves. And the associations evoked, reinforced by music and costume, made it all look transplanted, a dance overwhelmed by intrusive alien artifacts. The printed program noted that the dancer had studied in Japan. Granting the deep impressions of this experience, he would be well-advised to spend time exploring what he had gained before simply lopping off a hunk of exotica and presenting it as a dance.

I recall another dance, *Depicting the Cranes in Their Nests*, by Joan Finkelstein, who had also studied Japanese martial arts and used martial arts movement. It began with brash young warriors thrusting their swords, dodging, tumbling, striking until all are lying in postures of disorderly death. Then, one by one, they rise, silently struggling to precarious balance on one leg, reincarnated as harmless and vulnerable cranes. On one level it was a sensitive rendition of a folk tale, on another, a metaphor for all miraculous transformations, innocence into wisdom, life succeeded by spirit.

Cross-cultural influences are assuredly rich resources for dance. Think of Denishawn's dance travelogue,[5] Graham's works from Native American culture, of which she wrote: "A great deal of what I do today is not only American Indian but Mexican Indian. It is not that I tried to be either a Mexican or an Indian, but to gain the ability to identify myself with a culture that wasn't mine."[6] Think also of Cunningham's fascination with Zen, which led him to chance, indeed, his entire aesthetic. Art is generated by transformation, not by grafting.

PREDICTABILITY

Sometimes, while watching a dance, I find I know what the next moves will be. If this continues, I lose interest. It's not that I insist on being constantly surprised; but when the choreographer falls into such predictable patterns that I can't help but notice, I sneak a look at my watch.

CONSULTING YOUR INNER COURT

Value judgments, it seems clear, have emotional roots. Yet whatever your feelings about a dance, it's useful to attempt to rationalize them. Did you respond to the movement, action, concept, images, associations? Did the dance excite, intrigue, stimulate, touch, stir, disturb? And just how did the dance work its effects?

Try to view the dance as would a scholar, a historian, or a critic. If you were unmoved, try to figure out what the dance lacked. If you disliked it, try to identify its faults or ineptitudes. But if you were deeply disturbed, look again. Maybe it offered a true vision, which can agitate or infuriate, yet is precious and rare.

A TALE OF TWO TALENTS

There is a choreographer I'll call John. He polishes his dances with the zeal of a marine drill sergeant, spends every dime on costumes and lighting, and devotes endless hours to technical rehearsals. His concerts are gems of polished perfection. His dances, on the other hand, are pompous rehashes of ideas that were trite before he was born. You leave his concerts dissatisfied, but not doubting that he gave his all. His reviews are respectful, although seldom favorable.

Another choreographer, I'll call Richard, is bold and has command of craft. He *earns a living* choreographing trade shows and stock musicals— yet gives regular concerts, which obviously mean a lot to him. His concert dances crackle with daring and originality, yet always have a tatterdemalion look. Costumes are shabby, the lighting lacks character, and the dancing needs a good cleanup rehearsal. Richard gets scathing reviews and was once told in print by critic Clive Barnes to look for another line of work!

John's lack of creative talent is all too common. One leaves his concerts feeling sad. Richard's inability to get his act together makes people mad— yet that, too, is lack of talent. In his commercial work he has a rehearsal assistant, costume designer, lighting designer, and stage manager; but with his own company, everything's on his shoulders. Despite superior ideas, I don't think he really notices the sloppy dancing and shabby production. That's where his talent fails. You can't offer vacuous perfection in place of good ideas, but neither can you bury good ideas in sloppy production. John and Richard are real people, and neither respects the other. Yet, between them, they possess the talents of one really fine choreographer!

WHAT DOES A DANCE MEAN?

Dances offer frameworks within which we can find many meanings. But does this imply that they have no intrinsic meaning, and can mean just about anything?

A powerful dance, *Talking in Her Sleep,* performed at the American Dance Festival by the Guangdong Modern Dance Company, shows a woman in the throes of a nightmare. It is said that an earlier title inferred abortion and that authorities stepped in and forbade it. Yet that meaning can still be read into the dance. Although the present title allows other meanings, little, if anything is lost. To insist on knowing exactly what a dance means is like insisting on knowing what a flower means, or a human being.

WHAT DOES A DANCE DO?

A dance evokes, elicits, stimulates, enlivens, quickens, vivifies, excites, stirs, provokes. It wakens, kindles, arouses, opens, expands, enriches.

Does dancing motivate? Some educators believe so, and use it to help students. Does dancing teach? Certainly, although not didactically or Socratically. It teaches more immediately, at the same time circuitously, and in ways we have yet to comprehend completely.

In *The Grasp of Consciousness,* Jean Piaget describes how he gave children action tasks—walking on all fours, slinging a tethered object, spinning a ping pong ball, sliding down a slope—then asked each child to describe the task, and measured their cognizance of it. His conclusion: "Cognizance (or the act of becoming conscious) of an action scheme transforms it into a concept and therefore that cognizance consists basically in a conceptualization."[7]

How exciting to think that action leads to thought. And how does dance, far more complex than the actions devised by Piaget, become conceptualized in the mind of a ten-year-old beginner or a fifteen-year-old striving toward virtuosity? Piaget's work puts ground under the conviction that learning to dance is a powerful way to learn to think.

ENDNOTES

1. Martha Graham, *Blood Memory* (New York: Doubleday, 1991).

2. Christine Merz from Switzerland, Anat Danieli from Israel, Karel Vanek from Czechoslovakia.

3. Norman Lloyd, who is the composer of scores for Humphrey's *To the Dance, Invention,* and *Lament for Ignacio Sanchez Mejias,* also scores for José Limon, Hanya Holm, and Martha Graham, among others.

4. American Dance Festival, Duke University, Summer 1991.

5. It can be argued that Ted Shawn's dances were superficial in their use of exotica. Judging by photographs, he played everything from Adonis to St. Francis. Yet some of his works were penetrating and are still performed, and after all, exotica was far less familiar in that entirely different era.

6. Graham, *Blood Memory,* p. 143

7. Jean Piaget, *The Grasp of Consciousness* (Cambridge: Harvard University Press, 1976), p. 332.

CHAPTER 11

EXCURSIONS

All choreographers spend time in studios, but unless they make only solos, they will be there with others. Making dances is not solitary like painting, writing, or composing music. On the contrary, it is often down-right gregarious.

Dancemakers work with other dancers, with dance companies, with artists of other disciplines, with stage managers; they write program notes, devise titles, take bows, seek audiences, apply for grants, negotiate misconceptions about dance and dancers, and deal with concepts of elite and popular culture, multiculturalism, eclecticism, and ambiguity. They compete, face critics and criticism, and often yearn for time alone with their thoughts.

If making dances constitutes the legs of a grand tour, what follows now are side trips.

BOWS

Martha Graham once explained why performers take bows; they have such an advantage over audiences, who would be on the stage if they only could be, that a humble bow restores audience self-esteem. This view harks back to the days when performers played for powerful lords to whom they dared not act superior. Whether or not you take that approach, you make a statement with your curtain call.

Curtain calls come in two basic types: those that extend the dance and those that end the dance.

Dance-Extending Bows

Here performers stay in character and lighting retains the mood. The bows are as choreographed as the dance and some become a kind of coda. Such bows:

➤ Run the risk of looking egregiously stagy, cute, or melodramatic.
➤ Remind the audience that the choreographer is in control.
➤ Deny the audience a chance to meet performers as individuals, which bows can do in a small yet important way.
➤ Never balance out the unequal audience/artist relationship.

You may gather that I am uncomfortable with dance-extending bows. Yet sometimes they work, especially if they are followed by a final dance-ending bow.

Dance-Ending Bows

Special bow lighting bathes the stage in brightness; important roles get the most prominence. When a large cast is onstage, major players go front and center. For individual bows, major players go last. It's important that such bows be staged and rehearsed. In dances that create a powerful mood, the dance-ending bow can be used to relieve it. A good example of the dance-ending bow came after Eiko and Koma's *Rust*, performed in a setting that looked like an exotic garden with a shallow pool into which rain fell. The dancers, naked, moved like slowly growing things. After the lights had dimmed and come back up, they appeared in tunics and bowed deeply from the waist, a gesture of ritual obeisance that complemented their demeanor of distant dignity.

Some dancers develop such individual bows that audiences wait with anticipation and delight. Maya Plisetskaya summoned the grandeur of imperial Russia. Alicia Alonso made you feel she was thanking you, humbly and personally. Martha Graham became a small resilient figure making a sacrificial offering. Rudolph Nureyev bowed with a mysterious half-smile, as though amused by the roars he had generated. Merce Cunningham seemed caught in the light, like a deer in headlights. When he was in the Graham Company, Erick Hawkins strode into his bows with business-like efficiency; later, in his own company he approached the audience shyly, as if to offer humble thanks. Dancers from India bow with palms pressed piously together, which is exotic and attractive, although when tried by Americans, it can look phoney and pretentious. Antony Tudor's comic ballet *Gala Performance,* which takes place "backstage," includes a delicious spoof of bows.

As a practical matter, keep bows simple, at least until you have enough experience to know exactly what you want to project and how to project it.

*P*ROJECT 241 DISTINCTIVE BOWS.

1. Create a bow that communicates something to the audience. For example: humbleness, arrogance, sauciness, cuteness, solemnity, impatience, seriousness, humor, distance, friendliness, etc.
2. Experiment with your own bow. Seek ways to make it enhance your dance or the audience's perception of you, the dancer.
3. Make a dance study of bows alone. ■

TITLES, OR WHAT'S IN A NAME?

Kenneth King, Pilobolus, and others have made dances titled *Untitled;* Laura Dean titled one *No title;* Gus Solomons jr designed a logo—a music staff with a broken line through it—and put it where the title goes; and some have simply left a blank space where a title would go. You have the right not to title your dance, but dancemakers mostly do. The dance's title should rarely be the title of its music because it misses a chance to add to the dance's identity. Once, a graduate student turned in his program copy with the title *Masterpiece.* I asked, "Is your dance one?"

"One what?"
"A masterpiece."
He looked startled. "I didn't mean it that way."
"How did you mean it?"
"It's just the title of the song."

He hadn't even bothered to think what the word meant. Some important dances do use musical titles. When you can make a dance like Balanchine's *Symphony in Three Movements,* ignore this advice.

Left to right: Ernestina Day, Ted Shawn, and Ann Douglas in *Gringo Tango,* by Ted Shawn.

Jacob's Pillow Archives

Titles have different functions. Once, they tended to be descriptive. Audiences expected it and choreographers obliged: Ruth St. Denis, *Freedom, Dance of the Volcano Goddess, A Figure from Angkor Vat, When I Go Alone at Night;* Ted Shawn, *Savage Dance, The Crapshooter, Gringo Tango, General Wu's Farewell to His Wife;* early Martha Graham, *Heretic, Revolt, Four Insincerities, Lamentation, Lugubre.*

If Ted Shawn had used *General Washington's Farewell to His Wife,* you'd have anticipated a different dance. What happens *When I Go Alone at Night?* One smiles at *Gringo Tango* and is intrigued by *Four Insincerities.*

Descriptive titles are seen today; but don't expect them simply to illustrate what is described. One that does, spectacularly, is Trisha Brown's *Man Walking Down the Side of a Building.* Others set up dances: Laura Dean's *Square Dance;* Meredith Monk's *Education of the Girlchild;* Gus Solomons jr's *Warm-up Piece;* Valerie Striar's *Cosimo's Dream of the Adults.*

Poetic images resonate in the mind: Alvin Ailey, *Feast of Ashes;* James Waring, *Amethyst Path;* Martha Graham, *Mendicants of Evening.*

When Merce Cunningham was asked, "What does that dance represent?" he replied, "What do you represent?"—teaching us that dance can be a thing-in-itself. Many of his titles say that too: *Place, Story, Signals, Loops,* although others do not—for example, *How to Pass, Kick, Fall, and Run.* Yet neutral titles keep attention on the dance: Viola Farber, *Notebook;* Paul Taylor, *Tablet, Tracer;* Art Bauman, *Periodic;* Lucinda Childs, *Screen.* It can be harder to find a good neutral title than one that is descriptive or poetic.

Titles can cry out: Talley Beatty, *Come and Get the Beauty of It, Hot;* Manuel Alum, *Woman of Mystic Body . . . Pray for Us;* Remy Charlip, *More, More, I Want More.*

Wordplay sets up comedy: James Waring, *Pumpernickel and Circumstance;* Pilobolus, *Carmina Banana;* Jean Erdman, *Now and Zen;* Marian Sarach, *Debussey Watusi.*

Some titles are teasers: Deborah Hay, *Elephant Footprints in the Cheesecake;* Cliff Keuter, *Fall Gently on Thy Head;* Jack Moore, *Five Scenes in the Shape of an Autopsy.*

One-word titles can be potent: Murray Louis, *Hoopla;* Meredith Monk, *Juice;* William Dunas, *Bad* (long before Michael Jackson's album); Judith Dunn, *Motorcycle;* Simone Forti, *Huddle.*

Titles can be cute or obscure or both: *Spyrogyra, Dispretzled,* and *Walklyndon*—all in the repertory of Pilobolus, whose company name was first a dance title.

Some particularly apt titles: Martha Graham's *Part Real, Part Dream* sums up life as a dancer, maybe even life itself. Erick Hawkins's *Here and Now, with Watchers* sums up dance. Lois Bewley's *Pi R Square,* from the formula for the area of a circle, evokes brainy abstraction and intellectual pretension. Rachel Harms's *Toxic* describes a corrosive relationship.

Can you think of a word that could not serve for a title? Guess which of the following are actual titles before looking at the endnote.[1]

The   1¹1   its   %#&-#@?   Dental Floss cat#ccs70-10/13NSSR-gsj9M   Gluptch   Stock #17J-25 PYMMFFYPPMFYNM YPF   081052193Z

Poetry

Titles are like brief poems, even briefer than haikus. Searching for titles in poems is like digging for gold where something gleams. I have found titles in works by T. S. Eliot, W. H. Auden, James Joyce, D. H. Lawrence, and Frederic Prokosch, among others. You don't have to read the poem deeply—just browse. When a line jumps out, read more closely. Virtually all poetry blazes with title ideas.

Sometimes a title comes along with a dance idea; but I had completed a dance drawn from T. S. Eliot's *Love Song of J. Alfred Prufrock* and still had no title. I knew the poem by heart, yet went through it line by line to find *After the Teacups.*

A darkly grand poem by Frederic Prokosch, *Bird of Yearning,* gave me the title of a dance I finally made in Cologne, Germany. But the title's German translation, *Vogel Der Sehnsucht,* was not euphonious to my ear, so I made up another: It was an omen. *Der Türm* was a disaster.

Martha Graham completed a dance in 1948, but had no title; so she asked poet Ben Bellit to watch rehearsals. He wrote:

It is the place of the rock and the ladder, the raven, the blessing, the tempter, the rose. It is the wish of the single-hearted, the undivided, play after spirit's labor: games, flights, fancies, configurations of the lover's intention: the believed Possibility, at once strenuous and tender: humors of innocence, garlands, evangels, Joy on the wilderness stair: diversion of angels.

Graham picked *Wilderness Stair,* but a year later she changed it to *Diversion of Angels.* A poem from the dance-in-progress and two titles from the poem!

The Bible

Even if your dance is not on a Biblical theme, the inner experience with which dance is concerned is constantly illuminated in Biblical prose.

Brainstorming

Keep a notepad handy, even by your bed. Most of your jottings won't be right, but one day you may discover a perfect title in the curious collection you will gradually accumulate.

*P*ROJECT 242   TITLES.

1. You have a dance but no title. Sit down with a clean sheet of paper. Put down anything that could conceivably be a title—for anything. When you have filled the page, or several pages, look them over and extract, mix, match, revise.
2. At all times, jot down imaginary titles for imaginary dances. When you have filled a page, buy a notebook, and fill that.   ■

WHEN IS A DANCE DONE?

Knowing when any work of art is done is not easy. It's harder for playwrights than novelists, and hardest of all for poets, who must wring maximum meaning from the fewest words. Dancemakers, whose materials are infinite and evanescent, are certainly in a class with poets.

There is one practical way. A dance is done when presented to an audience. To those who see it, it is a done dance. Of course, it can always be redone.

What about the Work-in-Progress?

A work-in-progress belongs in the studio. Show it to colleagues, classmates, friends, special invited audiences, but not to a general audience. To bring in an audience—then hope to evade judgment by saying it's unfinished—is a cop-out. If you're stuck with a deadline, take your medicine, as Martha Graham did with *Wilderness Stair,* which got a dismissive review from *New York Times* critic John Martin. Graham knew the dance wasn't ready but didn't whine, "work-in-progress." There are exceptions, but most often, that disclaimer on a program earns no respect.

FRED ASTAIRE AND HERMES PAN

Lives there a dancer with soul so bare,
Who has never exulted in Fred Astaire?

Astaire credits his choreography to Hermes Pan; but in his autobiography, *Steps in Time,* you learn that Astaire himself played a big part.

Hermes Pan had been a Broadway chorus dancer. In Hollywood he met Astaire in a studio. Astaire needed a step, Pan offered one, and they became a team. You can see Hermes Pan dancing in the film *Coney Island;* he's Betty Grable's partner in the big number near the end. The dances Pan and Astaire made are far more than star vehicles. They are wonderful dances! In his biography Astaire wrote:

> When working on my own choreography I am not always receptive to outside suggestions or opinions. I believe that if you have something in mind in the way of a creation, such as a new dance, or an effect, you are certain to come up with inaccurate criticism and damaging results if you go around asking for opinions. It is the easiest thing in the world to become discouraged by a well-meant suggestion which may throw you off your original train of thought. Your idea can be so completely distorted that it never gets back on the beam.[2]

I had occasion to learn a dozen or so Astaire dances, captured painstakingly, move-by-move, from the screen. They were not his virtuoso tap numbers, but duets he danced with Ginger Rogers (page 264), Rita Hayworth, Eleanor Powell, Jack Buchanan, and George Murphy. It was like having a distant, yet sublime, apprenticeship with the master. If a theorist could explain why Astaire's dances are so good, it wouldn't likely enable you to make one. But learning a few of his dances might help.

*P*ROJECT 243   FRED ASTAIRE STUDY.

Art students sit in museums copying great masters before trying their own ideas. Rent some Astaire films on video and watch the dances enough to get a feel for them. Learn a few steps, a whole dance, more. Show your work, and in the afterglow, assay a dance of your own. ■

Picture Collection, The Branch Libraries, The New York Public Library

Ginger Rogers and Fred Astaire dance to "Smoke Gets in Your Eyes" in *Roberta*.

ANTIPODES: AN AMERICAN DANCE TRADITION

American modern dance had two pioneers: Isadora Duncan and Ruth St. Denis. They could hardly have been more different. Duncan was a nonconformist, repudiated marriage, advocated free love, had children by different fathers. St. Denis, on the other hand, was a decorous conformist, married her partner, Ted Shawn, ran a businesslike company and school, and graciously fulfilled society's expectations.

Artistically they were just as different; Duncan looked within for inspiration; St. Denis turned to exotic dance forms. Yet both were originals with magical stage personas and both left an indelible stamp. They were polar opposites or *antipodes,* a word Yves Musard used to title a powerful solo dance.

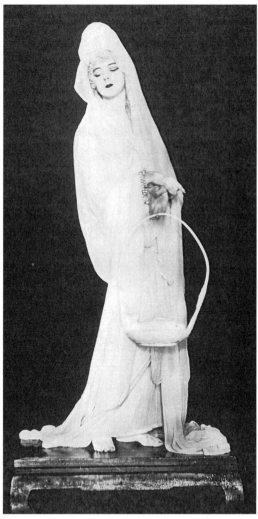

New Dance Group Archives

Ruth St. Denis's *White Jade,* clearly inspired by a carving.

How lucky to have had them both! Duncan left no methodology other than the sweeping concept of dance as personal expression. With Duncan alone, would modern dance have survived? And with only St. Denis, whose dances drew on exotic forms, would American dance have been able to lift the blinders that for so long kept it in thrall to European traditions?

Having had both, American choreographers gain the broadest canvas, most varied landscape, most nurturing climate. We seek within and also draw from the world. And American audiences are ready for anything. They adore virtuosity, admire craft, rise to ideas, love surprises and beautiful movement—even if what results looks like nothing ever before called dancing. Give them a shock and they will flock to the concert halls!

DANCE COMPETITIONS

Competition ballroom dancers are to recreational ballroom dancers like chess grandmasters are to patzers. Irish step dancing gained a new audience when network TV ran *Riverdance* and *Lord of the Dance,* whose stars and corps dancers are competition veterans. Competition is the high road to success in these two forms; winning builds reputations, brings teaching opportunities, paid exhibitions, and lately, mass audiences.

Classical ballet competitions are well-established in Europe, drawing participants from all continents, and there is an effort to establish them in the United States. There are also choreography competitions. I served as judge for one, the Vestris Prize, whose winning entry was performed by the Boston Ballet.

Martha Graham liked to say, "One competes only with the image of the ideal dancer one can become," which is like the personal best in sports. But once she said, "I want to be first and I want to be best," which is all-out head-to-head competition.

All dancers compete for space in dance class, for the notice of teachers, for jobs at auditions, for roles in companies; choreographers compete for commissions and grants. In class, dancers often try to outdance one another, and there's a sense of competition in performances of tap, break, hip-hop, flamenco, and other forms. But a distinction needs to be drawn between such competition and formal competitions with designated winners and losers. When dance is placed into a primarily competitive arena, it takes on aspects of a sport. Some dance-competition organizers even term it "sport dance" or "dancesport."

As in gymnastics and figure skating, dancing lacks an absolute objective like finishing first or sinking baskets. So, judges must rate skills. This can be reasonably objective, but they must also rate artistry, which is inherently subjective. Sports officialdom tries to break artistry into components, such as interpretation, elegance, fire, and other intangibles, which judges then score. But the scores still derive from subjective responses, so it's only an illusion of objectivity. I recall a spectacular pair of Canadian ice dancers in the 1990 Olympics, whose unusual transitions and distinctive physicality marked them out from the rest. They got top marks for skills but were downrated for artistry. In a postcompetition interview they said they supposed they had been too avant-garde. They were a breath of fresh air, and I regret not seeing anything like them since; but then, why would other skaters emulate "losers"? Thus, judges often play a defining role in the artistic/aesthetic course of such a sport, as they do in competition dance.

For years I was troubled by the very idea of art competitions, but rethought my position after considering something Martha Graham said in Singapore in 1955. The company had been invited to a reception that included a performance by an adagio team. The man wore formal attire and was steely strong. His partner was almost naked, and could fold her long torso, arms, and legs into alarming contortions while held aloft, whirled, tossed in the air, and caught inches from the floor. Throughout the most extraordinary acrobatic maneuvers they appeared to ignore each other completely. I found them appalling and fascinating.

Next day I asked Martha what she'd thought about them. She gave an approving answer, so I asked, challengingly, "Do you think what they do is as good as *Errand into the Maze?*"

She answered: "It's not worse. It's different."

Different is how I've come to see dance in competitions. Where most dances are shaped by an idea which may merely be the idea of dancing, competition dances are shaped by the rules and a consuming desire to win. After watching a series of competition ballroom dances, one is struck by their consistency. All have the same cast—one man, one woman. All are about the same length, and every couple earnestly tries to demonstrate virtuosity. Within these limits, every couple ardently seeks to show individuality.

Costumes vary but in predictable ways. For traditional waltz and foxtrot, men favor formal attire, women flowing gowns. Latin dancers like saucy Latin-look costumes, jazz couples, macho/boyish for the men, sexy/cute for the women.

Competition audiences demand virtuosity and authority, then seek the subtle differences in style and bearing that allow some to be rated above the rest. (The keen concentrated attention competition dancers get from audiences and judges alike would be cherished by any performer.) Concert audiences enjoy virtuosity and authority too, but are also alert for variety, depth, and new ideas. In modern dance ideas take precedence over everything.

For both concert and competition dancer, the moment of truth is in performance—magic time—after which, hopefully, there is applause. For the concert dancer, there may be reviews, which, if good, can help careers, if bad, can be ignored. For the competition dancer, applause is followed by the score, which cannot be ignored, and upon which careers depend. For the concert dancer a day comes when the teacher, though still essential, plays a secondary role. The competition dancer, like the athlete, maintains a career-long dependency upon a personal teacher, trainer, or coach. These are by no means all of the differences.

Competition satisfies a primal human need and there is no reason why dance should be denied it, just as there's no reason why one cannot enjoy every kind of dance. Those who promote dance competitions claim that they attract people who might otherwise ignore dance; certainly, what we see on television takes place in vast packed arenas.

But when an art submits itself to competition, it must narrow its focus so that judges can compare. The Vestris Prize, for example, limited cast size, length of dance, and music, which had to be by a seventeenth-century Italian composer. If a choreography competition comes along, by all means enter. Winning may open doors; but win or lose, it's a showcase. As for performing competitions, the first thing judges downgrade is less-than-perfect technique. After that, they venture into the world of artistry. If you possess flawless technique and are willing to submit your artistry to committees of experts, competitions may be your ticket to fame.

PRESERVING DANCES

Once, I remarked to *New York Times* critic Anna Kisselgoff that it's a shame the 1877 Moscow premiere of *Swan Lake* had come too early to be filmed. Kisselgoff replied that *Swan Lake* is still performed *because* it hadn't been filmed! Changes in style, technique, and interpretation can render a performance obsolete, even though the choreography is sound. Were we able to view the actual premiere of *Swan Lake* today, we'd likely think it hopelessly out of date.

A 1991 report by the Carnegie Mellon Foundation and the National Endowment for the Arts (NEA) argues that video is the principal way to preserve dances.[3] If so, future generations, wishing to revive today's dances, will have to extricate the choreography from past performances, styles, techniques, and interpretations. What would survive?

King Lear and many other great plays are available on video. Do directors watch them before going into rehearsal? Emphatically not, say those

I've spoken to. They go back to texts. Dance too has texts—notated dances—of which there are far too few, unfortunately. If the Carnegie Mellon/NEA view prevails, there will be always too few, condemning future audiences to see the great works of today only to the extent that they can be disentangled from past performances. As each video version, ever more distant from the original, becomes the authority for the next revival, eventually the choreography will be lost.

Video is a precious record of past performances and a great jog for the memory of choreographers or others who already know a work and are thus able to correct errors and fill in the blanks left by the camera's eye. But when the choreographer and original dancers are gone and when all memories have faded, videos, even assuming present formats can still be played, will offer only a multiplicity of performances, all differing, all obsolete.

To preserve dances for posterity, the solution, as in music, is notation, which produces scores free of stylistic, technical, and interpretive baggage, fully able to transmit the original movement to future interpreters. That there are not enough notators to go around should encourage those with the talent to study notation. And if you want your own dances to be seen by future audiences, have them notated!

$\mathcal{P}$ROJECT 244   DANCE NOTATION.

1. Take a course in dance notation.
2. Reconstruct a notated dance.
3. Notate a dance.   ∎

TAPESMANSHIP

In the 1970s, the Artists Foundation of Boston rented a theater and let applicants for commissions show their works live. This admirable process has given way to videos, which can be requested for college admissions, scholarships, fellowships, honors, awards, and grants, as well as commissions. To audition nowadays, your dance must look good on screen.

Even the largest full-color screens filter out subtlety, water down drama, and weaken impact. If the camera pans close, movement in space is lost; long shots flatten space and make figures tiny.

Video can show a dance from any angle, capture subtle moves in close-ups, zoom in and out. Yet panelists tend to become suspicious if there is constant cutting, shots from odd angles, superimposed images, and electronic gimmickry. They wonder if it is a cover for weak choreography. If the purpose of the video has to do with live choreography, don't let a videomaker run amok with your dance.

Judges want to see a dance clearly and without comment. But many fine dances just don't look good on a screen. If you have a dance like that, you can either adapt it for video or if that's not feasible, submit a dance that works on video. A dance on video needs to start fast, stay bright, and end high. A single dancer, a pair, or a small group is good, and moves should be swift and cleanly sculpted. A striking TV dance is always a kind of tour de force.

Break dancing, and to a lesser extent, hip-hop, both invented by TV-wise, inner-city youth, fulfill TV screen demands well. So did choreographer Charles Moulton, who said that he originally made *Nine Person Precision Ball Passing* to catch the attention of a grant-giving panel. It is also important to know something about the grant-making body and its objectives. Is it interested in dance outreach, pleasing audiences, experiments?

Some tricks of tapesmanship:

1. Keep screen titles and credits short.
2. Assume no more than 5 minutes of your dance will be viewed.
3. Get to the main action in less than 30 seconds. A masterpiece that takes time to establish mood won't be watched.
4. Avoid murky, dim, or overly dramatic lighting.
5. Submit a tape with what you want seen at the very beginning. If it is merely cued up, a wrong push of a VCR button can wreck your chances.
6. Eliminate shots of dancers warming up, rehearsing, having coffee, and so on.
7. Avoid video and electronic tricks.
8. Few points are given for broadcast-quality tape. Save your money.
9. Be sure to submit a format (VHS, 8mm, etc.) that the panel can view. If you're not sure, ask!
10. A dance on tape is just a dance on tape. Its purpose is to persuade panelists that you are the one. Once you have the commission, you can choreograph what you like.

*P*ROJECT 245 AN AUDITION VIDEO.

Make a 3- to 10-minute video that shows you to advantage. ■

What happened to the keen tango shown at a college festival in Kalamazoo, Michigan? to Cliff Keuter's moving *Brothers,* created with two nontrained dancers at Arizona State University? How many will see *Pack,* Lynn Shapiro's biting, joyous dance for men, Aydin Teker's zany, hilarious I.D., Sam-Jin Kim's poignant *Gok Doo,* dances that could add zing to many a repertory? Think how many good dances are performed a few times, then disappear. What if most fine novels were read by a few hundred people, then scrapped? Just that happens in dance, even though dance companies all over the world need repertory.

No other art form is so heedless of its treasures. Yet dance people aren't to blame because dances, unlike novels and films, can't be packaged for mass consumption; and since notation is hard to come by, few dances are recorded as texts to await revival. Nor can they be recorded like music and decently played back because dances made to be seen live in three dimensions are greatly degraded on video or film. So good dances continue to disappear from the face of the Earth. If some of the following strategies seem far-fetched, it is because they reflect the urgency of the need.

A Dance-Company Tip Sheet

COMPANY CALL, a market newsletter for dance companies. It should be in hard copy, with an edition for the World Wide Web. There are some 200 professional U.S. dance companies and as many college groups. There is also a growing market abroad in companies that span traditional and modern forms, many eager for repertory, particularly from the United States.

COMPANY CALL respondents would cover all dance concerts, submitting reports to include basic facts: length, casting, music, set, availability, etc., and also limited value judgments, but not criticism or the self-absorbed smarting-off that sometimes passes for reviews. Respondents' value judgments would be directed toward assisting company directors in deciding if a given work would be useful in repertory and good for their audiences.

Income would come from subscriptions and possibly from a small commission on each dance mounted. It is not likely to become self-supporting, so it would depend on volunteers and support by a university with a good dance or dance-scholarship program.

Dances As Salable Works of Art

Dances are works of art. Wealthy people like to own works of art. Why not own a dance? The owner would get title and specific rights. The dance would always be performed with the owner's name attached, gaining for the owner a place in dance history. The owner could sell performance rights, or the dance itself, which, like other works of art, might appreciate. Like any work of art, the owner would not have the right to alter or deface it, and for restaging, would have to employ the services of the choreographer or a designated surrogate. Such matters would be spelled out in the sales contract and certificate of ownership.

Dance Auction

This is a performance followed by an auction, in which the dances performed would be auctioned off. Admission to the auction would come with a ticket to the performance, with an extra charge for a bidding paddle and the right to bid. Each dance could be auctioned immediately after it is performed, or all dances could be auctioned after the final curtain. A professional auctioneer would add ambience and the added excitement of the auction should interest the press and attract audiences. Dance ownership would be made official through legal documents granting rights as described.

Corporate Dance Companies

In China the railroad industry has a dance company; in Mexico the army has had one. The Russian Army has a chorus. The U.S. Army spends more on bands than the NEA spends on all the arts combined, but one doubts there will ever be a U.S. Army dance company. Yet why not one sponsored by Exxon or Citibank? There's corporate arts support, and you can't watch public television without getting an eyeful of corporate logos. The logical next step is hands-on corporate dance company sponsorship. A dance company would be cheaper and more prestigious than most institutional advertising, and go over big abroad, where corporate America can always use a boost.

As to artistic matters, in 1948, a perfume company commissioned Ruthanna Boris to make a ballet with the title *Quelques Fleurs,* the name of its new perfume. The dance turned out to be a pleasant bit of fluff. Certainly, blatant commercialism would get little respect, like infomercials on late-night TV. Corporate America should be smart enough to recognize the value it could get through identification with a genuine dance company and real works of art. After all, the medieval church didn't do so badly with Leonardo da Vinci, et al. Imagine touring with: *THE IBM BALLET • THE PEPSI JAZZ DANCERS • MACDONALD'S MIME TROUPE • THE TOYOTA TAPPETS • THE MICROSOFT MODERN DANCE TROUPE • THE J. C. PENNEY FOLK DANCE ENSEMBLE • THE L. L. BEAN COUNTRY CLOGGERS.*

DANCE CRITICISM

My kindly view of critics was nurtured by Louis Horst, who published and wrote for *Dance Observer.* Musician, composer, critic, and above all teacher, Horst's criticism was written for the dancers themselves! In 1986, thinking how nice it would be to spend three weeks watching and writing about dance, I jumped at an offer of a fellowship at the Critics Conference of the American Dance Festival. When Paul Taylor and Daniel Nagrin found out why I was there, both asked, "Have you become one of *them*?"

Some artists consider critics to be their natural enemies, but I've always thought of them as part of the dance community. Dance critics in particular perform yeoman service advancing dance and building audiences. The great teacher Bessie Schoenberg said that New York City became the nation's dance capital "because all the dancers came here!" And were written about by critics, I would add.

In 1947, my first year with Martha Graham, two weeks before the opening of her Broadway season, Graham left evening rehearsals for "dinner with John," rolling her eyes. The same thing happened a few days later "with Walter." They were John Martin, dance critic of the *New York Times*, and Walter Terry of the *Herald Tribune*. Mark Ryder put it this way: "She explains the dances to them so they can look wise and all-knowing in print. It doesn't hurt her reviews either."

If you get a good review, should you write a thank you note? In 1965, after a good notice in a London paper,[4] I decided that a brief thank-you note was appropriate. A couple of years later I met the critic, Clive Barnes, who had come to this country to write for the *New York Times*. I asked him if it was okay to write a thank-you note. He said, "I get plenty of letters telling me how terrible I am, so I don't mind an occasional one telling me I'm not so bad."

Can you learn from reviews? I've never read a review, other than by Louis Horst, from which I learned more than the writer's opinion. Most newspaper dance critics are reporters with a specialty, like those who write about fashion or food, although good dance writing, like good sports writing, can be a fine thing. Edwin Denby, a model for many dance critics, was a sensitive dance lover who produced eloquent prose. Although I would say that dancers have as much chance of learning from dance writers as athletes have from sports writers, Twyla Tharp writes, "Even if a review is negative, reading it helps me better understand what exactly it is I think I'm doing in dance."[5]

What about scathing reviews? All writers write to be read, which encourages some to get cute. In the late 1940s, prefacing a review of Martha Graham, a critic for the *New York Daily Mirror* wrote, "A company of twisted bagels has come to Broadway," hoping, I guess, to be mistaken for clever. Another boob wrote, "*Diversion of Angels* should be titled 'Angels at Angles.'"

I got a scathing review in 1951 from Anatol Chujoy, editor and publisher of *Dance News*. After seeing my solo titled *Flak*, Chujoy wrote, "He looked like a man in the last stages of cerebral palsy."[6] Such a sentence would never be written today, but at the time I didn't mind because it was a strong response, and far better than something bland, or no review at all.

Scathing reviews are part of the game. And if you should meet your antagonist, there is a special pleasure in presenting a serene face. Above all, never do as Clive Barnes said choreographer Brian MacDonald did. MacDonald accosted Barnes at a party, saying, "Why have you got a knife in my back?"—to which Barnes replied, "It's not in your back. It's in your front!"

What is the difference between reviews and criticism? Roughly—the difference between hamburgers and *haute cuisine.* Reflective pieces appear in *Ballet Review, Movement Research Performance Journal, Attitude,* and other journals, yet, in my opinion, we have little dance criticism comparable with good literary criticism. It's not a put-down to say that most dance criticism is on a par with food criticism, which is interesting and useful, after all; but a bright exception is Susan Leigh Foster's *Reading Dancing,*[7] a work of lucidity and depth. You may not agree with all she says, but it's keen criticism and a must-read. On the other hand, there's penetrating dance writing that can't be called criticism, like Judith Lynne Hanna's *Dance, Sex, and Gender* and *To Dance Is Human.*

Dance Publications

The dance community is growing and now extends to much of the world. Artists work best in awareness of others, and dance publications provide a needed link. The Internet is exploding with dance newsletters, dance web pages, bulletin boards, and chat rooms, but these cannot substitute for printed journals like *Attitude, Ballet Review, Dance and the Arts, Dance Magazine,* and *Movement Research Journal,* all published in New York. Many other worthwhile publications have come and gone, but all can still be found under "Dance Periodicals," in the Dance Collection of the New York Public Library at Lincoln Center. Overseas magazines include *Dancing Times* (London), *Dance Australia* (Sydney), and *Danser* (Paris).

*P*ROJECT 246   EXPLORE DANCE CRITICISM.

1. Collect writing by specific critics or publications, or collect all that is written about specific artists.

2. Explore dance archives—now available on the Internet!—to get a sense of how critics have viewed new artists and new dance forms. Early criticism of modern dance may surprise you.

3. See if you can find out which critic on a New York City tabloid in the late 1940s described Martha Graham's troupe as "a company of twisted bagels." Start with the *Daily Mirror*. ■

$\mathcal{P}$ROJECT 247   A DANCE FROM DANCE CRITICISM.

Critics attend dance performances, then write their impressions in words. Reverse the process. Read criticism, then make a dance from it.

- Use dance criticism read aloud as a sound score. The reader can be a dancer, another stage performer, or a disembodied recorded voice.

- Some critics attempt to describe movement: Jack Anderson of the *New York Times*, Deborah Jowitt of the *Village Voice*, or Marcia B. Siegel, who is collected in several books.[8] Might a dance be made by extracting movement descriptions, then trying to do the moves as described?

- Collect extreme reviews, adoring and worshipful, or nasty and panning. The negative ones won't be so easy because as a group, dance critics love dance, respect dancers, and don't like to say bad things about them. Yet even the most benign sometimes go for the jugular. You can also research publications that, lacking full-time dance critics, assign reporters who know little about dance or consider it beneath them. Put together a script that is doting or vicious or a mélange, and make a dance to it. ■

Dance has an anomalous place in human affairs. It was the first form of religious expression, yet today is an art millions consider a sin. Sects of three major religions forbid it and one can even understand why; they sense that dance has sacramental power and fear it will compete for a devotion they view as belonging only to God.

* * *

With the rise of personal computers, the world became aware of programs that create so-called "virtual reality." A few are practical, simulating the view from an automobile or airplane, and can be used for teaching or training; but most are computer-generated cartoonlike games made to amuse. If this is virtual reality, we need another term for the deep inner reality generated by works of art.

* * *

A dance is performed and the instant you see it, opined critic Marcia Siegel, it vanishes. But isn't that true of all performances? Because plays and scores can lie upon library shelves, their performances are no less ephemeral than those of dance.

A play or symphony lies dormant until brought to life in performance, thereafter to take its place in the deeply interior sanctuary of personality, along with poems, novels, and for that matter, the love of family and friends. When you see a dance, it enters your experience to become part of your life, ever to remain an integral part of yourself.

* * *

For a time I questioned whether I should dance. It seemed selfish and frivolous in a world so desperately in need. My doubts persisted even though Martha Graham, my polestar, constantly affirmed the importance of art. Of the Philistines she liked to say, "They had no poets, so they died."

Doubts were resolved in 1955 after a long tour through Asia and the Middle East, when the director of an Israeli theater troupe asked me to stay and work with his company. Anxious to get home, I said, "If I did stay in Israel, I'd want to plant trees and build houses." He shook his head, sadly. "Then you'd waste yourself. We have plenty of people who can plant trees and build houses. We need people who can dance!"

* * *

Deborah Jowitt made a dance titled *Palimpsest,* inspired by archeological artifacts that bore the signs of one civilization atop another. Her dance has remained in my mind because it generated an insight; the dance studio is the ultimate palimpsest.

* * *

Architect Sverre Fehn "has described the act of building as an attack by culture on nature," noting that in this confrontation "a new consciousness arises."9 The word "attack" is apt for the assaults on nature by bulldozers and urban sprawl, and unfortunately, not all architects are as nature,9 friendly as Sverre Fehn or his predecessor, Frank Lloyd Wright.

Dance, also an expression of culture, exalts nature in its very existence, as all dances, one way or another, renew our consciousness of nature. I especially delight in the fact that dances are environmentally pure. They need space, but far less than does a parking garage. They don't pollute, and no matter how much they use a dance studio, they never use it *up.*

* * *

There are those who dance and to whom little else matters. As long as I knew Martha Graham, she considered herself a dancer. Jerome Robbins's life is summarized by the occupations he is said to have listed on passports: "dancer," then "choreographer," then "director," then, "ballet master." On my passport, I listed "dancer" until 1969, then "choreographer/ teacher." Eventually I learned I was more interested in the work of others than in my own. Passports no longer list occupations. If they did, I suppose I'd say "teacher."

NEW MAPS

Martha Graham titled a dance *Dancing Ground*, which seems to describe the world all dancemakers enter and some seek to enlarge.

Laura Foreman and John Watts conceived *Skydance* for a helicopter that dropped balloons over the Sheep Meadow in Central Park while a skywriting airplane wrote "Hi," and drew a smily face. The same two artists entered an entirely different landscape with *wallwork* (page 278), which consisted wholly of the poster that advertised it. Stephan Koplowitz made a dance by preparing a web site, www.webbedfeats.org, and through it gathering materials for a dance in Bryant Park. In the coming millennium, expect people to dance in gravity-free environments and, yes, on the Moon! But ordinary dancing grounds—stages, studios, village squares—will forever present the infinite frontiers within.

Bessie Schoenberg had students reexamine ideas long taken for granted. "What's a jump?" she would ask, seeking danced answers.

Claire Porter uses language to evoke images and the structures of language to create frameworks with which her students make highly personal dances. After observing a session, I came away unsure of what had happened and can only conclude that Porter herself is part of the process.

The teacher as part of the process is glimpsed when Martha Myers unleashes a mischievous animus, dislodging dancemakers from comfortable paths. After enticing two dancemakers to dance their sturdy solos in close proximity, revealing an impromptu and startling duet, one asked, "What are we going to do next?"

"I don't know what I'm going to do!" Myers replied, and though not denying that a work of art is the singular issue of order wrought from disorder, affirmed that the creative spirit is never completely controlled.

If Foreman and Watts illustrate the drive of dancemakers toward new environments, Koplowitz seeks new ways to evoke the creative process, while Schoenberg, Porter, and Myers, along with unsung legions of ardent mystagogues, guide and goad dancemakers toward new landscapes

JOHN WATTS / LAURA FOREMAN
PRESENT
wallwork

Stroke of genius. . . .One of the
new strain of creative talents.
A WINNER.
— New York Times

John Watts is the one
American who has
made the strongest
impression.
— Dagens Nyheter, Stockholm

Perhaps if I were rich, I'd
contrive to have a work by
Laura Foreman quietly going on
in some room in my house all
the time. . .tremendously
exciting.
— Village Voice

. . .compelling.
— New York Times

. . .held the audience
spellbound.
— Musical America

With the theatricality of Fellini
and the imagery of Magritte,
Foreman has given life, soul
and mystery to our cityscape.
— Dance Magazine

The most moving
thing on the
program. . . .
— Village Voice

Ingenious. — WBAI-FM

Superbly and brilliantly creative.
— Houston International Film Festival

. . .a spaced-out,
intoxicating
communication.
— New York Daily News

. . .among the most innovative
and inspired work of our time.
— Art + Cinema

John Watts. . .
a wizard.
— Soho Weekly News

[One of] the people who
created the future. . .inspired
the free-form holographic living
theatre art.
— 21st Century Five Star Final

. . .other-worldly
beauty.
— The New Records

[One of] the people
who created the
future.
— 21st Century Five Star Final

SOLD OUT

PHOTO: GWEN THOMAS

94 Chambers Street
New York City

Friday / Saturday,
May 29 & 30, 1981

Continuous performances
7:00 p.m. till midnight

Gwen Owen

RESERVATIONS RECOMMENDED, 925-3721 / ADMISSION, S6.00

wallwork, by Laura Foreman and John Watts. The poster *is* the dance.

within. Immediately upon publication of this book, one or many will discover a landscape undreamt of here, for maps are ever-changing and the MAP OF MAKING DANCES will never be completely drawn.

WHY DANCE?

I had a loving uncle, who in my fifth year as a dancer, asked, "When are you going to stop this dancing and go to work?" I said, "Dancing *is* my work," but in my heart I wondered. If you've never wondered, you're lucky. Forty-some years later, I still wonder—but with joy, not angst. I had promised myself to get off the stage before people muttered that I should, yet still find myself there from time to time, taking comfort in the fact that Ruth St. Denis danced in her eighties and Merce Cunningham is dancing as this is written. I don't put myself alongside such luminaries, yet all dancers share the need to dance. When you dance, you transcend ordinary existence.

I still perform with my wife, Elizabeth, who began as a ballet dancer and now does a show, *Dancing on Air,* in which I am her dream partner, the immortal Fred Astaire. After a performance at a senior center, a grandmotherly woman asked, "Are you two married?" I said we were. "How wonderful!" she said, "To go dancing through life together!"

* * *

The world needs dances! Each one offers a look into the heart of a unique world. The more a dance succeeds in revealing that world, the better dance it is. That is the true measure of a dance's worth. Form is immaterial, technique incidental, and the potential is dazzling. Making a dance is no less than a chance to add meaning to life.

THE BEGINNING

ENDNOTES

1. Actual titles: *The,* a 1915 Dadaist work by Marcel Duchamp; *cat#ccs70-10/1 3NSSR-gsj9M,* a dance by Gus Solomons jr (1970); *PYMMFFYPPMFYPNM YPF,* a dance by Twyla Tharp (1970); and *081052193Z,* a dance by Reijo Kela (1989).
2. Fred Astaire, *Steps in Time* (New York: Harper, 1959), p. 7.
3. William Keens, Leslie Hansen Kopp, Mindy N. Levine, *Images of American Dance: Documenting and Preserving a Cultural Heritage* (Washington DC: National Endowment for the Arts, 1991).

4. *London Times,* 24 February, 1965, following the premiere of *Abyss,* Harkness Ballet, Cannes, France.

5. Twyla Tharp, *Push Comes to Shove* (New York: Bantam, 1992), p. 115.

6. The line sticks in my memory, as you can understand; yet I cannot locate it, for it was not in Anatol Chujoy's own journal, *Dance News,* whose review by Winthrop Palmer was highly approving.

7. Susan Leigh Foster, *Reading Dancing* (Berkeley, CA: Univ of Calif, 1986).

8. Marcia B. Siegel, *At the Vanishing Point* (New York: Saturday Review, 1972), *Watching the Dance Go By* (Boston: Houghton Mifflin, 1977), *The Shapes of Change* (Boston: Houghton Mifflin, 1979).

9. *New York Times,* 14 April 1997, p. C7.

$\mathcal{I}$NDEX